366 Days of Truth in a Nutshell

Daily bites of Biblical wisdom to challenge and encourage

John Mollitt

Kingdom Publishers

Copyright© John Mollitt 2024

All rights reserved. No part of this book may be reproduced in any form by photocopying or any electronic or mechanical means, including information storage or retrieval systems, without permission in writing from both the copyright owner and the publisher of the book. The right of John Mollitt to be identified as the author of this work has been asserted by him in accordance with the Copyright, Designs, and Patents Act 1988 and any subsequent amendments thereto.

A catalogue record for this book is available from the British Library.

All Scripture quotations have been taken from the New International version of the Bible

ISBN: 978-1-916801-28-8

1st Edition 2024 by Kingdom Publishers, London, UK.

You can purchase copies of this book from any leading bookstore or at: **www.kingdompublishers.co.uk**

Contents

FOREWORD	7
BIBLE READINGS JANUARY	9
BIBLE READINGS FEBRUARY	45
BIBLE READINGS MARCH	79
BIBLE READINGS APRIL	114
BIBLE READINGS MAY	149
BIBLE READINGS JUNE	186
BIBLE READINGS JULY	221
BIBLE READINGS AUGUST	257
BIBLE READINGS SEPTEMBER	294
BIBLE READINGS OCTOBER	331
BIBLE READINGS NOVEMBER	369
BIBLE READINGS DECEMBER	407

FOREWORD

Christian anecdotes are addictive and there is something wonderfully helpful about them interspersing an exposition or a talk. It is certainly helpful to have an entire year's supply of them, which we can read daily. They help us to understand the great doctrines of the faith as well as basic Christian living and practice. They give us a glimpse into others' lives, families and ministries, assuring us that our own experiences and problems are not so peculiar after all. These nutshells of truth have blessed me, both as a pastor and as a Christian.

This book is one man's collection of observations, anecdotes and reflections which will not only bless his contemporaries but will kindle a curiosity and affection from a people yet unborn. From having the briefest of conversations with the late Duke of Edinburgh, to memories of feeding the birds as a child, and receiving an idyllic-looking jigsaw as an older man, John deftly weaves wisdom and truth into his recollection of a life well lived. As you read this book, you will smile often. This is not just because John is a likeable man with a loving, supportive wife, and a range of interesting and amusing situations which he recalls, but because every one of these anecdotes, points to One even better- the Lord Jesus Himself.

ALAN MARSDEN (Pastor)
Salem Chapel
Martin Top
Clitheroe
Lancashire

BIBLE READINGS JANUARY

1 January

> 'The Lord replied, "My Presence will go with you and I will give you rest". Then Moses said to him, "If your Presence does not go with us, do not send us up from here". Exodus 33:14-15

Suggested Reading Joshua 1:1-9

It was a great honour for Pat to be invited to a garden party at Buckingham Palace and an honour for me to accompany her. It was over twenty-five years since we had last visited London, and we knew that travelling by tube to our accommodation on Drury Lane would be for us 'country yokels' a considerable challenge.

Arriving at King's Cross station, we bought tickets for Covent Garden but were somewhat disorientated by the hustle and bustle of our capital city. We made our way to the appropriate platform and Pat approached a well-dressed man. 'Can you help us?' She said. 'We are from the Yorkshire Dales and want a train to Covent Garden'. The man, a solicitor from South Africa, could not have been more helpful, telling us to 'stick with him' as he would be alighting at Holborn Street, the previous station.

He advised Pat to conceal her purse as this was London, not the Yorkshire Dales, and within minutes, we boarded the train together. We chatted, and then to our delight and slight embarrassment, he did not get off at Holborn Street, but got off with us at Covent Garden and escorted us to our accommodation on Drury Lane. What a lovely man, and he literally went out of his way to help us.

The believer is on a journey from earth to heaven---a journey which can be fraught with dangers and difficulties. But we are never on our own. That which was promised to Moses and to Joshua during the days of their pilgrimage, has been promised to every child of God. His Presence will go with us. At the beginning of a new year, what a comfort and encouragement to know we have a Guide and a Friend, who accompanies us every step of the way.

Peace comes not from the absence of trouble but from the presence of God

(Alexander Maclaren)

2 January

> 'Surely, I was sinful at birth, sinful from the time my mother conceived me'. Psalm 51:5

Suggested Reading Romans 3:9-20

My son told me the first two words spoken by our youngest granddaughter, after the usual 'mummy' and 'daddy' and they were significant words. She picked up a toy, held it tightly to her chest and then, when approached by her older siblings, said 'mine, mine.' But when her siblings picked up their toys, she approached them and said, 'share, share.'

Her parents had never sat her down and said 'today we are going to teach you how to be selfish and jealous'. They had no need to for, although there is an attractive innocence about young children, they are still born with a sinful nature.

Jealousy, envy selfishness are not vices which have to be taught; they are inherent in every human being. The Psalmist David fully recognised this and confessed 'I was sinful at birth, sinful from the time my mother conceived me'. How sad this biblical truth is so often denied and youngsters are not given the discipline and guidance they require.

Original sin is in us, like the beard. We are shaven today and look clean, and have a smooth chin; tomorrow our beard has grown again, nor does it cease growing while we remain on earth. In like manner, original sin cannot be extirpated (completely destroyed); it springs up in us as long as we live.

(Martin Luther)

3 January

> Jesus said, "The Kingdom of God has come near. Repent and believe the good news". Mark 1:15.

Suggested reading Acts 2: 22-41

For many years, Employment Exchanges/Jobcentres issued the British Visitor's Passport (BVP) on behalf of the Passport Office. It was a single-page cardboard document, valid for one year, and could be obtained on sight of an applicant's birth certificate.

One day, 'Ricky', a cockney was on 'passport' duty, when an elderly man arrived with his application form, photograph, and birth certificate. As he was leaving, he asked Ricky, 'Do I need a jab?' This was a reasonable question as inoculations were necessary for travel to certain countries. Being a cockney, Ricky thought the man was asking, 'Do I need a job?'

His response was unequivocal. 'A jab? What do you need a jab for? You are on holiday, aren't you? Just go and enjoy yourself.'

The biblical gospel cannot be preached without repentance being emphasised, and yet some would seek to do that. They offer a therapeutic Jesus who can make sinners happy, not a crucified Jesus who died to make them holy. But our hearts need to be jabbed, cut, and convicted of sin before we can ever truly trust Jesus as Saviour. And it is then our deeds which prove the reality of our repentance.

Men will never come to Jesus and stay with Jesus unless they really know why they are to come and what is their need. Those whom the Spirit draws to Jesus are those whom the Spirit has convinced of sin. Without this conviction of sin, men may seem to come to Jesus and follow for a season, but they will soon fall away and return to the world.

(J.C. Ryle)

4 January

> 'An inheritance that can never perish, spoil or fade. This inheritance is kept in heaven for you, who through faith are shielded by God's power until the coming of the salvation that is ready to be revealed in the last time'. 1 Peter 1:4-5

Suggested reading Matthew 6: 19-24

We had a Blue Badge for Aaron's Motability vehicle, and when it needed renewing, we made an application to the County Council. The replacement came, but within weeks, I detected that the ink on the badge was starting to fade. This did not pose a problem until I received a parking ticket because the details were ineligible. I appealed against the decision but got short shrift from the parking company, who assured me that blue badges do not fade. I contacted the County Council and received an apologetic response. They had never known it to happen before, but the ink used on a batch of Blue Badges had proved faulty and had resulted in numerous complaints. The council asked for details of the parking company and subsequently the parking ticket was rescinded. Disappointingly, I heard nothing from the parking company, who had all but accused me of tampering with the Blue Badge.The hymn-writer said 'change and decay in all around I see' and on earth that is true of all our possessions, even our prized possessions. With the passing of time, everything perishes, spoils or fades. But what characterises earth does not characterise heaven. Our reward, our inheritance---Jesus and His salvation---that will never change or decay. It will be fresh and new, bright and shining throughout the eternal ages

> Fading is the worldling's pleasure
> All his boasted pomp and show;
> Solid joys and lasting treasure
> None but Zion's children know
>
> (John Newton)

5 January

> 'Nothing in all creation is hidden from God's sight. Everything is uncovered and laid bare before the eyes of him to whom we must give account'. Hebrews 4:13

Suggested reading Matthew 22:23-32

A young man, well known to me, came into the Jobcentre, desperate for any kind of work. This was a pleasant surprise because when I had interviewed him in the past, he had shown no appetite for work. He assured me that he was prepared 'to consider anything' and I arranged for him to be interviewed for work as a builder's labourer. He got the job and I rejoiced at his change of heart and my success in getting him into employment.

My joy, however, was short-lived, as browsing through the local paper a few weeks later, I read that this man had been in court, charged with a serious offence. The judge was of a mind to send him to prison but having heard from his defence lawyer, he had decided on a suspended prison sentence.

Why this change of heart? The lawyer explained that his client, having been unemployed for almost two years, had at last obtained work and was now able to support his family. For this reason, he pleaded with the judge not to impose a custodial sentence. Shortly afterward, having deceived both me and the judge, the man gave up his job and was again on benefits.

We can be deceived. The 'wool can be pulled over our eyes', but that can never be the case with God. He sees right through the excuses, the pretence, the hypocrisy---he knows the 'real' me and the 'real' you. He knows whether I am truly sorry for my sin and if my repentance is sincere. The Lord is omniscient, and therefore he is the only judge whose verdict will be fair and indisputable.

How few of us live one life and live it in the open! We are tempted to wear a different mask and play a different role according to each occasion. This is not reality but play-acting, which is the essence of hypocrisy.

(John R.W. Stott)

6 January

> 'Let the message of Christ dwell among you'. Colossians 3:16

Suggested reading Psalm 119: 97-112

I went with my brother to preach at the harvest thanksgiving services in a Yorkshire Dales village. We took the afternoon service and were told where we would be having tea, prior to the evening service.

When we arrived at the house, the lady said, 'I am sure, on such a beautiful afternoon, you don't want to come inside just yet. Go for a drive and come back at 5pm.' We did as she suggested, and when we got back a most acceptable tea was set before us. But instead of engaging in conversation, the lady sat in her chair and watched a television programme. We got the distinct impression that we were not altogether wanted and we certainly did not feel at home.

Does the Word of God feel at home in our hearts? Not if we ignore or doubt it. Not if we resent or resist it. But if we welcome and obey the Word, even when we are humbled and rebuked by it, then the Word of God will feel at home.

I want to know one thing, the way to heaven…. God, himself has condescended to teach the way… He hath written it down in a book. Oh, give me that book! At any price give me the book of God.

(John Wesley)

7 January

> Jesus said: 'So you also must be ready, because the Son of Man will come at an hour when you do not expect him'.
> Matthew 24:44

Suggested reading 2 Peter 3: 1-10

I am sure that all banks today have a wide array of security systems, but in the 1960s, things were not quite as sophisticated. At the sub-branch, where I worked, we pressed a button, a light flashed and the alarm sounded. The system was tested monthly and there were occasions when the alarm went off unintentionally.

What was the response of passers-by to the alarm going off? The truth was--- no response. No one ever telephoned the police or took any kind of action. People just assumed it was a practice or a false alarm and so continued with their shopping or whatever else they happened to be doing.

Warnings are given in the Scriptures and the alarm is constantly given by preachers but they are largely ignored by the majority of people. 'God will not intervene. Jesus will not come again. There will be no Day of Judgement'. That is the general consensus. We have been warned about these things but they have not happened in the past---why should we expect them to happen in the future?

How we need to understand that no alarm in Scripture is a false alarm. True, we do not know the timing, but we do know every warning will be fulfilled. God will intervene. Jesus will return. We shall be judged. Are we ready and prepared for these momentous events?

I am daily waiting for the coming of the Son of God.

(George Whitfield)

8 January

> 'Religion that God our Father accepts as pure and faultless is this: to look after orphans and widows in their distress and to keep oneself from being polluted by the world'.
> James 1:27

Suggested reading Matthew 9:18-25

As a child and as an unconverted teenager, I heard my grandfather preach and pray. And yet, it was something else which made a deep impression upon me. Well into his eighties, he spent two or three afternoons a week, visiting the sick and those in need. On Wednesdays, when he visited us in Morecambe, after lunch he would catch the bus to Heysham. Here he called on an aged aunt, before walking the three miles back to our home. On route he visited sick and housebound people whom he knew in Morecambe.

At a quarter past five, the door would open and Grandad had returned---having been a signalman on the railway, you could set your watch by him. We would then sit round the fireside, whilst he updated us on all the people he had visited.

According to the New Testament, this is authentic Christianity, demonstrated by the Lord Himself. Jesus not only preached to the multitudes but had compassion on them and fed them. Having trusted Christ as our saviour, we must now follow Him as our example.

I would not give much for your religion unless it can be seen. Lamps do not talk but they do shine.

(Charles H. Spurgeon)

9 January

> ' For the wages of sin is death, but the gift of God is eternal life in Christ Jesus our Lord'. Romans 6:23

Suggested reading Ephesians 2:1-10

Afternoon tea with Pat at the quaintly named Cock Pit Farm Tea Rooms in Burley in Wharfedale was something I had greatly anticipated and I was not to be disappointed. Quiche, freshly made sandwiches, natural yoghurt sundae, scone with jam and clotted cream, home -made cakes and a cup of Yorkshire tea---what was there not to like? On a scorching summer afternoon, it went down a treat.

There was, however, something which added to the joy of the occasion. I did not have to pay a thing, as it was a Father's Day gift from my daughter. Having confided it was not easy to know what to get dad and, wanting a change from book tokens and subscriptions to magazines, I can only say she made an excellent choice. One she can repeat whenever she wants.

A gift is given as a result of the generosity of the giver. God's gift of eternal life is the 'gift of gifts' as it is not temporal but everlasting. A free gift to all who will repent and trust in Christ but not a cheap gift. It was purchased only through the substitutionary death of Christ for sinners on the cross of Calvary. Free to us but supremely costly to the Godhead.

Everlasting life is a jewel of too great a value to be purchased by the wealth of this world.

(Matthew Henry)

10 January

> 'And my God will meet all your needs according to the riches of his glory in Christ Jesus'. Philippians 4:19

Suggested reading Matthew 6:25-34

As a pastor with a wife and two young children, money was often tight, and yet again and again we were to prove the goodness of God. One morning the car needed a new tyre and so off we went to Kwik Fit. As Pat and I sat in the waiting room, drinking coffee, the mechanic came with news that we did not want to hear. The car needed not one new tyre but four! Our hearts sank because we knew that, once we had paid for the tyres, there would be nothing in reserve.

As we travelled back to Ingleton, Pat said there was now no alternative ---she would have to find a job. This was something we had never wanted, as the children were still young and Pat wanted to be available to work within the church. It seemed, however, to be a case of 'needs must'.

We had lunch and that afternoon we received a phone call from social services. A few months earlier we had been accepted as foster parents and there was now a baby requiring parental care. We gladly took in the child, and as a result of the fostering allowances received, there was no need for Pat to find work outside of the home.

Our material needs can cause us anxiety and yet Jesus assures us that such anxiety is both unnecessary and unprofitable. We have his promise that, if we are his followers, then we will be provided for. 'Your heavenly Father knows' says Jesus and it is as we rest and trust in him, that our anxieties are eased and our needs are met.

What a serene and quiet life you might lead if you would leave providing to the God of providence. If God cares for you, why need you care too? Can you trust him for your soul and not for your body?

(Charles. H. Spurgeon)

11 January

> 'For he has clothed me with garments of salvation and arrayed me in a robe of his righteousness'. Isaiah 61:10

Suggested reading Matthew 22:1-14

On receiving the invitation to a Royal Garden Party at Buckingham Palace, Pat graciously asked me to accompany her. Weeks were spent in dress shop after dress shop, looking for that special outfit. Eventually she found what she was wanting and very nice it looked to. So much time had been spent concentrating on Pat's outfit that I mistakenly thought I had passed 'under the radar'---but I hadn't.

One Sunday morning, just a few weeks before the special day, I said to Pat, 'I think this suit will be alright for the garden party'.

I immediately sensed I had said the wrong thing. A look of disgust came over her and she almost snapped, 'You are not going to the palace dressed like that'.

What I thought was good enough was, apparently, not good enough for the Queen, and within days, I was choosing not just a new suit but all the accessories as well.

Many think they are alright and can appear before God just as they are, but the Bible says no. 'All our righteous acts are like filthy rags' (Isaiah 64:6) Even our best deeds are all spoiled and tainted by sin. We each need a new suit which God provides when we come to repentance and to faith in his Son. The new suit being nothing less than the righteousness of Christ Himself.

God has charged or imputed the guilt of our sin to his Son, Jesus Christ and has imputed or credited Christ's righteousness to us.

(Jerry Bridges)

12 January

> 'For it is by grace you have been saved, through faith---and this is not from yourselves, it is the gift of God---not by works, so that no-one can boast' Ephesians 2:8

Suggested reading 2 Samuel 9

My father was born in Yorkshire but I was born and raised in Lancashire. However, for over 40 years I have lived in the white rose county, first in North Yorkshire and now in West Yorkshire.

Yorkshire is known as God's own country and anyone born in the county is proud of where they come from and what it has to offer. This pride is not without good reason as Yorkshire is the largest county and incorporates cities, seaside towns and the beauty of the Yorkshire Dales.

It is also the birthplace of many notable people, from almost every walk of life. Amy Johnson, the aviator, William Wilberforce, the slave emancipator, Len Hutton the cricketer, Charlotte Bronte the author, Percy Shaw, the inventor of cat's eyes---and many, many others.

This pride in the county was reflected when I was recently in a café in Otley. At the next table, there was an elderly gentleman with these words on his T-shirt 'British by birth, Yorkshire by the grace of God'.

My testimony and the testimony of every true believer is very different---'Sinner by birth, citizen of heaven by the grace of God'. We can rightly be proud of the county of our birth but we are even more excited by heaven---the country that God has prepared for his people. We do not deserve or merit heaven. We cannot earn or work for it. Salvation and heaven are only ours through the grace of God.

Amazing grace, how sweet the sound. That saved a wretch like me.

(John Newton)

13 January

> 'Rejoice always, pray continually. give thanks in all circumstances; for this is God's will for you in Christ Jesus'.
> 1 Thessalonians 5:16-18

Suggested reading Matthew 6:5-13

When our daughter was at university, we arranged for her to have a telephone installed in her student accommodation. The phone was installed on 21st September but when she received her first bill, she was being charged for calls that had been made from the 7th September---a fortnight before the phone had been installed.

It fell to dad to try and sort out the problem. Thankfully, at that time, you could still speak to a BT supervisor, and over a period of time, I spoke to a most helpful man. Indeed, I developed quite a relationship with him. We were on first name terms and we chatted about our wives, our children, our work and many other things. The relationship developed because the problem was not resolved right away.

We might think how wonderful it would be if every request was granted, every situation resolved and every need met the first time we brought it to the Lord in prayer. But would it be? I suspect not, because it would mean that little time was spent in his presence. We would make the request and not think about the One to whom we were praying.

No, because prayer is not immediately answered, it necessitates going to the Lord again and again. We then spend time in his presence, and as we do so, our relationship with Christ grows and develops.

We must learn to spend quality time with God.

(Derek Copley)

14 January

> 'Encourage one another and build each other up' 1 Thessalonians 5:11

Suggested reading Jeremiah 1:4-10

I was a nervous young man when I took my first faltering steps as a preacher. To be faced with a 'sea of faces' was not something I had ever previously experienced. I could identify with the prophet Jeremiah 'I do not know how to speak; I am too young'. (Jeremiah 1:6)

There was, however, one country chapel where I immediately felt at ease. Towards the front, there sat a man with a shining, beaming face, and throughout the service, he would nod approvingly. What an encouragement to a novice preacher.

'Uncle John' had preached but rather than now preach, he felt his calling was to encourage and reassure other preachers. This was a ministry he faithfully fulfilled until he was called home in his nineties. Many a preacher can testify as to how much they were helped by this godly man.

As preachers, we hope to encourage the congregation, but the congregation can also encourage the preacher. A smile, a nod, a heartfelt 'amen' can make all the difference to a preacher who is tired and struggling. 'Uncle John' was a 'Barnabas' and we thank God for all who are encouragers in the church today; those who seek not only to encourage the preacher but every believer.

More people fail for lack of encouragement than for any other reason.

(Anon)

15 January

> 'Jesus said-----"For the Son of Man came to seek and to save the lost". Luke 15:9-10.

Suggested reading Genesis 3:1-10

One warm summer evening after school, my friends and I were playing cricket in the street, outside the home of a bachelor school master. Each morning, he went for his train at seven and did not return until six in the evening. All was going well until a wayward shot sent the ball over his wall and broke a window.

We stopped the game of cricket and then amused ourselves with hopscotch or other such games that occupied children in the 1950s. We continued---or we did----until 6pm, when, there, in the distance turning into the street, we saw Mr. R, the schoolmaster. What happened next? Well, we scarpered. You could not see our feet for dust. And why? We had no desire to meet the man, we had offended; the man whose window we had broken.

In Genesis 3, Adam and Eve hide from God for the very same reason. They had no desire to face the One whose commandment they had broken. It is not---as some think---God who hides from men and women but rather men and women who, because of their sin and disobedience, hide from God. That is why Jesus had to come into the world ---he came 'to seek and to save the lost'.

The chief reason people do not know God is not because he hides from them but because they hide from him.

(John. R. W. Stott)

16 January

> 'Be alert and of sober mind. Your enemy the devil prowls around like a roaring lion looking for someone to devour'.
> 1 Peter 5:8

Suggested reading 2 Corinthians 11:21-29

In order to help the family budget, I became a paperboy, and for several years, whatever the weather, I was up at 6 am and ready for the morning delivery. The money was not great---twelve shillings a week, I seem to recall---but it was my first taste of work and something which I very much enjoyed.

There was only one downside and that was the likelihood of being bitten by a dog. I was invading their territory and they had every right to retaliate. Dogs outside posed the greater danger, but some dogs were waiting inside, ready to pounce as the paper came through the door. Only hand dexterity sometimes ensured that one finished the round with all fingers still intact.

I was bitten twice and until my daughter got her own canine pet, those experiences caused me, for years afterwards, to be wary of dogs. The first occasion, a barking mongrel ran at me and bit my leg, whilst on the second occasion, the dog was rather more subtle. A non-barking corgi slowly came towards me before, unexpectedly, sinking its teeth into my ankle.

In parts of the world today, Satan is not barking as a dog but roaring as a lion. Believers are being persecuted, imprisoned, and martyred as the devil attacks the body of Christ. In the west, for generations we have been spared such attacks, but there is evidence that Satan is now beginning to bare his teeth.

However, such is his subtlety, the 'roaring lion" can become an 'angel of light'. He introduces false teaching into the church which is attractive but deceptive, and the undiscerning are led away. We are back to the Garden of Eden, where the fruit was attractive but Satan used it to deceive Adam and Eve. We must ensure that 'we are not unaware of his schemes'.

Satan does far more harm as an angel of light than as a roaring lion.

(Vince Havner)

17 January

> 'Are not two sparrows sold for a penny? Yet not one of them will fall to the ground outside your Father's care. And even the very hairs of your head are all numbered. So, don't be afraid; you are worth more than many sparrows'.
> (Matthew 10:29-31)

Suggested reading Psalm 23

My grandfather, and to a lesser extent my grandmother, were cat lovers, and I cannot remember a time when there was not a feline in their home. A variety of 'moggies' including a tortoiseshell, a Manx cat without a tail and even a cat with three legs were all long-term residents.

Grandmother was not sentimental about animals and I can recall cold winter nights with cats purring in front of an open fire---or they were until half-past eight. Then grandmother would, unceremoniously, get hold of the cats and put them out of the back door. No cat slept overnight in her house.

My grandparents lived on a busy road and, inevitably there were cats which fell victim to the traffic. My grandfather coming across any dead cat would pick it up and bring it home to be buried. A small area of his garden became a cat cemetery.

The concern which my grandfather had for cats is but a pale shadow of the concern which God has for all of his creation. Sparrows, we would say are 'two a penny' but they are still the objects of His care. How much more are believers---made in his image, redeemed by his Son---objects of his care and watchfulness? The very hairs of our head are all numbered and are of some value to him. Let us rejoice that we have such a Father in heaven.

God who made all things; on earth, in air, in sea
Who changing seasons brings. He cares for me.

God who sent His Son, to die on Calvary
He, if I lean on Him, will care for me.

(Sarah Betts Rhodes)

18 January

> 'When your words came, I ate them; they were my joy and my heart's delight'. (Jeremiah 15:16)

Suggested reading. Psalm 19: 7-11

When Desmond--our daughter's dog--was two, to my shame, Pat encouraged me to get in on the act and to at least send him a birthday card. My knowledge of the canine world is somewhat limited but as far as I know, dogs cannot read. It, therefore, seemed sensible to get him a card with a difference--a card he could eat.

Pat has spent years card making but this one was quite unique as strips of dog beef were attached to the front of the card. Losing all sense of reason, I even composed a verse for inside the card.

Desmond is two today
And so we want to say
As a special treat
A card you can eat
Woof-woof, Hip-hip, Hooray

Desmond duly arrived and after the singing of 'happy birthday', he totally ignored my verse and scoffed the meat. Probably the best card he has ever received. An amusing incident but it reminds me of the words of Jeremiah:

He DISCOVERED the WORD. 'When your words came'. Have we discovered that the Bible is the greatest book of all? It is the word of God. He DIGESTED the word. 'I ate them'. Do we 'eat' the word of God or do we just 'taste' it or 'pick' at it? As we 'read, learn and inwardly digest' the Bible, so our souls are strengthened and nourished. We need to meditate upon the Scriptures, to hide them in our hearts, for then the word becomes to us what a life sustaining meal is to a hungry man. He DELIGHTED in the word. 'they were my joy and my heart's delight'. As we DISCOVER and DIGEST the word, all the more we DELIGHT in the word, finding treasures which thrill and satisfy the soul.

Read it to get the facts, study it to get the meaning, meditate on it to get the benefit.

(David Shepherd)

19 January

> 'The law is holy and the commandment is holy, righteous and good'. (Romans 7:12)

Suggested reading Exodus 20:1-17

Our daughter had a hamster in a cage and she regularly took it out for exercise and to clean the cage. On this particular day, the hamster saw the chance to escape and she disappeared under the floorboards. Joanna was heartbroken and for the next forty-eight hours, every effort was made to find the missing pet.

All attempts failed until there was a knock on the back door and there stood our neighbour with the errant Henrietta in his hands.

'Do you know what this is?' He asked, 'I almost stepped on it.'

I tell you there was great rejoicing in our household over the hamster that had been lost but was now found.

Some might think that putting a hamster in a cage is very restrictive, perhaps even cruel. The truth is, however, that within the confines of the cage, the hamster is far safer than anywhere else. Indeed, for the next few days, Henrietta filled her pouches with food, lest she should go missing again.

To some the Ten Commandments might seem narrow and restrictive, but God knows that it is only within those boundaries that society can be civilised, content and safe. How sad that many children are now exposed to moral danger, being brought up without any boundaries, because a previous generation has abandoned the Ten Commandments

There is nothing in the law of God that will rob you of your happiness; it only denies you that which would cause you sorrow'.

(Charles H. Spurgeon)

20 January

'The church of the living God, the pillar and foundation of the truth'. 1 Timothy 3:15)

Suggested reading Galatians 1:6-12

The old Employment Exchanges could be depressing places, often scruffy and poorly decorated. This was certainly true of the premises I worked at during the early 1970s but in the mid-1970s, the government had a change of strategy. Employment Exchanges had been responsible both for finding the unemployed work but also the paying of unemployment benefit. It was now decided to separate the two functions.

Consequently, Jobcentres came into being and what a contrast they were to the old Employment Exchanges. In Morecambe, we went into a new building with carpets and modern furniture---quite unrecognisable from the 'wooden hut' in which I had worked for the previous four years. It was a building welcomed by both staff and the public.

Unfortunately, the Jobcentre opened in Morecambe at a time of high unemployment and also at the end of the summer season. This meant that, though we had an impressive building, embarrassingly we had very few jobs to offer. I remember the manager saying, 'it is like opening a new bakery when there is a shortage of bread'. It was for this reason that some Jobcentres became known as 'joke-centres' because jobs were almost non-existent.

A church without the gospel is like a bakery without bread, a Jobcentre without jobs. It serves no real purpose and deserves to be shut down. And whilst it is always sad when a church closes, it is just as sad when a church stays open but does not preach the gospel. How we need gospel churches, Bible-believing churches---churches which are 'the pillar and foundation of the truth'.

Wherever we see the Word of God purely preached and heard, there a church exists, even if it swarms with many faults.

(John Calvin)

21 January

> 'Clothe yourselves with the Lord Jesus Christ, and do not think about how to gratify the desires of the flesh'. (Romans 13:14)

Suggested reading Colossians 3:12-17

When I started in the banking sector in the late 1960s, the dress code was still very strict, with a suit and white shirt being the order of the day from Monday to Friday, whilst a sports jacket was permitted on a Saturday morning.

After a six months probationary period, I was required to have an interview with the regional general manager, at the head office in Liverpool. Dressed in a smart suit, a white shirt, and with a recent haircut and polished shoes, I waited nervously for my appointment. To say the interview did not get off to the best of starts would be an understatement.

'Don't you think it is time you had your hair cut'? Was the opening question. The visit to the hairdresser, which had satisfied me, obviously did not satisfy Mr. M.

Sadly, the interview did not get any better when he spied a fountain pen in my breast pocket. 'Take that out of there', he said 'we are members of a profession and we must dress accordingly'.

I cannot recall how the conversation then progressed, but as I was appointed permanently on to the staff, I can only presume things got better.

'We are members of a profession and must dress accordingly'. Writing to the Colossians, the Apostle Paul said something very similar. As believers, our profession of faith is in Jesus Christ and therefore, care must be taken with our 'spiritual wardrobe'. There are things I must not wear---anger, rage, malice etc. and things I must wear---compassion, kindness, humility etc.

This is only possible as we 'clothe ourselves with the Lord Jesus Christ'. Instead of being preoccupied with temporal earthly matters, our chief concern is to be more and more like Jesus. Having trusted him as saviour, we now follow him as our example, so that increasingly, we may live as Jesus lived. Is my 'spiritual wardrobe' more important to me than my 'physical wardrobe'?

The world takes its notions of God from the people who say they belong to God's family.

(Alexander Maclaren)

22 January

> 'Righteousness exalts a nation but sin condemns any people'. (Proverbs 14:34)

Suggested reading Psalm 11

All the sewage pipes were being renewed, and for our four-year-old son, the diggers, the wagons and the earth removers provided much excitement. Before work and after work, I had to take Andrew to see the men, the machinery and the deep holes.

The work went on for several weeks, and one evening we were watching television downstairs when there was a deafening sound upstairs. Cautiously investigating the noise, I was shocked to discover that the plaster ceiling in our bedroom had come crashing down. If anyone had been in bed at the time, the consequences could have been much more serious.

We were convinced, as were many others, that the foundation of the house had been disturbed by the roadworks but our conviction was not shared by the insurance company. For Andrew, it all added to the excitement, but from then onwards, taking him to see the workmen did not have, for me, quite the same appeal.

The Psalmist asked 'when the foundations are being destroyed, what can the righteous do'? The biblical foundations of creation, marriage, work, the Lord's Day are being eroded and destroyed; the effects of which are increasingly to be seen in our broken and secular society. What can the righteous do? We can pray. We can maintain a consistent Christian witness and we can continue to trust in a Sovereign God, whose ultimate purposes will never be thwarted or overthrown. 'The earth will be filled with the knowledge of the glory of the Lord, as the waters cover the sea'. (Habakkuk 2:14)

The man who measures things by the circumstances of the hour is filled with fear; the man who sees Jehovah enthroned and governing has no panic.

(G. Campbell Morgan)

23 January

'God sent the Spirit of his Son into our hearts, the spirit who calls out "*Abba* Father". So, you are no longer a slave, but God's child; and since you are his child, God has made you also an heir' (Galatians 4:6-7)

Suggested reading Romans 8:9-17

Pat and I became foster parents with Lancashire Social Services in 1985. Initially, we cared for two babies; one we picked up from hospital when he was five days old, and the other came to us as a six-month-old baby. Christopher stayed with us for five weeks, and Michelle for six months. We were sad when the time came for them to move on.

In November 1987, we were asked to foster a multi-handicapped baby boy. Aaron came to us when he was ten weeks old and we fostered him for the next sixteen years. Friday 2nd April 2004 was a momentous day--- it was the day Aaron stopped being fostered and was adopted into our family. He became a Mollitt, and on that day everything changed. He took our name and our address. He became our child and the inheritor--- for what it was worth---of all that we possessed. And he entered into a relationship that was now permanent and not temporary

As believers we have been adopted---not fostered---into the family of God. It is a permanent arrangement, not temporary. How amazing! By nature, we are the children of the devil but, through grace, God has adopted us into his family. We needed a father but God did not need any more sons because he already had a Son who was perfect, a Son who was the apple of his eye.

How amazing that he should adopt us and grant us a change of name, a change of address, a change of status. We are now called Christians, heaven is our home, and as the children of God, we are joint heirs with Jesus and the possessors of innumerable riches. Appreciate afresh the wonder of your adoption.

I am a pilgrim and stranger on earth but I am not an orphan.

(Vance Havner)

24 January

> 'The Lord's servant must not be quarrelsome but must be kind to everyone---not resentful'. (2 Timothy 2:24)

Suggested reading Acts 11:19-26

My physics teacher was an able scientist, but one of the most ill-tempered men I have ever met. A piece of chalk or the blackboard duster often being flung at a pupil with whom he was displeased.

The treasurer of the church I attended, as a boy was the assistant manager of a building society and I am sure he was a conscientious banker. However, most Sundays, he was never at worship but arrived at the end of the service to collect the money.

There was a footballer who I greatly admired for his goal-scoring achievements, but his private life left a lot to be desired.

An able teacher, a professional banker, an exceptional sportsman---all admired and respected because of their gifts, even though their personal behaviour was sometimes questionable.

Men and women, irrespective of their characters, can often excel in their chosen occupation or interest because they are gifted. Christian service is altogether different because, beside gifts, there is the need for graces. Whatever their position in the church, the person must be qualified and capable, but the necessary graces are even more important. A covetous minister, a self-centred treasurer, or a bad-tempered Sunday School teacher, irrespective of their natural abilities, can do much harm to the cause of Christ. Barnabas was an apostle, a missionary, a teacher---a gifted man---but just as important 'he was a good man, full of the Holy Spirit and faith'. (Acts 11:24) Gifts and graces are both necessary for effective Christian service.

It is not great talents that God blesses, so much as great likeness to Jesus.

(Robert Murray McCheyne)

25 January

> 'It was not with perishable things such as silver or gold that you were redeemed from the empty way of life---but with the precious blood of Christ, a lamb without blemish or defect'. (1 Peter 1:18-19)

Suggested reading Isaiah 55:1-7

The family were coming to stay for a few days at Christmas and so off we went on a twenty-mile journey to a supermarket in Carnforth. The supermarket was heaving with people, but eventually, with a trolley full of 'goodies', off we went to queue at the checkout. I helped to pack the food into carrier bags and Pat prepared to settle the bill. Oh dear---a frantic search in her bag and purse but no bank card. She looked to me but I had neither card nor money.

All we could now do was take the shopping out of the trolley, whilst a member of staff was summoned to return the goods to the shelves. How embarrassing and how disappointing. Yorkshire puddings, meat, ice cream, biscuits, chocolates, drinks---a plethora of good things but no one to pay for them. No card. No money. No receipt.

Forgiveness of sin, peace with God, an eternal home in heaven---these all had to be paid for. As sinful people, we had nothing to offer; the debt was far too great ever to be paid for by us. We needed someone to pay the price on our behalf. And that is why Jesus came---to redeem us, to pay the price of our salvation. He went to the cross of Calvary and he paid the price 'not with perishable things such as silver or gold' but with his own 'precious blood'.

He died that we might be forgiven. He died to make us good.
That we might go at last to heaven, Saved by His precious blood.

There was no other good enough. To pay the price of sin:
He only could unlock the gate. Of heaven and let us in.

(Cecil Frances Alexander)

26 January

> The Lord God said to the serpent---"I will put enmity between you and the woman, and between your offspring and hers; he will crush your head and you will strike his heel". (Genesis 3:14-15

Suggested reading Matthew 4:1-11

In the 1960s, wrestling was a regular part of the Morecambe entertainment scene, with bouts being held, every Thursday night, in the Winter Gardens ballroom. As a teenager, I remember seeing wrestlers such as Jackie Pallo, Mick McManus, Les Kellett, and Kendo Nagasaki inciting the crowds, as they apparently inflicted torture upon each other.

Of course, it was entertainment rather than sport, and though popular in the 1960s and 1970s, wrestling declined as it became known that bouts were stage-managed and predetermined. However, this did not mean that all the physicality was fake, as broken bones and bloody noses were not an unknown occurrence. I saw wrestlers seriously injured and needing treatment before returning to their dressing rooms.

In the Bible, the great contest is between Jesus Christ and Satan, and it is true to say that the result was predetermined. It was predetermined in eternity and pronounced by God in the opening chapters of the Bible.

God predetermined Christ's victory over Satan but that does not mean that the contest was not intense and agonising. The 'heel' of Christ would be struck, implying pain and suffering but the 'head' of Satan would be crushed, implying conquest and victory. At Calvary, the outcome was never in doubt but we must never underestimate what it cost Christ to defeat Satan and to save us from our sin.

There are references in the Bible to the devil's wiles and his shrewdness. But when he gambled on his ability to unseat the Almighty, he was guilty of an act of judgement, so bad as to be imbecilic.

(A.W. Tozer)

27 January

> 'What does the Lord require of you? To act justly and to love mercy and to walk humbly with your God'. (Micah 6:8)

Suggested reading Luke 22:24-30

The man who mentored me when I first started preaching was one of the most humble men I have ever met. He never spoke about himself, so my knowledge of his past was very limited. However, at his funeral service, we learnt what we had not known before. He was a Master of Arts from Cambridge, had a distinguished war record, with medals for bravery, and had been employed as a British diplomat. He had also served on a number of influential bodies and committees. After the service, someone commented 'I never knew we'd had such a man amongst us'.

Humility is one of the greatest of all Christian virtues. In this fallen world, the prize often goes to the assertive who put themselves before anyone else. This should never be true of the child of God. He is the disciple of One who 'made himself nothing, by taking the very nature of a servant, being made in human likeness. And being found in appearance as a man, he humbled himself by becoming obedient to death---even death on a cross'. (Philippians 2:7-8) Jesus was humility personified, and as we wrestle with pride and self-seeking, we must ever keep our eyes upon him.

They that know God will be humble: they that know themselves cannot be proud.

(John Flavel)

28 January

> 'For false messiahs and false prophets will appear and perform great signs and wonders to deceive, if possible, even the elect. See I have told you ahead of time'. (Matthew 24:24-25)

Suggested reading Matthew 7:15-23

After years of having vehicles which ran on petrol, I purchased a van which ran on diesel. I put fuel in the van and we had a trouble-free ride to Hexham in Northumberland.

Having parked the van, we had lunch and an enjoyable afternoon in the town, but when we wanted to return to Ingleton, the vehicle would not start. I eventually telephoned the R.A.C. but whilst I waited for them to come, I realised what the problem was. Yes, I had put petrol not diesel in the tank, and in so doing, I had done potential damage to the engine.

The immediate remedy was to fill the tank with diesel and trust that no permanent damage had been done. Thankfully, the van did restart and we were able to get back to Ingleton.

It is a sobering thought, but Jesus said that teachers can travel far on the wrong fuel. Many have been deceived and before Christ returns, many more will yet be deceived by false teachers and false prophets. They might have impressive, successful CVs, but in their ministry, they use 'deception' and 'distort the word of God'.

One day, it will be revealed that they have been running on the wrong fuel---not the right spirit-- but in the meantime, what potential damage they are doing to the souls of men and women. We need always to be on our guard against false teachers.

Error preached as truth, has contributed to the delusion of multitudes who are lost.

(Ian. H. Murray)

29 January

> 'I, even I, am he who blots out your transgressions, for my own sake, and remembers your sins no more'. (Isaiah 43:25)

Suggested reading Matthew 12:30-37

As my grandparents grew older, every Christmas, we had a family party at their home. Around a dozen of us assembled and, it was always a happy evening, as we ate food and enjoyed games together. I remember it, also, because as a young boy, it was the one time in the year when I stayed up until after midnight.

One year, my uncle brought with him one of the first tape recorders and he hid the machine behind a chair. Later in the evening, he played it back, and Grandma was quite adamant, 'That's not me. I don't shout. I never said that',

She protested but her protests were in vain because it was her, she had said that. All her words had been recorded.

How sobering to realise that all our thoughts, words and deeds have been recorded by the Lord, and that nothing is hidden from His all-seeing eye. This is a record we would not want any of our family or friends to see but it is known to God. 'Everything is uncovered and laid bare before the eyes of him to whom we must give account' (Hebrews 4:13)

Thankfully, that need not be the end of the story. For all who repent and turn to Jesus, there is a wonderful promise. 'I am he who blots out your transgressions---and remembers your sins no more'. In Christ the tape is wiped clean.

Release! Signed in tears, sealed in blood, written on heavenly parchment, recorded in heavenly archives. The black ink of the indictment is written all over with the red ink of the cross: 'the blood of Jesus, his Son, purifies us from all sin'

(T. De Witt Talmage)

30 January

> 'For you know the grace of our Lord Jesus Christ, that though he was rich, yet for your sake he became poor, so that you through his poverty might become rich'. (2 Corinthians 8:9)

Suggested reading Ephesians 1:3-10

When our son was born, we opened a Building Society account in his name and handed him the passbook when he was a teenager. At the time there was a balance of just over £200. He put the book in the back of a drawer and forgot all about it, until he came across it some ten years later. He went into the local office of the building society to have the book brought up to date, and to his amazement discovered he now had a balance of almost £3000. In the intervening years the building society had become a bank and its customers had benefitted from a windfall payment. Our son was far richer than he had ever imagined himself to be.

I visited an elderly lady who, though she lived in a detached bungalow, was far from wealthy. She was on welfare benefits and kept selling items of furniture to help with household expenses. One afternoon, she said she had some money which she wanted me to count, and she produced three envelopes from a cabinet. I was astounded to discover £3000 in the first envelope, £4,000 in the second envelope and in the third envelope---£5,000.

On expressing my surprise, the lady told me that the money was not hers as it belonged to her sister. This might have once been the case, but as her sister had died some years previously, the money was now hers. She was living in relative poverty, having no idea just how rich she really was.

I fear that can also be true of believers. How rich we are in Christ---our sins are forgiven, we are reconciled to God, we are indwelt by His Spirit and we have the promise of an eternal home in heaven. We are heirs of God, joint heirs with Christ. How rich we are and yet at times, we walk in this world as though we are spiritual paupers.

Shame on us for being paupers when we were meant to be princes'.

(D. Martyn Lloyd-Jones)

31 January

> 'Ascribe to the Lord the glory due his name; bring an offering and come before him. Worship the Lord in the splendour of his holiness'. (1 Chronicles 16:29)

Suggested reading Matthew 15:1-9

In 1985, I was speaking at a missionary conference in Harrogate. The conference ran from the Friday night till Sunday lunchtime, and the organisers kindly invited my wife and children to join them for the weekend. The Saturday afternoon was delegated as 'free time' and this was more than agreeable to me as, on that day, Manchester United were playing Everton in the FA Cup final. However, I was faced with a dilemma---how could my twelve-year-old son and I watch the match, when there was no TV in our accommodation?

And so it was that I came up with a somewhat devious plan. Pat had an aunt and uncle in the town, and I suggested that we call on them and hopefully, Uncle Ted would be a football fan. It was around 2.45 pm when we knocked on their door and we got a most enthusiastic reception, but the TV was not switched on. As kick-off time approached and there was no movement towards the TV, I politely asked whether it would be possible for Andrew and I to watch the cup final.

Although Uncle Ted was not interested in football, they were only too happy to oblige. Consequently, we watched a match which was to be historic, even if not for the best of reasons. It was the first FA Cup Final in which a player had been dismissed.

My motives for calling at the house of Uncle Ted and Aunty Peggy were not entirely pure, but what about when we come to the house of God? Do we come to worship the Almighty, to meet with him, to hear his Word or have we alternative motives? Do we come out of habit or to ease our conscience? Do we come just for the music or to meet with friends? What is our motive? Jesus said of the Pharisees, 'these people honour me with their lips, but their hearts are far from me'.

Without the heart it is no worship. It is a stage play. It is an acting a part without being that person, really. It is playing the hypocrite'.

(Stephen Charnock)

BIBLE READINGS FEBRUARY

1 February

'He has set a day when he will judge the world with justice by the man he has appointed. He has given proof of this to everyone by raising him from the dead. (Acts 17:31)

Suggested reading John 3:16-21

In the late 1960s, when I worked in a bank, the doors always shut promptly at 3pm. If the doorbell rang at 3.05, there was always a panic amongst the staff. It meant the bank inspectors were in town and immediately they would set about checking what money was in the tills and in the safe. If anyone had been dishonest, there was no opportunity to put things right---the inspectors had come.

On one occasion, an inspector was known to some of the staff because prior to being promoted, he had worked in that particular branch. He was the same man, but his role was now very different. He was not there to help or assist, as he might have done before, but rather to inspect and pass judgement on what the staff had done.

When Jesus comes again, He will be the same Jesus. This was promised by the angels when Jesus ascended. 'This same Jesus who has been taken from you into heaven, will come back in the same way you have seen him go into heaven'. (Acts 1:11) He will be the same Jesus but his role will be very different. He came the first time to save---He comes a second time to judge. Today we stand between his first and second comings, so how vital it is that we trust Jesus as Saviour before we face Him as our Judge.

If we are believers in Jesus Christ we have already come through the storm of judgement. It happened at the cross.

(Billy Graham)

2 February

> 'Your Father knows what you need before you ask him'. (Matthew 6:8)

Suggested reading 1 Kings 17:7-16

Our honeymoon was booked in North Wales but a rail strike meant we were dependent upon the kindness of a neighbour to take us to Llandudno in his car. The arrangement being that he would then come back for us on the following Saturday.

However, during the course of the week, the rail strike was settled and so we would be able to come back by train. The night before we were due to return, we went down to the railway station but to our consternation, we discovered that we did not have sufficient money for the tickets.

That evening, in the Christian guest house, we prayed specifically for this urgent need to be met. The following morning, I went to settle up with the proprietor of the guest house, who greeted me with the words, 'my, you've kept that quiet. I didn't know you were on honeymoon'. I then discovered that he had knocked a few pounds off our bill and that was sufficient for us to buy the rail tickets and to get back home.

Our Father in heaven, knows every need and is able to supply every need. Sometimes, the need is met in surprising and unexpected ways but always in ways which ultimately are for our spiritual growth and benefit. We lay our requests before the Lord and wait for Him to answer, knowing that He will do what is best for His children.

He who feeds his birds will not starve his babes.

(Matthew Henry)

3 February

> 'Jesus said: "Truly I tell you, unless you change and become like little children, you will never enter the kingdom of heaven". (Matthew 18:3)

Suggested reading Luke 18:9-17

Pat was always eager to have plenty of toys and activities to keep our grandchildren amused, whenever they were staying with us. Reluctantly, I agreed we could have a children's slide in the back garden, but regretted the decision when the equipment was far larger than I had anticipated. This made mowing the lawn difficult, as each time the grass needed cutting, the slide had to be manoeuvred into a different position. However, I could not deny that the slide gave our grandchildren hours of amusement.

One day, we invited a group of elderly people from a church, some miles away to come for lunch. It was a beautiful day but, before we ate, one lady---nearer to eighty than seventy---commented 'I would love a go on that slide'. I was unsure whether it was a good idea, but with no health and safety warnings on display, I let her go ahead. There were several steps to climb, which she cautiously mounted, and then she came down the slide at a far greater pace than she had gone up. She landed on the grass with a shout of triumph and was far more excited than any of our grandchildren had been.

When Jesus said 'unless you change and become like little children, you will not enter the kingdom of heaven', he was not advocating childishness but rather childlikeness. Little children are characterised by simplicity, humility, obedience and trustfulness, and these qualities must be seen in all who wish to enter the kingdom of heaven.

There is a vast difference between childlike faith and childish faith. A childlike faith calls the believer to remain forever in a state of awe and trust of the heavenly Father. A childish faith balks at learning the things of God in depth. It refuses the meat of the gospel, while clinging to a diet of milk.

(R.C. Sproul)

4 February

> 'We know that we are children of God and the whole world is under the control of the evil one'. (1 John 5:19)

Suggested reading Matthew 13; 18-23

From childhood, I have always enjoyed feeding the birds. I threw out crumbs and scraps of bread as a boy, but in more recent times, I have bought seeds from the garden centre. This pleasurable activity became even more enjoyable when, during the Covid pandemic, we were largely confined indoors.

I had two feed-holders in the garden, but I was puzzled by how soon they needed refilling. Indeed, we bought seeds in bulk to save unnecessary visits to the garden centre. Either the birds in West Yorkshire were strangely hungry, or there was another explanation.

The mystery was solved when, early one morning, looking out of the window, I saw a squirrel enveloped around the feed-holder. Unlike, the birds he had not just come for a peck; he had come for his morning breakfast. Further observation confirmed the squirrel was not a sole diner but was accompanied by his friends. Whilst not objecting to feeding the squirrels, it grieved me that this was at the expense of the birds.

A remedy was found at the local garden centre by purchasing a squirrel-proof birdfeeder. So, there are now feeders for both birds and squirrels, but one of the feeders can only be accessed by the birds. This means the squirrels can still feed but cannot snatch seeds away from my feathered friends.

Satan swiftly takes the word from hard and unresponsive hearts. It never penetrates because the devil convinces the unbeliever that what is being heard is of no importance. Preoccupied with temporal, earthly things, they never reflect or meditate on the word of God. How we need to pray for understanding minds and softened hearts whenever the Bible is expounded and the gospel preached.

Satan commonly stops the ear from hearing sound doctrine before he opens it to embrace corrupt.

(William Gurnall)

5 February

'I will dwell in the house of the Lord for ever'. (Psalm 23:6)

Suggested reading Hebrews 11: 8-16

Forty years had passed by since we had last bought and sold a house, and estate agents in 2018 were unrecognisable from what they were in 1978. In those far-off days, estate agents did not have websites and the publicity material was very basic---not much more than typed particulars with small photographs glued on to a piece of cardboard.

Today things are very different. Every house merits a professionally produced brochure with stunning images, skilfully drawn floor plans and a narrative designed to grab the attention of any prospective buyer. Indeed, when our house went on the market and we received the brochure, I scarcely recognised it. I commented to Pat 'Why ever are we selling? Who would want to move from a house and garden as beautiful as this'?

A buzz phrase today is a 'forever home'---a house so perfect that it is where a person intends to live for the rest of their lives. Strangely, I have met people who have bought their 'forever home' but within years the 'forever' has become 'temporary' and the search for the 'ideal 'home has recommenced.

The only truly 'forever home' is the one provided by Christ in heaven for those who have trusted Him on earth as Saviour. It is a home we cannot move from and never would want to move from because it is perfect. For the real attraction of heaven is not just the absence of pain and sorrow but the immediate presence of Christ. Jesus said, 'Father, I want those you have given me to be with me where I am and to see my glory'. (John 17:24) Heaven is to be with Jesus, where He is and that is why it will be our 'forever home'.

In our first paradise in Eden, there was a way to go out but no way to go in again. But as for the heavenly paradise, there is a way to go in but no way to go out again.

(Richard Baxter)

6 February

'Submit yourselves then to God. Resist the devil and he will flee from you'. (James 4:7)

Suggested reading 1 Corinthians 10:1-13

I once attended a meeting of Alcoholics Anonymous---I hasten to add as an observer and not as a member. At the time I was trying to help a man with an alcoholic addiction.

In the meeting I was most challenged by the testimony of a recovering alcoholic. He explained that, as a successful businessman, he and his wife had enjoyed three or four foreign holidays every year. But he testified that he had now not been out of the country for over three years.

The reason was this: he had always had a fear of flying and so each time before he boarded a plane, he had always had a few stiff drinks. Now he dare not take the risk of touching alcohol and was not prepared to put himself in the way of temptation.

What a challenge to the believer. Are there not times when we put ourselves in the way of temptation? We go to places or we engage in activities, where it is easy for Satan to 'gain an advantage over us'. It is no use praying 'Lead us not into temptation', if we then run right into it.

If you don't want the devil to tempt you with forbidden fruit, you had better keep out of his orchard'.

(Doug. Barnett)

7 February

> 'Brothers and sisters, stand firm. Let nothing move you. Always give yourselves fully to the work of the Lord, because you know that your labour in the Lord is not in vain' (1 Corinthians 15:58)

Suggested reading Romans 16: 1-16

As a teenager, for several years, I was a member of Lancaster Chess Club. It was a well-attended club with team matches and individual tournaments. Our secretary was a retired college lecturer but besides being our secretary, he was also the club captain and our best player.

One evening, we were returning from a tournament where the team had been beaten and unusually Mr. Turner had also lost his match. As we travelled, he sighed and said 'I don't wish to make excuses but it isn't conducive to good chess when someone says "Mr. Turner, the kettle is boiling'. The poor man; not only was he our secretary, captain and best player---he was expected to brew the tea as well.

There are believers in churches who are 'weary in well doing' because they are overworked---having to do everything---whilst others 'sit at ease in Zion', not willing to accept any responsibility. More than ever, the church of Jesus Christ today needs men and women who will give themselves 'fully to the work of the Lord'.

Since my heart was touched at seventeen, I believe I have never awakened from sleep, in sickness or in health, by day or by night, without my first waking thought being how best I might serve my Lord.

(Elizabeth Fry)

8 February

> 'Then Peter got down out of the boat, walked on the water and came towards Jesus. But, when he saw the wind, he was afraid and, beginning to sink, cried out "Lord save me". (Matthew 14:29-30)

Suggested reading Acts 16:25-34

Pat and I were courting and had taken a day trip by train to Dumfries. It was a sunny July afternoon and what could be better than a boat ride on the River Nith? We paid the boatman and I took the oars. 'Do you know what you are doing?' asked a nervous Pat. 'Of course I do' was my response, keen to impress my fiancée.

'The truth will out' and it did not take too long to emerge. As we drifted ever further from the bank and headed towards the river bridge, the boatman began to gesticulate. He then came towards us shouting 'you should have told me if you did not know how to row'. Attaching a rope to the boat, he towed us to safety and the young man who got out of the boat was much humbler than the confident man who had got into the boat.

'Are you saved?' Was a question I remember being asked as a teenager but not a question that is often asked today. Are you a Christian? Are you a believer? These are perhaps the equivalent questions being asked today. And yet, it is the question 'are you being saved?' that emphasises our true condition.

Our situation is even more desperate than being saved from drowning. We have rebelled against God, broken His commandments and are heading for judgement---we desperately need to be saved. And that is what Jesus came to do. He left heaven for earth, became a man and went to the cross, all because He loved us and desired to save us from our sins. Have we thanked Him and trusted Him as our saviour?

The casting out of demons is ascribed to God's finger; his delivering of Israel from Egypt to his hand; but when the Lord saves a sinner, it is his 'holy arm' which gets him the victory'.

(W. Pink)

9 February

> 'We do not have a high priest who is unable to feel sympathy for our weaknesses, but we have one who has been tempted in every way, just as we are---yet he did not sin. Let us then approach God's throne of grace with confidence, so that we may receive mercy and find grace to help in time of need'. (Hebrews 4:15-16)

Suggested reading Mark 6:45-52

In the Department of Employment, I worked with a fraud investigator who was collecting evidence on those who were working, yet claiming benefits. I am sure that investigators now have far more sophisticated equipment at their disposal but nevertheless, this man used his ingenuity.

He sat in his car, reading his newspaper, but he had cut out two squares in the paper, so that he could see the man who was painting, building or cleaning windows. To the casual passer-by, he appeared to be just reading his paper, but his eyes were constantly on those who were defrauding the public purse.

In the gospel account, Jesus was praying, on a mountain, to His Father in heaven but He saw His disciples as they toiled and struggled on the sea. One eye was on His Father but His other eye was on His disciples. Now, in heaven, Jesus intercedes to His Father but His heart is still with His followers on earth. We are never abandoned or forsaken. We will never be tried beyond what we are able to bear. Our sympathetic Saviour watches, knowing how much we can and cannot endure.

If I could hear Christ praying for me in the next room, I would not fear a million of enemies. Yet the distance makes no difference; he is praying for me.

(Robert Murray McCheyne)

10 February

"Return faithless people", declares the Lord, "I will cure you of backsliding". (Jeremiah 3:14, 22)

Suggested reading Revelation 2:14-22

Ted, from a non-Christian background, had only been converted a few weeks, when an elderly believer kindly invited him and me to spend an evening with her and her husband. It was a most enjoyable occasion with good food and lively conversation.

As we prepared to leave, this godly lady took Ted to one side and whispered 'It's all very sad, but my husband has grown rather cold'. Ted was not familiar with 'evangelical jargon' and was somewhat taken aback, wondering why she was sharing with him the state of her marriage. As we travelled home, I explained to Ted that she was referring to her husband's walk with the Lord.

Charles Spurgeon, the 19th century preacher, speaking about the church at Laodicea said: 'They were not cold, but they were not hot. They were not unbelievers, yet they were not earnest believers. They did not oppose the gospel, neither did they defend it. They were not working mischief, neither were they doing any great good. They were not disreputable in moral character, but they were not distinguished for holiness. They were not irreligious but they were not eminent for zeal. Their condition was one of mournful indifference and carelessness.

Is this a description of my heart or my church? The remedy today is still what it was in Jeremiah's day. We need to return to the Lord who has promised, 'I will cure you of backsliding'. The Lord who saved us is the only one who can restore us, and in His compassion and mercy, He has promised to do so.

If you find loving any pleasure more than your prayers, any book better than the Bible, any house better than the house of the Lord, any table better than the Lord's table, any persons better than Christ, or any indulgence better than the hope of heaven----be alarmed.

(Thomas Guthrie)

11 February

'It is God who judges: he brings one down, he exalts another' (Psalm 75:7)

Suggested reading Romans 13:1-7

We were on holiday with my brother and his family at Greystoke, near Keswick. The accommodation was adequate but not too spacious for four adults and five children. Most days the weather was wet and trips out were necessary in order to preserve family harmony.

Returning home one evening, with tired and hungry children, we counted an unexpected problem and yet one not without precedence in the Mollitt household— we could not find the house key. As the search intensified and the frustration increased, the tenseness was broken by one of the children. 'Can't Margaret Thatcher help us'? The eight-year-old was not joking---so prominent and powerful was 'Maggie' in the 1980s, the youngster obviously thought she could do anything.

Eventually---without the help of 'Maggie'---the key was located and access gained to the cottage.

There are times when kings, presidents, emperors and prime ministers can seem all-powerful, but we must remember that their power comes from God. In a moment they can be deposed and in a relatively short time be forgotten. How much better to trust in the Eternal God than to have confidence in mortal man. The Psalmist was right: 'It is better to take refuge in the Lord than to trust in man. It is better to take refuge in the Lord than to trust in princes'. (Psalm 118:8-9)

Alternatives confront us, and between them we are obliged to choose; either God governs, or he is governed; either God rules, or he is ruled; either God has his way, or men have theirs. And is our choice between these alternatives hard to make?

(A.W.Pink)

12 February

> 'When God created man, he made him in the likeness of God. He created them male and female and blessed them' (Genesis 5:1-2)

Suggested reading Psalm 8

Our daughter and family were away for the weekend in London, and we had agreed to look after their guinea pig. On the Friday morning, I noticed Pat was clearing my desk. 'What are you doing?' I enquired. 'That is where the guinea pig's cage is going'. My mild protest fell on deaf ears, and I had to accept that for three days, I was below Daisy in the pecking order.

My daughter bought a Boston terrier puppy, and though never a dog lover, Desmond soon won me over. However, I have to admit to being astonished when I visited the local pet store. Advent calendars for cats. Flat caps for dogs. And almost anything you can buy for a baby, you can also buy for a pet. I did not know whether to laugh or cry.

Animals are God's creation, a source of great pleasure, and should never be ill-treated. But it is man who is the crown of God's creation. Increasingly this is being forgotten with man being seen as just another animal. It is man alone who has the capacity to know and worship God, because he alone has been made in God's image and after God's likeness. It is a back-to-front world when some would rather worship a d-o-g than worship G-o-d.

Man is a creature, because he is made by God. But he is a unique creature, because he is made like God.

(Edmund P. Clowney)

13 February

> 'All have sinned and fall short of the glory of God and all are justified freely by his grace through the redemption that came by Christ Jesus'. (Romans 3:23-24)

Suggested reading Titus 3:3-8

I was not too surprised when the examiner informed me I had failed my driving test. Pulling out to pass a stationary vehicle, I misjudged the speed and distance of a car coming in the opposite direction. We were a bit too close for comfort and I noticed an immediate change in the examiner's demeanour.

Before my second attempt, I made an appointment with the optician, and being diagnosed as short-sighted, I began to wear glasses. This, perhaps, aided my driving and shortly afterwards, I successfully completed the driving test. What a thrill when I was handed the 'pass' certificate. I now had a full licence, no longer needed to be accompanied, and was a qualified driver.

I qualified as a driver because I passed a test and came up to a required standard. It was my eventual competence and ability which brought it about. Sadly, there are those who think this is how salvation is obtained, but nothing could be further from the truth. Because of our sin and rebellion, we have forever disqualified ourselves from heaven and God's salvation. Even our very best works and efforts are tainted by sin and fall short of God's perfect standard. Salvation is all of God's grace--- unmerited and undeserved.

Amazing grace! How sweet the sound,
That saved a wretch like me!
I once was lost, but now am found;
Was blind but now I see.

'T was grace that taught my heart to fear,
And grace my fears relieved;
how precious did that grace appear
the hour I first believed.

(John Newton)

14 February

> Again Jesus said, "Simon son of John, do you love me?" He answered, "Yes Lord, you know that I love you". (John 21:16)

Suggested reading Luke 7:36-50

Our son works in Singapore and due to Covid, we had not seen him or his family for two years, but they were finally able to get back for Christmas and the New Year. Facetime is most welcome in maintaining contact 'across the miles' but as Pat says 'you can talk with your grandchildren but you cannot cuddle them' Consequently it was a joy to be reunited with the family and to spend special time with our grandchildren.

The three weeks passed by all too quickly and in no time at all, we were having to say our farewells. Before embarking on the return journey, they all had to take a Covid test at the airport, and we could not but be moved by a text from our ten-year-old granddaughter. 'I love you Nana and Granddad. The test was negative. I was hoping it would be positive and then I could have spent more time with you'. An expression of love that brought a tear to our eyes.

We can demonstrate our love for Jesus in many ways: by telling Him, obeying Him and by loving others. But do we ever show our love for Jesus in an extravagant way, as the sinful woman did? A sacrificial act? A generous deed? A magnanimous response? As believers, we too have been forgiven much---we should therefore love much.

You must love Christ with a sincere love, with a new love, with an entire love, with a superlative love; and you must love him for himself, and not for anything you get from him.

(James Renwick)

15 February

> 'Oh the depth of the riches of the wisdom and knowledge of God! How unsearchable his judgements and his paths beyond tracing out'. (Romans 11:33)

Suggested reading Isaiah 55

One of my church members faithfully handed out gospel leaflets in Ingleton and distributed *Challenge,* an evangelical monthly newspaper to certain houses in the village. The paper had details of Ingleton Evangelical Church attached to it. One of the homes 'challenged' each month was that of Ernest and Beatrice, a couple who had retired to Ingleton.

One late September afternoon, Beatrice was out, when friends from the Methodist church were distributing harvest produce in the village. Calling at her home, fruit and flowers were handed to Ernest and, when Beatrice returned, she just assumed that the harvest gifts had come from the Evangelical Church. Consequently, the following Sunday, Beatrice decided to attend the church, in order to express her appreciation.

Our harvest thanksgiving services had been at the beginning of September and so we were somewhat perplexed by what Beatrice was telling us. Eventually, the confusion was sorted out and Beatrice began to attend the services regularly. She listened most attentively as the Word was preached and having professed conversion, she was baptised and received into the membership of the church.

'God moves in a mysterious way. His wonders to perform'. So wrote William Cowper, the hymn-writer, and that was certainly true in the conversion of Beatrice. The Challenge newspaper, the distribution of harvest gifts and a misunderstanding all being used to bring Beatrice to a knowledge of the truth.

God's ways are behind the scenes but he moves all the scenes he is behind.

(John Nelson Darby)

16 February

> 'Therefore, since we are surrounded by such a great cloud of witnesses, let us throw off everything that hinders and the sin that so easily entangles, and let us run with patience the race marked out for us. Let us fix our eyes on Jesus, the author and perfecter of our faith'. (Hebrews 12:1-2)

Suggested reading Colossians 3:1-11

A friend was driving in the countryside when he saw a pheasant lying in the road. He stopped, picked up the bird and put it in the back of his car. After a few minutes, he heard a stirring, and to his shock, he discovered the pheasant was not dead but stunned. Stopping the car, he released the bird back into the open.

Having a shower, I noticed a daddy long legs coming to a sudden halt, as it was overtaken by the water. I turned off the shower, gently picked up the lifeless insect and placed it carefully on the window sill. I continued my shower and minutes later, the daddy long legs was still not moving. However---much to my surprise and delight—he was not dead for later, as I cleaned my teeth, he was climbing the bathroom wall.

We might sometimes think that we have mastered a particular sin and that, as far as we are concerned, it is now dead. How sobering and humbling it is, to discover that the sin is not dead but still alive and active. Where sin is concerned, there is never room for complacency or confidence in self. We must constantly 'fix our eyes on Jesus, the author and perfecter of our faith'.

I find not one corruption of my vile heart is dead, though some seem now and then asleep.

(John Newton)

17 February

> 'Whoever claims to live in him must walk as Jesus did'.
> (1John 2:6)

Suggested reading Titus 2:11-14

In the 1970s, many a Saturday in September and October was spent witnessing on the promenade at Blackpool. It was the time of the illuminations and crowds flocked from all the country to the resort every weekend. At times, it almost felt as though one was witnessing in Sodom and Gomorrah but nonetheless, never a weekend passed by without some profitable conversations.

One afternoon, I got talking to a young man who was not hostile; on the contrary he understood and agreed with what was being said to him. I was hoping that I was challenging him, but then he said something which challenged me. 'I am outside the church', he said 'because my dad is on the inside'.

Apparently, his father was a well-known lay preacher but his son was so ashamed of how his dad treated his mother and children, he had vowed never to go to church again.

I had no reason to doubt the truth of what the young man was saying, but what a challenge to all pastors, preachers and professing Christian believers. Am I a hypocrite---one thing in church on a Sunday and something altogether different, the rest of the week? Having trusted Christ as my Saviour am I now following Him as my example?

It is the mark of a hypocrite to be a Christian everywhere, except at home.

(Robert Murray M'Cheyne)

18 February

> 'Taste and see that the Lord is good; blessed is the man who takes refuge in him'. (Psalm 34:10)

Suggested reading John 6: 41-51

As an itinerant preacher, I have been entertained in numerous homes, where I have enjoyed excellent food and fellowship. One Sunday, we were having a meal, when our host and hostess insisted that we had a piece of apple pie. Apparently, this was no ordinary apple pie, because the previous day, this hospitable couple had travelled over twenty miles to a bakery where, in their words 'they make apple pies to die for'. With such a recommendation, we willingly accepted their invitation and were not disappointed---the apple pie was delicious.

But how did we prove that the apple pie was delicious? By checking the ingredients or by accepting the enthusiastic re-commendation of our friends? No, we only proved the quality and richness of the apple pie by tasting it for ourselves.

Jesus is the One who satisfies, the One who gives eternal life but we can only prove it to be so, when we personally trust him for ourselves. Sadly, there are many who will never take that step of faith. They will debate Him, scrutinise Him, question Him but only those who trust him as Saviour experience the wonder of his salvation. We have to 'taste' and it is then we 'see that the Lord is good'.

It will not save me to know that Christ is a Saviour: but it will save me to trust him to be my Saviour.

(Charles H. Spurgeon)

19 February

> 'We must go through many hardships to enter the kingdom of God'. (Acts 14:22)

Suggested reading 2 Corinthians 1:8-11

Accompanied by Aaron in his wheelchair, we got on the train at Clitheroe and alighted at Bolton. To leave the station, one had either to use the lift or the stairs, but having the wheelchair, there was, for us, only one option. It was then that the problems started, as the lift was 'out of order'.

I went to an office on the station, to be met by a most unhelpful man. His only solution being, that we caught a train to Salford and then a train back from Salford to Bolton. We would then be on a platform where the lift was working. At first, I thought he was being humorous, but no, he was deadly serious.

I declined his advice and went back to Pat and Aaron. We were pondering what to do when we were approached by a young man who, recognising our dilemma, asked if he could assist. To get off the platform, there were numerous steps to mount, but obtaining the help of two other men, we eventually managed to get the wheelchair up the stairs and onto the streets of Bolton. How grateful we were to those men who put 'health and safety' considerations to one side and came to our rescue.

It is rare for a person to be saved and then immediately be 'lifted' to heaven. We set out on a pilgrimage and we soon find there are 'stairs' to mount. 'Stairs' which are steep and 'stairs' which cause us to feel tired and weary. We need helpers, who will help by prayer and support, when the way is uphill and strenuous. We need helpers---can we be a helper to others?

Christ went by the cross to the crown, and we must not think of going any other way.

(Matthew Henry)

20 February

> 'Dear children, continue in him, so that when he appears we may be confident and unashamed before him at his coming'. (1 John 2:28)

Suggested reading Matthew 24:36-44

As a small boy, if I was misbehaving, my mother would sometimes say, 'your dad will be home soon'. I did not know whether dad would be home early, at his normal time or whether he would be working overtime, in which case I would be in bed when he got home.

The important thing was not the timing of his coming but rather the certainty of his coming. The actual timing was uncertain but his coming was indisputable. This fact was usually sufficient for me to change my ways and to be a better-behaved young child.

It is the same with the Second Coming of Christ. Christians can get caught up with the timing of His coming, which is uncertain, rather than with His actual coming which is certain. He may come today, next year or it may be in a hundred years' time, in which case, we shall all be in our beds when he comes! But he is coming and because he can come at any time, we need to be ready all of the time. This, of itself, should cause us to walk in this world in such a way that we shall be 'unashamed before Him at His coming'.

He who loves the coming of the Lord is not he who affirms it is far off, nor is it he who says it is near. It is he who, whether it be far or near, awaits it with sincere faith, steadfast hope and fervent love.

(Augustine)

21 February

> 'Prophecy never had its origin in the will of man, but men spoke from God, as they were carried along by the Holy Spirit'. (2 Peter 1:21)

Suggested reading 2 Timothy 3: 10-17

During my ministry in Ingleton, I officiated at a number of weddings. These were special but often nervous occasions as all involved were anxious for the day to go ahead without mishap. At one wedding, I had an added responsibility for, not only had I to conduct the wedding but I was asked, by the father of the bride, to write the speech, he was to give at the reception.

In some ways, this was more demanding than taking the actual service but eventually I put something together and later listened when the speech was given. It was a strange experience for, whilst it was my speech, it had the mannerisms and personality of the bride's father stamped upon it.

The Bible was written by forty human authors over a period of two thousand years, but they were not setting out their own thoughts or ideas. Rather they spoke and wrote as they were moved by the Spirit of God. They were real people, not robots and stamped their own individual style and personality on their writings.

The Gospel of Mark is different to the Gospel of Luke, just as the Epistles of Paul are different to the Epistles of Peter. But 'carried along by the Holy Spirit' means that what they wrote is perfect, consistent and without error.

If there be any mistakes in the Bible, there may as well be a thousand. If there be one falsehood in that book, it did not come from the God of truth.

(John Wesley)

22 February

> 'But when the kindness and love of God our Saviour appeared, he saved us, not because of righteous things we had done, but because of his mercy. He saved us through the washing of rebirth and renewal by the Holy Spirit'. (Titus 3:4-5)

Suggested reading Luke 18:9-14

I don't mind admitting it, but I am among the worst when it comes to DIY. Pat's father was able to turn his hand to anything and prior to our marriage, she assumed that all men were the same. In that sense, I have been a big disappointment to her.

One day I was attempting to knock a nail into a wall in the hall, but by the time I had finished, the wall in the hall had almost been replaced by a hole in the wall. I am lethal with a hammer, recognising that in my hand, it can be a weapon of mass destruction.

The advantage is I am never nagged by Pat as to why some 'job' is still outstanding---she is happy for me to leave it well alone and to let others more competent do the work.

There is, however, one area of DIY where we all fail and that is DIY salvation. Sadly, there are multitudes like Cain in the Old Testament and the Pharisees in the New Testament who feel that by their own works and efforts, they can make themselves acceptable to God. This is an awful delusion for even our very best works are all tainted and spoiled by sin. We are entirely dependent on the perfect, finished work of Christ on the cross, for our salvation.

I have taken my good deeds and bad deeds and thrown them together in a heap and fled from them both to Christ, and in him, I have peace.

(David Dickson)

23 February

> 'Always be prepared to give an answer to everyone who asks you to give the reason for the hope that you have'. (1 Peter 3:15)

Suggested reading Colossians 4:1-7

Table tennis is a game I have played all my life. It began at school and continued throughout my days in the civil service. Since then, at family gatherings or Christian conferences, I have never been slow to pick up a bat and ball. I do not claim to be more than an average player, but it is a game which has brought me many hours of enjoyment.

The serve is one of the key skills a table tennis player can have, as the speed and spin of the ball can give the server an immediate advantage. Unfortunately, this is not a skill which I have altogether mastered. My strength is not so much in serving the ball but rather in being able to return it, and points are often won when opponents become frustrated, as their smashes are returned.

Whist few believers are called to preach, every believer is required 'to give an answer'. When we are challenged about our Christian faith, we have to be able 'to get the ball back'; to give reasons why we are Christians and why the faith we have embraced is relevant and logical. If questioned by the seeking or the cynical, are we able to do that?

Evangelism in the New Testament sense is the vocation of every believer. There is, therefore, something radically wrong, when we imply that personal evangelism is the province of those who have the time and/or inclination to take special courses and learn special techniques.

(Roland Allen)

24 February

> 'Strengthen the feeble hands, steady the knees that give way; say to those with fearful hearts, "Be strong, do not fear; your God will come---to save you". (Isaiah 35:3)

Suggested reading Exodus 17:8-16

It is four years since I broke my wrist, and due to the skill of the surgeon, I regained the use of my right hand. However, due to my failure to do the necessary physio, the wrist is far from being perfect. As a result, my grip is weak, and I have become something of a liability, especially in cafes and restaurants. Drinks knocked over, and a glass cup falling to the ground have embarrassed me and caused unnecessary work for the staff. Just a few days ago, I picked up three bottles of milk from the doorstep but only two reached the safety of the fridge!

Shaking hands, too, has also become a potentially hazardous activity. After one service, a man gripped my hand and gave it such a shake, I almost winced with the pain. I have never been a 'hugger'---not advisable anyway during the pandemic---but perhaps I ought to consider this less painful way of greeting.

There are times when our hands are weak, our knees are knocking, and our hearts are fearful. It is then we need the ministry of encouragement. We need others to come alongside us and to reassure us that the God who was faithful in Isaiah's day, is still faithful in our day. Whatever our present trials, the Lord will come to us and often, it will be through our brothers and sisters in Christ.

God does not comfort us to make us comfortable but to make us comforters.

(J.H.Jowett)

25 February

> 'If you, then, who are evil, know how to give good gifts to your children, how much more will your Father in heaven give good gifts to those who ask him'? (Matthew 7:11)

Suggested reading Luke 11:1-10

Before a busy Sunday, it was my usual custom to go to bed in good time the previous evening. One Saturday, just before midnight, we were awakened by a persistent knocking at the front door. I went downstairs and asked, 'Who is there'? 'You don't know me', came the response, 'but I am an evangelical'. I opened the door and there, before me, was a tramp wanting something to eat and a bed for the night.

Pat made him a snack and I then took him down to the church hall and made him comfortable for the night. The following morning, he had a cooked breakfast, came to the morning service, and after a roast lunch, he went on his way with a couple of pounds in his pocket. The accommodation must have been to his liking, as he was to visit us on further occasions.

On that first Saturday evening, he was a man in urgent need and the need was so great that he did not hesitate to get me out of bed at midnight. I think he would have been a Methodist, a Baptist or an Anglican---depending on whose door he was knocking.

Clifford was not ashamed to make his need known and to plead for help. In the parable of 'The Friend at Midnight', Jesus advocates a similar response. With confidence, urgent needs can be brought to our Heavenly Father, knowing that He will provide according to His good and perfect will. We are encouraged to 'ask', to 'seek' and to 'knock'.

The great tragedy of life is not unanswered prayer but unoffered prayer.

(F.B. Meyer)

26 February

> "I can do everything through him who gives me strength".
> (Philippians 4:13)

Suggested reading 2 Corinthians 12:1-10

Due to an unnerving childhood experience, my son-in-law has a phobic fear of flying. It was, therefore, ironic when his family received, as a Christmas present; a voucher for a thirty-minute scenic pleasure flight from Teesside Airport. The voucher was for three and with the two grandchildren immediately booking their places, the question was--- would the third seat be occupied by their mum or by their dad?

Holidaying together with them, one July afternoon, we all made the journey to the airport---the big issue of the day being still unresolved. My son-in-law was obviously very nervous but the staff and especially the pilot could not have been more reassuring. Eventually Al. took the courageous decision and was escorted to the light aircraft: no doubt feeling like a man being led to the gallows.

The aircraft took off and we all waved as it headed towards the coast. Half an hour later, the plane landed safe and sound, and Al got out a different man to the one who, just a short time earlier, had entered the plane. We bought him a PILOT badge, commending him for doing, what he thought he would never be able to do.

There are times when, for the believer, times can be hard and circumstances can be difficult. We cannot see a way out or a way forward. But Paul testified that, as he relied on the power of Christ, so he was able in every situation to endure and be content. We can take heart and be encouraged for, no matter how impossible our circumstances might seem to be, that same strength is still available today.

He giveth more grace when the burdens grow greater.
He sendeth more strength when the labours increase.
To added affliction, he addeth his mercy.
To multiplied trials, his multiplied peace.

(Annie Johnson Flint)

27 February

> 'The heart is deceitful above all things and beyond cure. Who can understand it'? (Jeremiah 17:9)

Suggested reading Psalm 139

Recently, I have been suffering from lower back pain and there are times when I find it difficult to get out of a chair. Diagnosing myself, I am sure the cause is Desmond the dog pulling in one direction and me trying, often unsuccessfully, to restrain him.

Back pains are amongst the commonest of complaints but it is not always easy for medics to discern whether patients are genuine or not. A doctor friend recalls how, on one occasion, he signed a man off work for a fortnight, only later to see the man in a pair of overalls and with a ladder on his shoulder. It appears the man just wanted time off work, in order to paint his house.

Our excuses can be similar to a bad back. Others cannot always discern whether they are real or whether they are phoney. But God can. He knows whether 'I am too tired' or 'I am too busy' or 'I cannot afford it' is the truth, or whether they are just selfish excuses. 'You are familiar with all my ways. Before a word is on my tongue, you know it completely, O Lord'. (Psalm 139:3-4)

There is a vast difference between an excuse and a reason. There may be some validity in the latter but not in the former'.

(Donald Grey Barnhouse)

28 February

> 'He who guards his mouth and his tongue keeps himself without calamity'. (Proverbs 21:23)

Suggested reading James 3:1-12

The hot summer of 2018 brought a huge moorland fire to an area of seven square miles above Bolton. The fire went on for forty-one days, and at its height, there were over thirty-five engines, supported by specialist wildfire fighting teams from other areas of the country. Night after night, it provided compelling viewing on the local TV news.

From his home, my four-year old great-nephew could see the apocalypse and was understandably concerned. One day, pausing for a moment, he enquired of his mother, whether he could take a cup of cold water on to the moor and put the fire out. Good for Jimmy that he wanted to extinguish the fire but sadly the blaze could never be put out with just a cup of water.

In a similar way, the tongue can start a fire which sometimes is never put out. How many unhappy, broken relationships begin when 'something is said' and a hurt is caused, which is never healed. The Bible has much to say about our mouths, our tongues, our lips and it is wise counsel which we do well to heed. Once spoken, a word can never be returned and the damage caused can be irreparable. Far better to keep silent than to speak in 'haste' and have to repent in 'leisure'.

One of the first things that happen when a man is really filled with the Spirit is not that he speaks with tongues, but that he learns to hold the one tongue he already has.

(J. Sidlow Baxter)

29 February

'The Lord will watch over your coming and going both now and for evermore'. (Psalm 121:8)

Suggested reading Acts 8:26-35

I first started preaching in 1969 but did not have a car until 1979. This meant that for ten years I was dependant on public transport or the kindness of relatives and friends to get me to preaching appointments.

One Sunday afternoon, I was due to preach at Clapham (North Yorkshire) and decided to take the train from Morecambe. All went well until the train developed a mechanical fault at Wennington station. Several minutes passed and then I asked the conductor when he thought the train would go again. His not-too-helpful response was 'Your guess is as good as mine'.

With time going on, I was now faced with a dilemma---did I stay on the train or get off and hitchhike to Clapham? I decided on the second option and coming out of the station, I put my thumb up and to my surprise the first car stopped. In the car, was a Christian young man, whom I knew and he was on his way to see his fiancée in Ingleton. Desmond put his foot down and I arrived at the church in Clapham with just two minutes to spare.

'Chance, coincidence', says the unbeliever, but was it? When Philip met the Ethiopian in the vast Gaza desert, was that chance or coincidence? If Philip had come five minutes sooner, the Ethiopian would have been reading Isaiah 52; five minutes later and he would have been reading Isaiah 54. But he arrived when the Ethiopian was reading Isaiah Ch.53---a chapter which more than any other speaks of the suffering and death of Christ. 'Then Philip began with that very passage of Scripture and told him the good news about Jesus'. (Acts 8:35) It was not coincidence---it was God, in his providence, bringing together at a precise moment, a preacher and a seeker after truth.

In a similar way, I believe that, outside Wennington station, the Lord brought a preacher and a car driver together.

God not only orders our steps; he orders our stops.

(George Muller)

BIBLE READINGS MARCH

1 March

'You shall not covet'

Suggested reading Mark 10:17-23

My wife and I attended the Summer Fete at the local school because, being a governor, I felt we ought to be there. It was an opportunity to meet staff, parents and children and, also to financially support the school. We bought various inexpensive items and then, at one stall for fifty pence, Pat was invited to guess the name of a large teddy bear. Pat, never having bought raffle tickets or entered such competitions, felt a little uneasy but somewhat reluctantly 'named' the bear.

At the end of the afternoon, to her great embarrassment, hers was the winning name, and before a multitude of watching eyes, she was presented with the cuddly toy. Not wanting to keep her 'ill-gotten gain', Pat gave it to a grateful young mother. Her husband---a fellow believer---enjoying Pat's obvious discomfort, immediately renamed the teddy bear 'Raffles'.

Was Pat coveting? Was this a breaking of the 10th commandment? Some might say 'yes' but I would say 'No' and for the following reason. Pat named the teddy bear not hoping to win it, but desperately hoping not to win it. There was no craving or longing in her heart for the teddy bear, rather the exact opposite

Covetousness is a serious sin, a breaking of God's commandment, but let us not be made to feel guilty when our motive was not gain, just a desire to help school funds.

He is much happier that is always content, though he has ever so little, than he that is always coveting, though he has ever so much.

(Matthew Henry)

2 March

> 'Jesus said to them, "Watch out! Be on your guard against all kinds of greed; a man's life does not consist in the abundance of his possessions". (Luke 12:15)

Suggested reading Joshua 7: 19-26

One Saturday evening in January, I took my son from Ingleton to watch an ice hockey match at the Blackburn Arena---a venue opened by Christopher Dean and Jayne Torvill. There was plenty of razzmatazz, and all in all, it was an enjoyable experience, until we returned to where we had parked our car. To our dismay, we discovered that the passenger side window had been smashed and the car radio ripped out. We were thankful that the car itself had not been stolen. However, it was a draughty ride back to Ingleton; the car heater not being able to compensate for the cold wind blowing through the window.

The next day I had a journey down the M6 to Wigan, necessitating an early morning temporary repair to the window. This was not altogether successful, and I was pleased when the full repair was done the next day. So much hassle and upset because someone coveted my car radio.

Covetousness is a sin which so often leads to other sins. With Achan, it resulted in theft, whilst David's coveting of his neighbour's wife, resulted in adultery and murder. (2 Samuel 11:2-5, 14-15) Covetous—the 10th commandment--- is, therefore not a minor sin but a deadly sin, because it spawns so many others. It takes us where we never intended to go. 'Be on guard against all kinds of greed'.

Beware of the beginnings of covetousness, for you know not where it will end.

(Thomas Manton)

3 March

> 'The kingdom of heaven is like a merchant seeking beautiful pearls, who when he had found one pearl of great price, went and sold all that he had and bought it'. (Matthew 13:45-46)

Suggested reading Matthew 20:1-16

Alec was born in the North East but was evacuated to Ingleton during the war. He had never doubted the existence of God but readily confessed to me that his busyness with other things, meant God had always been at the fringe and not the centre of his life. Work, together with family and community responsibilities, had preoccupied his time.

In retirement, Alec was determined to put things right and consequently, he began to attend church, not in any spasmodic way but every Sunday morning and evening. Sometime later, Alec asked to see me and calling at his home, he confessed his personal faith in Christ and requested church membership. It was a moving and joyous occasion, when he was welcomed as a church member.

Not long afterwards, Alec was diagnosed with terminal cancer and no further treatment was available. His last Christmas was spent in hospital being discharged on the 30th December. Imagine my surprise when at 11.15, the next evening, Alec arrived at the watchnight service. He was pale and weak but this could not break his resolve to end the old year and to start the New Year with God. Alec passed away in February and whilst I mourned the death of a dear friend, I rejoiced that having come to know the Lord, in later life, he was now in the presence of his Saviour.

With the passing of the years, work, business, family responsibilities, and time-consuming hobbies can become all-absorbing. And the things of God become ever more neglected. How amazing, even at the eleventh hour, men and women can repent and embrace the Saviour. No one can be saved at the twelfth hour, for then life is over; the day of grace has passed. But, at the eleventh hour, even after years of neglect, you can know the salvation of God. Don't delay a moment longer.

When God says 'Today', the devil says 'Tomorrow'

(Anon)

4 March

> 'Let your light shine before men, that they may see your good deeds and praise your father in heaven'. (Matthew 5:16)

Suggested reading Philippians 2:12-18

Whilst we were putting our shopping into the car at the supermarket, a vehicle drew up beside us and an elderly lady got out. What attracted our attention was the colour of the car: lime green but so bright, that we almost felt we needed sunglasses.

Pat commented on the colour and the lady had an interesting response. 'I got tired of parking my car in supermarket car parks and then not being able to find it, so I thought I would buy a car I could not avoid seeing'.

Having spent time trying to locate my car when coming out of supermarkets, football stadiums, agricultural shows etc., I knew precisely what she meant. In her case it was definitely 'mission accomplished'.

As believers do we stand out from those who have no Christian profession? Stand out, not because we are awkward and difficult but rather because something of Christ is to be seen in us. Joseph shone in the house of Potiphar. Daniel in the court of King Nebuchadnezzar. Stephen before the Jewish Sanhedrin. They were dark places but they stood out as men of faith. The same challenge and calling still comes to believers today.

One of the first songs I sang in Sunday School might sound simplistic to some but it is true whatever our age.

Jesus bids us shine with a pure, clear light
Like a little candle burning in the night
In this world of darkness, so we must shine
You in your small corner and I in mine.

(Susan B. Warner)

5 March

> 'Do not believe every spirit, but test the spirits to see whether they are from God, because many false prophets have gone out into the world'. (1 John 4:1)

Suggested reading Acts 17:10-15

Three or four times a year, we went with Aaron to the children's hospice. The respite break was always most welcome and one of the attractions was the sumptuous food provided. We never returned home without having added a few pounds to our weight.

One lunchtime, we were tucking into our apple pie and custard, when there was an anguish cry from the kitchen. 'Stop ---that isn't custard, it is cheese sauce'. The mistake had belatedly been discovered in the kitchen but apparently, none of the diners had noticed.

The cheese sauce was of similar colour and texture to the custard, but the taste, though different, was not sufficiently different for anyone to complain. Without the cry from the kitchen, I would have continued eating the apple crumble but now it was not quite as appetising as before.

False teachers can be both subtle and convincing. What they say can be so near to the truth, it is mistaken for the truth. In Acts 17, the Bereans 'examined the Scriptures every day to see if what Paul said was true'. We must do the same. Everything must be tested by the Scriptures, and if it is contrary to what is written in the Word of God, then both the man and his message must be rejected.

Discernment is not simply telling the difference between what is right and what is wrong; rather it is the difference between right and almost right.

(Charles H. Spurgeon)

6 March

> 'I know whom I have believed. And am convinced that he is able to guard what I have entrusted to him for that day'. (2 Timothy 1:12)

Suggested reading Mark 8:31-38

When I worked in a bank, a number of people had safe deposit boxes, in which were placed coins, jewellery, wills, documents, family heirlooms etc---things which were precious and of great value to them. These boxes were handed to us and then they were safely kept, under lock and key, in the vaults of the bank.

Significantly, the boxes were not left at premises more frequently visited---the corner shop or the public house. Why? They were too valuable. Others might lose them or destroy them but our customers had confidence that we could keep what they had committed into our care.

The most precious thing we have is our eternal soul. Jesus said it is of more value than 'the whole world' and yet how few recognise this. The devil wants our souls and therefore it is vital that we commit them into the care and keeping of One who is stronger than Satan. Thank God, the Lord Jesus Christ is not only able to save our souls but also to keep them. Committed into his care, they are safe and secure both for time and for eternity.

The soul is such a thing, so rich and valuable in its nature, that scarce one in twenty thousand counts of it as they should.

(John Bunyan)

7 March

> 'O Lord, you have searched me and you know me. You know when I sit and when I rise; you perceive my thoughts from afar'. (Psalm 139:1-2)

Suggested reading John 10:1-15

Working in the Jobcentre in the 1970s unemployment was high and it was difficult to place men and women in suitable work. However, one of my colleagues---a retired RAF officer---thought, wrongly, that most of the unemployed did not want to work. Thus, when conducting interviews, he saw it as a challenge between him and the person in front of him--- a challenge he was determined to win. One morning, he was interviewing a smartly dressed man and sitting at the next desk, I overheard the conversation.

'Have you tried getting work in a warehouse again?
"I have never worked in a warehouse'.
'Well, you told us you had. What about going back on the buses?
'I have never worked on the buses'.
'Well, it says here you have. Did you enjoy being a caretaker?
'I have never been a caretaker'.
'You are John Turner---aren't you'? 'John William Turner'?
'No I don't have a middle name'.

Only then did the 'penny drop' and my colleague realised he had the wrong documents. The John Turner before him was a redundant professional man.

It sometimes does seem that we are just a number or a statistic, and even when we have a name that does not always show our true identity. How different with the Lord. There can be no mistaken identity with Him. He knows *'when I sit and when I rise. He perceives' my thoughts from afar'*. He discerns *'my going out and my lying down'* and *'is familiar with all my ways'*. All our individual needs are intimately known to the Lord. What a comfort.

God knows us altogether and cares for us, in spite of that knowledge.

(J. Charles Stern)

8 March

> 'Always give yourselves fully to the work of the Lord, because you know that your labour in the Lord is not in vain'. (1 Corinthians 15:58)

Suggested reading 1 Corinthians 3:1-9

As enthusiastic young converts, a group of us set ourselves the task of placing a gospel leaflet into every home in Morecambe. It was a colossal undertaking, with thousands of suitable leaflets being purchased, together with a detailed street map of the town.

Every Monday evening, winter and summer, rain or shine, with zeal and enthusiasm, we took to the streets. One of our number even went out on Christmas Day, as it fell on a Monday.

In our naivety, we perhaps thought we would convert the town but the visible response was negligible. Just three people made contact with us---one of whom we were able to help, as he was having contact with the Jehovah Witnesses.

However, we had done what Jesus commanded us to do. We had attempted to take the gospel to the inhabitants of our town and though feeble our efforts we could leave the outcome in His hands. Paul reminds the Corinthians that we cannot convert anyone but we can and must 'plant the seed', knowing that 'only God makes things grow'. May we be faithful and not despondent, as we seek to share the gospel with needy people.

The gospel is not to be preserved like the Crown Jewels, locked in our ecclesiastical strong room. It is to be spread locally, and to the ends of the earth

(Herbert M. Carson)

9 March

'I, the Lord do not change' (Malachi 3:6)

Suggested reading Hebrews 13:1-8

Going to the dentist---whilst never an enjoyable experience---is much less daunting now, than it was when I was a child. Gas for tooth extraction was never pleasant, whereas today the anaesthetic is administered with little discomfort.

My dialogue with dentists has always been somewhat limited, as it is not easy to speak when sitting in a chair. However, there was one dentist with whom I had a particular rapport. As he himself attended church, he was intrigued to know I was a minister, so the conversation was often interesting.

As I got to know him, I felt able to pass on to him Bible and hymn verses, particularly apt for dentists! For example, Psalm 84:10 'Open your mouth wide and I will fill it' and 'Change and decay in all around I see'. (Henry F. Lyte). Light-hearted conversation which led to the discussion of more serious topics.

Immutability is a big theological word, but it simply means God is not susceptible to change. He is always the same. This attribute makes God so different from everything He has created. Not only our teeth, but all material things are subject to change and decay, as are a nation's moral and spiritual standards.

In a world of constant change and turbulence, we can rest in a God whose character will never change, whose power will never diminish, and whose glory will never fade. Praise him for His immutability.

God cannot change for the better, for he is perfect; and being perfect, he cannot change for the worse.

(W. Pink)

10 March

> 'Who can discern his errors? Forgive my hidden faults'.
> (Psalm 19:12)

Suggested reading Leviticus 5:14-19

Is there a cure for snoring? If so, my wife would be delighted to know it. To my grandchildren, if not to Pat, it is a source of great amusement, especially when we are together on holiday. And yet, I myself am quite unaware that I do snore because it is something I only do when I am asleep and not conscious.

I do not underestimate the problems associated with snoring, as I know that in the case of two elderly ladies, it caused a breakdown in their relationship. They were sharing a bedroom on holiday when one complained she was being kept awake by the snoring of the other. Her friend objected to this insinuation, assuring her companion, 'I never snore'. A somewhat presumptuous statement to make I would suggest.

I can snore without knowing it, but much more seriously, I can sin without knowing it. And, as with snoring, whilst I might be unaware what I am doing, others are only too aware. I might be blind to my pride, my bitterness, my boasting, my jealousy, but others are able to see it. They see the sin being manifested, but it is only God who truly sees the depth and depravity of my sin.

I have a record by Jim Reeves and it contains these words:

'Forgive the sins that I confess to Thee
Forgive those secret sins I do not even see'.

(M. Battersby)

This should be our daily prayer for as I confess 'those secret sins I do not even see', so I have the comfort and assurance of knowing that 'the blood of Jesus, his Son, purifies us (me) from *all* sin'.

The ultimate proof of the sinner is that he does not know his own sin'.

(Martin Luther)

11 March

'Where two or three come together in my name, there I am with them' (Matthew 18:20)

Suggested reading Luke 10: 38-42

One evening, we had invited a number of friends round for an evening meal. In total, there were to be seven of us, but Pat had inadvertently set out eight places. As Pat apologised for the miscalculation, a man in the group immediately put her at ease by making a most significant comment. 'No need to apologise, Pat', he said, 'it is a reminder to us that we have an Unseen Guest.

Appropriately, on the wall as you entered our home, there was a plaque with the well-known words 'Christ is the Head of this house, the Unseen Guest at every meal, the Silent Listener to every conversation'. As we ate and fellowshipped together, those words were more pertinent than they had ever been before.

For the believer the presence of Christ is both a sanctifying truth and a source of comfort and joy. He is with us every second of every day and what an incentive that is, so to live as not to grieve his Spirit. But it also means that, in our trials and troubles, we are never on our own. We have his promise. 'Surely, I am with you always to the end of the age.' (Matthew 28:20) 'Never will I leave you; never will I forsake you'. (Hebrews 13:7) We have 'a Friend who sticks closer than a brother'. (Proverbs 18:24). Let us be thankful today for the One who is the Head, the Unseen Guest, the Silent Listener.

Within your circling power I stand. On every side I find your hand.
Awake, asleep, at home abroad, I am surrounded still with God.

(Isaac Watts)

12 March

> 'Who is like you, Lord God Almighty? You, Lord, are mighty, and your faithfulness surrounds you. You rule over the surging sea; when its waves mount up, you still them'. (Psalm 89:8-9)

Suggested Reading Mark 4: 35-41

Yeadon Tarn is a short, scenic walk, just a ten-minute ride from our home and is popular with walkers, fishermen, water sports activists, and with children who can buy pellets to feed a variety of birds. It is situated next to the Leeds-Bradford airport and planes can regularly be seen getting ready for landing and take-off. However, as it is the highest airport in the country, strong winds are often a challenge to pilots. But, as I was to discover one autumn Sunday afternoon, it can also be a challenge to walkers around the tarn.

It was a blustery day, and I was well dressed for the occasion until a strong gust of wind whipped off my cap and deposited it on the tarn. A well-loved cap, but not worth the unnecessary risk of trying to rescue it from the water. Farewell to my cap.

I have no power or authority over the wind or the water---I could not even prevent my cap from being displaced. But Jesus 'rebuked the winds and the waves, and it was completely calm. No wonder the disciples were amazed and cried, 'What kind of man is this'? As yet, the disciples did not fully recognise that Jesus was not just a man but a God/man. Only one who is 'Lord God Almighty' could 'rebuke the winds and the waves'. By His power over disease, death and nature, Jesus demonstrated His deity. Jesus is God as well as man.

Jesus did not cease to be the Son of God when he became man. He did not drop his deity which is an impossible thought. He remained what he was and added what he had not had, namely a human nature, derived out of a woman, a human mother. He became the God/man.

(Richard C. H. Lenski)

13 March

> 'Repent and do the things you did at first. If you do not repent, I will come to you and remove your lampstand from its place'. (Revelation 2:5)

Suggested reading Revelation 3:14-22

There is a popular pathway behind our home used by runners, hikers and dog walkers. It is an attractive walk with trees, shrubs and flowers, whatever the season of the year. I walk my daughter's dog on the pathway most days and always enjoy its beauty and tranquillity.

And yet, as a railway enthusiast, I also feel a measure of sadness because for one hundred years, until it fell victim to the 'Beeching Axe' in 1965, the pathway was part of the Ilkley to Otley railway. Now, although a useful community facility, there is precious little left to indicate that it was ever a railway. The pathway no longer fulfils the purpose for which it was originally intended.

In many a village, town and city in the UK, there are buildings which were once churches----buildings where believers worshipped and the gospel of Jesus Christ was faithfully preached. Now, these buildings are homes or warehouses or business premises but they are not being used for the purpose they were originally built.

Sadly, sometimes, the 'lampstand' has been removed because churches failed to preach the gospel. The warning given by the risen Lord to C1st churches, is a warning every church needs to take to heart.

A church without the truth is not a true church, and a church without the Spirit is not a true church.

(Anonymous)

14 March

'The gift of God is eternal life in Christ Jesus our Lord'.
(Romans 6:23)

Suggested reading Acts 8:14-24

Jumble sales were frequently held on a Saturday afternoon at Ingleton Community Centre, in aid of charities and local organisations. Do not be misled by the word 'jumble' as many of the goods on offer were of the highest quality. Indeed, some people would travel quite a distance, in order to pick up a bargain.

From time to time, Pat went to the jumble sales and one Saturday, she came back delighted, having bought a tartan skirt that was 'as good as new'. She decided to wear it at church, the following morning but was somewhat deflated when a lady whispered in her ear 'if I'd known you'd wanted that skirt, I would have given it to you'. Yes, the skirt had been donated to the jumble sale by the wife of our church secretary.

Pat paid for what she could have had as a free gift. At least, Pat did purchase the skirt, but many people seek to do what is totally impossible. They try to earn, work for, or purchase God's salvation but it can never be obtained in those ways. It is a free gift, bought for us by Christ, and is received through repentance and faith. The Apostle Peter tells us that salvation, though free, it is not cheap. 'It was not with perishable things such as silver or gold that you were redeemed from the empty way of life handed down to you by your forefathers, but with the precious blood of Christ, a lamb without blemish or defect'. (1 Peter 1:18)

Everlasting life is jewel of too great a value to be purchased by the wealth of this world'.

(Matthew Henry)

15 March

> 'Restore to me the joy of your salvation and grant me a willing spirit, to sustain me'. (Psalm 51:12)

Suggested reading Psalm 42

We had been kindly invited to the opening of the Splash Zone at Ingleton open-air swimming stadium. We made excellent progress travelling from Burley in Wharfedale, arriving in good time for the 11 am ceremony. Getting out of the car, a passerby told me there was a 'hissing' sound and one of my front tyres was deflating.

He was right, and taking his advice, I drove straight to a local garage before the vehicle became undrivable. The car staggered onto the forecourt, with the puncture now very obvious. I interrupted the owner, working on another vehicle, and told him my predicament. He could not have been more obliging, and leaving what he was doing, he began to remove the tyre which had fallen victim to a nail.

Within minutes, he had replaced the tyre with a spare and told me there was no charge. I thanked him profusely for his help, but insisted he was recompensed for his kindness.

As believers, sometimes we are 'running' well but then some sin or circumstance causes us to deflate. We feel flat and spiritually depressed and like a car with a puncture, we cannot move forward. So, the Psalmist cried out in Psalm 42 'Why, my soul, are you downcast and disturbed within me'? He was feeling deflated and needed reviving.

Thankfully, the Psalmist did not lose heart, knowing that he had a sure and certain hope in God His Saviour. Though deflated now, he was quite certain that he would again 'praise him' in the future. As believers, in our times of spiritual depression, we can have the same hope and assurance.

Let us never despair while we have Christ as our leader.

(George Whitfield)

16 March

> 'For this reason he had to be made like his brothers in every way, in order that he might become a merciful and faithful high priest in service to God, and that he might make atonement for the sins of the people. Because he himself suffered when he was tempted, he is able to help those who are being tempted' (Hebrews 2:17-18)

Suggested reading Hebrews 4:12-16

I met Paul when our son Aaron was in hospital. Having been at school, with our older boy, he recognised the surname and asked if I was Andrew's father. Paul had been a ward clerk but was now training to be a physiotherapist.

Some months later, I saw him again and I asked how he was doing.
'I am fine now', he said 'but I have just had time off with a bad back'.
'That is not good for a physio', I joked.
'Oh it is', he responded, 'I can now sympathise with my patients'!

The writer to the Hebrews says, 'We do not have a high priest who is unable to sympathise with our weaknesses, but we have one who has been tempted in every way, just as we are---yet was without sin' (Hebrews 4:15) Jesus was fully human. He experienced all the struggles and sufferings of mankind and, therefore He has a unique understanding of our condition. Jesus feels for us in our temptations, understanding the weight of them, even better than we do.

Saviour, breathe forgiveness o'er us
All our weakness, Thou dost know.
Thou didst tread this earth before us,
Thou didst feel its keenest woe.
Lone and dreary, faint and weary,
Through the desert, Thou didst go.

(James Edmeston)

17 March

'I am the Root and the Offspring of David, and the bright Morning Star'. (Revelation 22:16)

Suggested reading Isaiah 14:12-23

The first payable job available to young boys was that of a paperboy. The money was not great and I recall twelve shillings and sixpence being my weekly wage. Wednesdays and Thursdays were heavy days, as in addition to the national papers, the local paper and popular women's magazines had also to be delivered.

My round was in a residential area of Morecambe, and this was reflected in the choice of papers. The greatest demand was for the Daily Mail and the Daily Express, whilst others opted for the Times, The Guardian and the Daily Telegraph, with just a few going for The Sun and the Daily Mirror.

There was, however, one newspaper which stood out because it was delivered to just one house and that was the Morning Star. Beginning life in the 1930s as the Daily Worker, it was renamed and relaunched in 1966. The paper described its educational stance as 'Britain's Road to Socialism---the programme of the Communist Party of Britain'.

In Isaiah 14, Satan is referred to as 'a morning star' whilst Jesus, in Revelation 22, is called 'the Morning Star'. Two morning stars but what a contrast. Satan is a fallen star, but Jesus is the 'bright and morning star'. Satan is but a poor imitation of One who is 'the light of the world' and at the return of Jesus, his light will be forever extinguished. It might sometimes seem that, in the world today, Satan is winning but we must never forget that 'Jesus is stronger than Satan or sin, Satan to Jesus must bow'.

The whole of Satan's kingdom is subject to the authority of Christ.

(John Calvin)

18 March

'Be filled with the Spirit' (Ephesians 5:18)

Suggested reading John 3:22-36

Moving house is a major life-changing event and thankfully, it is something we have only had to do four times, in over fifty years of marriage. Our move, four years ago, was the smoothest as we were relocating to the village, where our daughter already lived. This meant help was readily at hand.

Nevertheless, it still meant there were many tasks which had to be undertaken before our new 'house' felt it was our 'home'. For example, it was three years before my car was able to get into the garage. Previous to that, it was on the drive, whilst books, boxes and many other extraneous items occupied the garage space.

Eventually, shelves were erected, a bookcase was purchased, and after many visits to the recycling centre, the car could have its rightful place.

Now, the challenge is to ensure that the garage does not again get cluttered with other things.

John the Baptist said that Jesus had 'the Spirit without limit' and believers are exhorted to 'be filled with the Spirit' but there are conditions. We cannot ever 'be filled with the Spirit' if we are full of self. We need to be emptied of 'self' before we can ever be full of Christ. Pride, envy, bitterness, covetousness etc. all need to be discarded before I can be full of Christ and His Spirit.

Jesus always had 'the Spirit without limit' because He was sinless and, in all things, pleased His Father. That can never be true of any believer, but the more we are emptied of self, all the more we will 'be filled with the Spirit'.

I've never known a person whom I thought was truly filled with the Holy Spirit who went out and bragged about it or sought to draw attention to himself.

(Billy Graham)

19 March

> 'Anyone who eats a sacred offering by mistake, he must make restitution to the priest for the offering and add a fifth of the value to it'. (Leviticus 22:14)

Suggested reading 2 Samuel 12:1-14

After three and a half years in banking, I was 'cashing' up on my final day before going for theological training. There was a mixture of emotions: sadness at leaving colleagues but also the anticipation of what was ahead. Perhaps the day had got to me because my till seemed to be £20 short. I rechecked my calculations and recounted the money, but there was £20 less in the till than there should have been. It was not unusual for a cashier to have a discrepancy of a pound or two but rarely £20, which in 1970, was a considerable sum of money.

I had not pocketed the £20, but with this being my last day at the bank, I could not have felt guiltier, even if I had. My feelings were not helped by the wry comments of certain colleagues who I hoped trusted my integrity, despite enjoying my embarrassment. Thus, I left Barclays Bank, pondering on the missing £20 and not on the leaving gift which had been presented to me earlier in the day.

However, the £20 shortfall was an error, on my part, but not a sin. I had not stolen the money or knowingly given it to someone---it was a genuine, unintended mistake.

The Bible distinguishes between a 'mistake' and a 'sin' but sadly the word 'mistake' is often used today when what is being described is sin. For example, someone has an affair, or dishonestly obtains money and then says, 'I made a big mistake'. Sorry, but it was not a 'mistake'; it was adultery. It was theft. It was sin.

We sin and we make mistakes because of man's fall but let us never confuse the two. Sin is a choice to do something we know to be wrong, but a mistake is something done unintentionally, because of our imperfect human nature. Sin always needs the forgiveness of God, whilst a mistake might need the forgiveness of others.

If there is anything worse than our sins, it is our infinite capacity to rationalise it away.

(Charles Colson)

20 March

> 'I am torn between the two: I desire to depart and be with Christ, which is better by far; but it is more necessary for you that I remain in the body'. (Philippians 1:23-24)

Suggested reading Genesis 6:11-22

My father was a station master and therefore a proportion of my childhood was spent on railway stations. An early memory is of trains stopping at Bare Lane station, near Morecambe and a number of wicker baskets being taken out of the guard's van.

On the platform, the baskets were opened and a cloud of pigeons took off into the sky. These were homing pigeons, entered by pigeon fanciers into races, and they were now beginning their journey home. Quite a sight for a young boy to see and how remarkable that an 'inner map and compass' got them to their destination. Is this not why animals and birds made their way to Noah's ark? The same instinct implanted in homing pigeons was also planted in them.

Believers have a homing instinct and that is for their home in heaven. There are many things on earth which bring us pleasure and satisfaction, and yet here we can never find true fulfilment. David the Psalmist said, 'you will fill me with joy in your presence, with eternal pleasures at your right hand. Now we have fellowship with and enjoy the presence of our fellow believers, but in heaven we will have communion with Christ and enjoy His immediate presence. We have a homing instinct to be 'in the house of the Lord forever'.

Heaven will mean the realization of all the things for which man was made and the satisfaction of all the outreaching of his heart.

(Ernest F. Kevan)

21 March

> Jesus asked them----'Do you still not see or understand? Are your hearts hardened? Do you have eyes but fail to see, and ears but fail to hear'? (Mark 8:17-18)

Suggested reading Matthew 18:1-6

The preacher had been speaking about the meeting of the Apostle Paul and King Agrippa. As they walked home from the service, my mother asked my brother---who was four at the time---what the preacher had been speaking about. His answer was quite specific: 'Paul and a tin of kippers'.

Pat and I were in the car with our grandson, when a police car raced by with lights flashing and siren sounding.

'O dear', said Pat, 'someone must have had an accident'.

With childlike innocence, the three- year- old asked 'Why---have they wet their pants'?

Children don't always get it right, but neither do we. There were times when the disciples just could not see what Jesus was trying to teach them. Their hearts were hardened, their minds slow to understand and we are no different. Nevertheless, if we are humble and maintain a childlike trust in Christ, His Spirit 'will guide us into all truth'. (John 16:13) We have a gracious tender saviour who is patient with us in our weaknesses. 'As a father has compassion on his children, so the Lord has compassion on those who fear him'. (Psalm 103:13)

Better to be slow of head to understand than slow of heart to believe.

(Vance Havner)

22 March

> 'What is your life? You are a mist that appears for a little while and then vanishes'. (James 4:14)

Suggested reading Psalm 90

Mrs. A, was a dear believer who had been a great help to Pat in her early Christian walk. Hearing that she had reached the grand old age of one hundred, we decided to visit her. As I saw the card she had received from the queen and congratulated her on becoming a centenarian, Mrs. A. remarked, 'Oh, that is nothing----there is a woman a few doors away and she is two hundred'!

'Two hundred'? I said, 'whatever do they feed you on around here'? When her granddaughter came into the room, I questioned her about this lady who was apparently two hundred. I was not too surprised to learn that she was, in fact, a hundred and two. But Mrs. A. was still not altogether convinced.

To us, one hundred years is a great age---and it is---and yet nothing at all, compared to eternity. Methuselah lived to be 969 but even his time on earth was just a speck when compared to the vastness of eternity. Time is short but its importance can never be underestimated, as our years on earth are preparation for eternity. Thank God, there is eternal life for all whose trust is in Jesus.

Spend your time in nothing which you know must be repented of; in nothing on which you might not pray the blessing of God; in nothing which you could not review with a quiet conscience on your dying bed; in nothing which you might not safely and properly found doing if death should surprise you in the act.

(Richard Baxter)

23 March

> 'Grow in grace and knowledge of our Lord and Saviour Jesus Christ' (2 Peter 3:18)

Suggested reading John 15:1-8

I had been speaking at an over 55s coffee morning and afterwards, it was the annual visit to a local restaurant. Pat and I were invited to the meal and we sat down to Yorkshire fish and chips at their best.

As I was eating a lady leant forward and said 'Can I ask you a question'?
'By all means', I said, 'provided it is not too difficult'.
'How long have you had your beard'?
Not a question, I was expecting but not too difficult to answer. 'I have had it', I replied, 'since 1976'.
At this point a man quipped, 'Well, it hasn't grown much'.

An amusing response but later it set me thinking. I have been a believer for longer than I have had a beard but have I grown and if so, by how much.

The irony is that what stops my beard from growing is the very thing that causes the believer to grow. I shave, I trim, I 'prune' my beard in order to satisfy my wife and to prevent growth. But what, prevents growth with my beard---pruning---it produces fruit in the believer.

Jesus said, 'every branch that does bear fruit, he prunes so that it will be even more fruitful'. (John 15:2) Whatever inhibits spiritual growth---worldly activities, ungodly practices, besetting sins---has to be removed. It may be a painful process but necessary if we are to bear more fruit.

The growth of grace is the best evidence of the truth of it; things that have no life will not grow.

(Thomas Watson)

24 March

> 'I resolved to know nothing while I was with you except Jesus Christ and him crucified'. (1 Corinthians 2:2)

Suggested reading 1 Corinthians 11:23-32

In a BBC poll of 2002, Winston Churchill was voted the greatest Briton who ever lived. Perhaps not too surprising, as twice Winston Churchill was Prime Minister, and as an inspirational statesman, he led Britain to victory in the Second World War. He was also a renowned writer, orator and artist.

And yet, for a strange reason, it is not so much the life of Winston Churchill I remember but rather his death. As a family, we never had a television but that changed when a set was installed on 23 January 1965 and I looked forward to a weekend of uninterrupted viewing. But the next day, Winston Churchill died and the scheduled programmes were all cancelled.

They were replaced by sombre music and the notification of a special programme. 'With the news of Winston Churchill's death bringing the nation to a standstill, BBC Television presents an obituary to a beloved man and a much-respected statesman'. Not quite the weekend I had been expecting.

Most people rightly remember the life rather than the death of Winston Churchill, but as believers, we are told to remember the death rather than the life of Jesus. That is not, in any way, to devalue His life, His teaching or His example, but to emphasise the supreme importance of His death. For it is through the death of Christ that our sins are forgiven and we are reconciled to God. With the Apostle Paul, may our thoughts always be centred on ' Jesus Christ and him crucified'.

I wish that our ministry---and mine especially---might be tied and tethered to the cross.

Charles H. Spurgeon)

25 March

> 'Woe to those who call evil good and good evil, who put darkness for light and light for darkness, who put bitter for sweet and sweet for bitter'. (Isaiah 5:20)

Suggested reading Jeremiah 8:4-12

We were having an afternoon drive in the Cumbrian countryside when we came to a signpost at a T junction. Sedbergh to the right was five miles and Kirkby Lonsdale to the left was six miles. I immediately felt disorientated, for I was sufficiently acquainted with the area to know that the town of Sedbergh was to the left and the town of Kirkby Lonsdale was to the right.

On returning home, I telephoned the Highways Department and they later confirmed that the sign had been placed the wrong way round. I hope not too many went astray but how confusing, both for those who knew the area and especially for those who did not.

Tragically, many of the moral signposts in our nation are now pointing in the wrong direction. Behaviour that the Bible condemns as evil is now considered to be good, whilst conduct which the Bible commends, is now considered to be undesirable. When evil is presented as being good and good as being evil, our nation is in a desperate plight. Little wonder that youngsters now use the word 'wicked' to mean 'good' or 'awesome'. When people abandon the Bible, thinking they know better than God, the outlook is bleak indeed.

Everything that is really worthwhile in the morality of today has come to the world through Christ. Dismiss his standards of right and wrong and try to draw up your own ethical code, and see where you will be.

(Campbell Morgan)

26 March

> 'Salvation is found in no one else, for there is no other name under heaven given to men by which we must be saved'. (Acts 4:12)

Suggested reading Mark 2:1-12

Peggy had been christened as a baby, and confirmed as a teenager but was now just an occasional church attender. She was, however, anxious for her grandchildren to be instructed in the Christian faith and started to bring them to the children's meeting at our church. Most parents or grandparents dropped their children off and picked them up again an hour later, but as one of her grandchildren was very young, Peggy stayed for the entire meeting.

She very much enjoyed the meetings and over the months, as the Gospel was explained in simple terms to the children, Peggy herself began to think more deeply about spiritual things. As a result, she began to attend church regularly on a Sunday night and in due course, she was converted, baptised and became a member of the church.

When Peggy first attended church, her concern was not her soul's salvation but the spiritual well-being of her grandchildren. But, with the passing of time, her priorities were changed and she saw her greatest need was her personal need of salvation.

The paralytic man in Mark 2 was brought to Jesus not because he wanted forgiveness but because he wanted to be healed. Jesus changed his priorities and though he came to be healed, he went away saved and healed. People come to churches for many different reasons and with many different motives but Jesus is able to change their priorities. They might come, initially for food or friendship but through the grace of God, they find something far greater---forgiveness of sin, peace with God and an eternal home in heaven.

Man, made in the image of God has a purpose---to be in relationship to God who is there. Man forgets his purpose and thus he forgets who he is and what life means.

(Frances Schaeffer)

27 March

> 'Even to your old age and grey hairs I am he, I am he who will sustain you. I have made you and I will carry you; I will sustain you and I will rescue you'. (Isaiah 46:4)

Suggested reading 2 Corinthians 4: 7-18

Mrs. P. was a delightful believer, greatly loved by all within the church and it was a joy to call at her home. Widowed for a number of years, she was a faithful attender at all the meetings in the church.

However, as she approached the age of ninety, her memory began to fail and it was necessary for Mrs. P. to move into a nursing home. At first, she knew and conversed with those who visited her but later, this was not the case. Sadly, as her condition deteriorated, she became ever more difficult and uncooperative----quite unrecognisable from the lady we had previously known.

This was a cause of distress to her church family but even more so to her own family. What had happened to Mrs. P. the gracious godly lady, we knew, loved and respected?

Sometimes the body breaks down and the mind weakens, and this can be most upsetting for those who witness it. But, as believers, we know there is a part of us which is not subject to decay. The Apostle Paul said 'I know whom I have believed, and am convinced that he is able to guard what I have entrusted to him, until that day (2 Timothy 1:12) Our souls have been entrusted to Jesus and with Paul, we know that they are forever safe in His keeping. This truth is reassuringly emphasised in the words of the old hymn:

The soul that on Jesus has leaned for repose,
I will not, I will not desert to its foes;
That soul, though all hell should endeavour to shake,
I'll never, no never, no never forsake. ('K' in Rippon's Selection 1787)

Never did a believer in Jesus die or drown in his voyage to heaven.

(Robert Traill)

28 March

> 'Fathers, do not exasperate your children; instead bring them up in the training and instruction of the Lord' (Ephesians 6:4)

Suggested reading Matthew 18:1-6

A young couple had been wonderfully converted from the world and the change in them was most dramatic. Paul said 'if anyone be in Christ, he is a new creation; the old has gone and the new is come' and this was visibly true in this man and his wife.

One Saturday, they went out for the day and it was one of those occasions when everything went wrong. It was a hot day, the trains were late and the children were arguing and bickering. Suddenly, tired and frustrated by the day's events, the father swore at his boy.

'Daddy', his son responded, 'I didn't think you used that word now that you know Jesus'.

The father was stopped in his tracks. He felt awful, having been humbled and rebuked by a child.

There are times when we all need to be humbled and rebuked, especially if we are putting obstacles in the way of children and young people. Jesus in Matthew 18:6 is severe with anyone guilty of such a thing. 'Better for him to have a large millstone hung around his neck and to be drowned in the depths of the sea' In our homes and churches as we interact with children and young people, may we be extra careful in all that we say and do.

Whatever parent gives his children good instruction, and sets them at the same time a bad example, may be considered as bringing them food in one hand and poison in the other.

(John Balguy)

29 March

'And being in anguish, he prayed more earnestly, and his sweat was like drops of blood falling to the ground'. (Luke 22:44)

Suggested reading Matthew 26:36-46

Going to the dentist is never pleasant but not quite the traumatic experience it was when I was a child. In those days, I always suffered twice. First, I suffered in the waiting room, as I listened for my name to be called out and I anticipated the ordeal that lay ahead. What I would have given for the appointment even then to have been cancelled.

I suffered in the waiting room but then I suffered in the chair as the dentist got to work with his drill and other implements. However, what I suffered in the waiting room---though real---it never solved my problem. My problem was only solved as I sat in the dentist's chair.

In no way, am I comparing Gethsemane and Calvary with a visit to the dentist---it would be blasphemous to do so. But did not Jesus suffer twice? In Gethsemane, he sweat drops of blood as he wrestled with the enormity of what was ahead of him. On Calvary he shed his blood as he bore the wrath of God in dying to save sinners.

Jesus suffered twice, and whilst we must never underestimate his sufferings in Gethsemane, neither must we forget that we are redeemed not by sweat shed at Gethsemane but by blood shed at Calvary.

In Gethsemane, the holiest of all petitioners prayed three times that a certain cup might pass from Him. It did not.

(C.S. Lewis)

30 March

> 'Christ redeemed us from the curse of the law by becoming a curse for us, for it is written: "Cursed is everyone who is hung on a tree". (Galatians 3:13)

Suggested reading Mark 15:21-39

Visiting a recently opened shopping mall, we decided to have a coffee at a restaurant on the first floor. Having Aaron with us, in his wheelchair, meant that we had to use the lift. It was not the most spacious of facilities and so I climbed the stairs, whilst Pat and Aaron got into the lift.

I reached the restaurant first because, half-way up the lift had stopped and Pat and Aaron were suspended between the two floors. Not a desirable but rather a disturbing situation in which to find oneself. Thankfully, help was at hand and soon we were all united in the restaurant.

When Jesus died upon the cross, He was suspended between earth and heaven, and that was significant. It indicated that Jesus was rejected both by earth and heaven. Rejected by earth because His purity and perfection exposed human sin and, in their malice, they preferred Barabbas to Jesus. Rejected by earth but why rejected by heaven? Rejected because, bearing our sin, Jesus became 'a curse for us' and God turned His back upon Him. Rejected by earth and heaven---how great was His suffering.

We may not know, we cannot tell
What pains He had to bear
But we believe it was for us,
He hung and suffered there.

(Cecil Frances Alexander)

31 March

> 'He was delivered over to death for our sins and was raised to life for our justification' (Romans 4:25)

Suggested reading Hebrews 10:1-14

Our first home was in Morecambe and was a pleasant three-bedroom semi. It was bought in 1971 for the princely sum of £3,650, which seemed a considerable amount at the time. However, by the time we moved to Ingleton in 1979, the price of the house had almost quadrupled.

Buying a house in Ingleton was not straightforward as, at that time, there were few houses on the market and those that were for sale required the buyer to put in an offer. Seeing a house that was suitable for our needs, we made what we considered to be a fair offer but it was turned down by the vendors. An improved second offer was accepted and work then began on renovating the property.

The experience taught me that an offer is only of value if it is accepted---otherwise an offer is a worthless thing.

On the cross, Christ offered Himself as a sacrifice for our sin, but if the offer had not been acceptable to God, then it would have been of no value. During the time that Jesus was in the tomb, heaven must have been in suspense---would the offer be accepted? Praise God, the answer came on Easter Day. The empty cross and the empty tomb are proof that his sacrifice for sin was fully acceptable to God. God raised Jesus from the dead and received him back into heaven because he was satisfied with the offering that Christ had made. 'Delivered over to death for our sins' and 'raised to life for our justification'. Hallelujah.

The resurrection of Christ is our receipted bill.

(Donald Grey Barnhouse)

BIBLE READINGS APRIL

1 April

> 'Jesus said to them, "why are you troubled and why do doubts rise in your minds? Look at My hands and My feet, it is I Myself! Touch me and see; a ghost does not have flesh and bones, as you see I have". When He had said this, He showed them His hands and feet. (Luke 24:38-40)

Suggested reading Luke 24: 13-35

Mr. R. was a retired man who was always willing to enter into a theological discussion. Sadly, it was not with a 'seeking' spirit but a desire to disprove the Bible and the Christian faith. One Spring evening, surrounded by daffodils, I likened the bursting forth of the flowers to the resurrection of Jesus.

Mr. R. was not impressed and had an immediate answer. Jesus was a twin, and once crucified, his brother had taken over. I explained to Mr. R. that there was a very real problem with his theory. After His resurrection, Jesus showed His wounds to His disciples, but how could the 'second' twin have wounds if He had never been crucified?

I am a twin and when we were young, if my brother had 'tummy' ache, I might have come out in sympathy, but when I broke my arm, his arm was not broken, and when he dislocated his finger, my finger was not dislocated. So, even though there may have been a certain telepathy between us, it certainly did not extend to actual physical injuries.

Sceptics are getting rather desperate when, without any evidence at all, they suggest that Jesus was a twin. Jesus invited the disciples to investigate the reality of His resurrection. And, they were certain, beyond doubt, that the Jesus who came out of the tomb was the same Jesus who had gone into the tomb. There was no deceit and even Thomas, who at first doubted the resurrection, was to be filled with joy, as he, too, was convinced by the print of the nails.

In an age of abounding unbelief and scepticism, we shall find that the resurrection of Christ will bear any weight that we can lay upon it'.

(J.C. Ryle)

2 April

> 'To this you were called, because Christ suffered for you, leaving you an example, that you should follow in his steps'.
> (1 Peter 2:21)

Suggested reading Romans 8:28-39

His parents are both teachers and so Pat asked our eleven-year- old grandson, 'Do you want to be a teacher when you grow up'? His answer was devastatingly honest.

'What, be a teacher? You go to school for fourteen years and then go back to teach things nobody needs to know'.

He obviously has no ambitions in that particular area and yet it is a natural question to ask. 'What do you want to be when you grow up'? As a five-year old, my answer was never in doubt. Living in a station house and with the Ulster express roaring through at 6.30 every morning, my only ambition was to be an engine driver.

Forward a few short years and alas, steam having been replaced by diesel, my ambition had changed. Football mad and with Preston North End my favourite team, I now wanted to be the next Tom Finney. Just one thing prevented the dream from ever being fulfilled: a distinct lack of ability. Later, as a typical teenager, my ambitions were less noble as I desired to be wealthy, popular and influential.

It is not wrong for a Christian to have ambitions, both for himself and for his family. And yet, the believer has an overriding ambition---to be more and more like Jesus. Any earthly ambition which dims the desire 'to be conformed to the likeness of his Son' (Romans 8:29) must be abandoned.

What is my ambition? What do I want to be? I want to be more like Jesus.

I know of nothing which I would choose to have as the subject of my ambition for life than to be kept faithful to my God till death.

(Charles H. Spurgeon)

3 April

> Jesus came to them and said "All authority in heaven and on earth has been given to me. Therefore, go and make disciples of all nations". (Matthew 28:18-19)

Suggested reading Luke 14: 25-35

As a boy in Morecambe. One of my favourite walks was the path behind Happy Mount Park, which continued by the side of Morecambe Golf

Club and ended by the canal in the village of Hest Bank. The walk was treelined and had magnificent views of Morecambe Bay.

It was popular with local youngsters because it was a treasure trove for mishit golf balls which, when retrieved, could be handed into the Golf Club for a small monetary reward. However, as a railway enthusiast, the walk had, for me, another attraction. It was necessary to cross the single-track railway line between Morecambe and Carnforth, and though rarely used, it required extra care. The need for care being emphasised by the sign: STOP, LOOK, LISTEN. BEWARE OF TRAINS. A sign still popular amongst those who collect railway memorabilia.

Discipleship starts when we STOP---when we are still, and perhaps, think seriously about God and eternal issues for the first time. 'Be still and know that I am God'. (Psalm 46:10)

We then LOOK to Christ and trusting Him as our Saviour, we set out on the road of discipleship. 'Look unto Me, and be saved. All you ends of the earth! For I am God and there is no other'. (Isaiah 45:22; NKJV)

The road of discipleship continues until we get to heaven, as we LISTEN and seek to be obedient to all that Christ has to say in the Bible. 'A voice from the cloud said, "This is my Son whom I love; with him I am well pleased. Listen to him". (Matthew 17:5)

A disciple is one who STOPS, LOOKS and LISTENS.

As the soldier follows his general, as the servant follows his master, as the scholar follows its master, as the scholar follows his teacher, as the sheep follows its shepherd, just so ought the professing Christian to follow Christ

(J. C. Ryle)

4 April

> 'While people are saying, "Peace and safety", destruction will come on them suddenly, as labour pains on a pregnant woman and they will not escape'. (1 Thessalonians 5:3)

Suggested reading Revelation 6:12-17

Our son Andrew, through being in the same team, became friendly with a Sri Lankan cricketer and during the winter months, when Shani returned home, they kept in regular touch.

On Boxing Day 2004, Andrew was perplexed to get a message from Shani, 'the tide is coming in---it is like a horror movie'. Switching on the television, we soon understood what Shani was talking about.

The day had begun calm and peaceful with many people enjoying the sea and sand of Sri Lanka's coast but suddenly the tsunami struck with great devastation. Shani escaped but over 230,000 people died on that day, which will forever be remembered.

It is an awesome and disturbing truth but when Jesus comes again, He will usher in the day of judgement. And it is the clear teaching of the Bible that, as with the tsunami, His coming will be sudden and will catch multitudes unprepared. That is why both Jesus (Matthew 24:43) and the Apostle Paul (1 Thessalonians 5:2) compared it to 'a thief in the night'.

Thank God that the suddenness of His return need not catch us unprepared. Jesus comes a second time to judge but He came the first time to save and if through repentance and faith, the purpose of His first coming is accomplished in us, then we are prepared for His return. Paul can say of us what he said of the believers in Thessalonica 'You brothers are not in darkness so that this day should surprise you like a thief'. (1 Thessalonians 5:4)

If we are believers in Jesus Christ we have already come through the storm of judgement. It happened at the cross.

(Billy Graham)

5 April

'By faith we understand that the universe was formed at God's command, so that what is seen was not made out of what was visible'. (Hebrew 11:3)

Suggested reading Psalm 8

I was asked to speak at a Harvest Supper and in preparation for the meeting, I got Pat to bake me an apple pie. At the supper, I explained that this apple pie was most amazing because it had made itself.

The ingredients had come together to form the pastry, the apples had sliced and fallen into the pastry, the pastry had jumped into the oven and then, after half an hour, the pie had emerged brown, cooked and ready to eat. Quite amazing---unbelievable.

The people looked at me as though I was talking nonsense---and of course I was. An apple pie does not make itself----behind this apple pie, there was a baker, a person. There was my wife. She had made it and later, at the supper, the pie was enjoyed by those who ate it.

Is it not astounding that people can think that this universe---so majestic, so beautiful, so intricate, so ordered---just happened? No Creator---there was just a 'big bang' and something came out of nothing. Surely, this is far more incredible than an apple pie making itself, and yet that is what multitudes have been taught and believe. 'Big bangs', explosions result in chaos not in order!

The probability of life originating by accident is comparable to the probability of the complete dictionary resulting from an explosion in a printing factory.

(Edwin Conklin)

6 April

> 'Whatever you do, work at it with all your heart, as working for the Lord, not for men, since you know that you will receive an inheritance from the Lord as a reward. It is the Lord Christ you are serving' (Colossians 3:23-24)

Suggested reading 2 Thessalonians 3: 6-15

I had only been working in the bank for a few weeks when a celebration was held to mark forty years of service by the chief cashier. His words to me on the morning of the meal were not very encouraging. 'Forty wasted years---forty wasted years'. That was how he summarised his time in the bank.

What a contrast to a testimony I once heard, as a boy, at a meeting in Morecambe. A man got to his feet and simply said 'I am a dustman for Jesus'. Some days later, I saw this man outside my house taking a tea break with his workmates. As they were reading the morning newspapers, he was reading the New Testament.

It is, of course, true that some jobs are more interesting and rewarding than others, but for the believer the work years have never been wasted; not if we have worked conscientiously, always seeking to commend the Lord Jesus by our conversation and our conduct.

A false distinction is sometimes made between Christian work and secular employment. Paul made no distinction, telling the slaves in

Colossae that they were serving the Lord Jesus. They were working for an earthly master but first and foremost, they were serving Jesus. May we never lose sight of that truth.

A dairymaid can milk cows to the glory of God.

(Martin Luther)

7 April

> 'Everyone who competes in the games goes into strict training. They do it to get a crown that will not last; but we do it to get a crown that will last forever. Therefore, I do not run like a man running aimlessly; I do not fight like a man beating the air. No, I beat my body and make it my slave so that after I have preached to others, I myself will not be disqualified for the prize' (1 Corinthians 10: 25-27)

Suggested reading Hebrews 10:19-25

In my form at secondary school, there was an Olympic contestant. Mary was the youngest athlete to compete in the 1964 Tokyo Summer Olympics, reaching the semi-finals of the 800 metres. I remember seeing Mary in the annual sports day at school and not surprisingly, she lapped many of the other competitors.

We saw a superb athlete but what we did not see was all the 'blood, sweat and tears' that went into making her the athlete she was. No doubt she had an innate ability, but that had to be complemented by many hours of early morning and late-night training in all kinds of weather. What we saw in public was the result of private disciplined training.

There are no shortcuts to becoming a sanctified, godly believer. There is no 'once and for all' experience that makes it happen; rather it requires self-denial and discipline. The discipline of regular church attendance, of daily prayer and Bible study. In running the Christian 'race', am I prepared to pay the price in order to obtain the prize?

The great need in the Christian life is for self-discipline. This is not something that happens to you in a meeting; you have got to do it.

(D. Martyn Lloyd-Jones)

8 April

> 'Give thanks in all circumstances; for this is God's will for you in Christ Jesus'. (1 Thessalonians 5:18)

Suggested reading Psalm 136

I was preaching at a church and on being told that one of the elderly members had just come out of hospital, I called to see her. Mrs. M. was in good spirits and for her age, was making a wonderful recovery after surgery.

Her room was full of cards to which I added my 'get well' card and I commented on how lovely it was to receive so many greetings. My comment brought an unexpected response, as Mrs. M, instead of expressing thanks for the cards she had received began to castigate those who had not sent a card. The miscreants were both 'named and shamed'.

I felt sad but not superior----perhaps on birthdays or at Christmas, I have been guilty of the same thing.

It is a sad trait of human nature but how often we find it easier to complain than to give thanks. The Apostle Paul tells us that to 'give thanks' is not just the polite thing to do; it is 'God's will'. We rightly seek God's will for major decisions in life---work, marriage, Christian service, etc. But by being a grateful person, I can daily be in the will of God. Today, let us not complain but be thankful.

As the Lord loves a cheerful giver, so likewise a cheerful thanksgiver.

(John Boys)

9 April

> 'For we are God's workmanship, created in Christ Jesus to do good works, which God prepared in advance for us to do'. (Ephesians 2:10)

Suggested reading Matthew 25:31-46

Pat's parents were retired but both still had part-time jobs. One afternoon, having telephoned them, Pat was concerned because neither of them was well. The next morning, I suggested that we made the twenty- mile journey to see them.

On arriving, we were relieved to find there was nothing about their health that was too disturbing and yet we were not prepared for what happened next. After ten minutes, Pat's father left for his job to be followed by Pat's mother, fifteen minutes later.

The result was Pat and I were now in the house, talking to one another but her parents---the ones we had come to visit—were nowhere to be seen. If we had come half an hour later, we would not have seen them at all. Nevertheless, our motive was good for we had come to visit the sick, even if Pat's original diagnosis had perhaps not been accurate.

In His description of the final judgement, Jesus emphasises the importance of feeding the hungry, giving drink to the thirsty, housing the stranger, clothing the naked, looking after the sick, visiting the prisoner. However, He is definitely not saying that it is by doing these things that we will gain access to heaven. 'Believe in the Lord Jesus and you will be saved' (Acts 16:31) ---that is the only way to heaven and yet Jesus says that all believers should be known for their daily acts of kindness and compassion.

This is not 'salvation by works'---it is 'salvation by His work on the cross' but a salvation whose reality is shown by the good works of believers.

Justification never results from good deeds; justification always results in good deeds.

(John Blanchard)

10 April

> 'We are taking pains to do what is right, not only in the eyes of the Lord but also in the eyes of men' (2 Corinthians 8:21)

Suggested reading Romans 13:1-7

Having stayed overnight in London, we had a taxi booked for half past nine to get us to the railway station. Waking early, we went across the road to a cafe advertising 'Croissants and Coffee'. This light breakfast was most enjoyable and afterward we went for a short walk before collecting our luggage and waiting for the taxi.

As we waited, I asked Pat, 'Did you pay for the croissants and coffee'?

'No', she replied, 'did you'?

To our consternation, we realised we had walked out of the café without paying. Pat rushed back whilst I guarded the suitcases. The proprietor was quite unaware we had not paid, thinking one of his assistants had taken the money. He was astounded that Pat had returned to pay, and he could not recall this ever having happened before. Pat returned just in time for the taxi and we began the journey home with an easier conscience.

In all their dealings, believers must be scrupulously honest and beyond reproach. For the Christian, honesty is not just the best policy, it is the only policy; a conscious decision, whatever the circumstances, never to steal, cheat or deceive. It is in this way that we can be different and distinctive from many in our society today.

If faith does not make a man honest, it is not an honest faith.

(Charles. H. Spurgeon)

11 April

> Jesus said, "I am the light of the world. Whoever follows me will never walk in darkness, but will have the light of life" (John 8:12)

Suggested reading John 3:16-21

Beamish Museum is an open-air museum in County Durham, which I have visited on numerous occasions. Recently, accompanied by grandchildren, I took a guided tour down the coalmine and saw the dark and cramped conditions where men had to work. Miners often had to work, lying on their backs and sides while chipping away at the coal seam.

The most memorable moment for the grandchildren was when our guide turned off the lights and we were plunged into total darkness. After that, there was not a glimmer of light and I must confess, it was not only the grandchildren who were relieved when the light was restored.

Years before, I had a similar experience in Ingleborough Cave at the heart of the Yorkshire Dales National Park. The floodlights had enabled us to see the amazing stalactites and stalagmites but when switched off, we were quite incapable of seeing anything. Vision is only possible when light is present.

The Bible has a lot to say about darkness and light. Jesus is 'the light of the world' but men and women avoid Him because their sins are exposed in His presence. But those who come to Him in repentance and faith have their sins forgiven, and light shines on their pathway. It is in the darkness that we stumble or take the wrong direction, but why walk in darkness when we can have Jesus the light of life besides us.

Don't be fearful about the way ahead, don't worry about where you are going or how you are going to get there. Believe in the one who came as the Light of the World, not only to die for people but to light the way. This one, Jesus Christ, is himself the light and will guide your footsteps along the way.

(Edith Schaeffer)

12 April

'The Word became flesh and made his dwelling among us. We have seen his glory, the glory of the Only Begotten Son, who came from the father, full of grace and truth'. (John 1:14)

Suggested reading John 8:1-11

'Can we put a tent up'? This was the request made by friends of our son, Andrew. We readily agreed and eventually a largish tent was erected in our back garden.

During the day, children enjoyed running in and out of the tent and as evening approached, two adults and five children decided to spend the night in the tent.

We were wakened just before midnight by one child having a change of heart and opting for the warmth and comfort of a bed indoors. The others survived the night and in the morning we all feasted on a full English breakfast.

Jesus 'made his dwelling among us' and the phrase literally means that he 'pitched His tent amongst us'. Jesus did not come to a stately palace outside Jerusalem---as the wise men expected---but rather to a stable in Bethlehem. And He did so in order that He might live, work, pray, suffer and die amongst us. Within hours of His birth, the shepherds had been to see Him. He is the approachable Jesus; the Jesus who wants to be known. And, because He is the 'friend of tax collectors and sinners' (Matthew 11:19), He will receive all who come to Him in repentance and faith.

The Son of God---came to seek us where we are in order that he might bring us to be with him where he is.

(J.I. Packer)

13 April

> 'You received the Spirit of sonship. And by him we cry "Abba Father" The Spirit himself testifies with our spirit that we are God's children. Now if we are children, then we are heirs---heirs of God and co-heirs with Christ'. (Romans 8:15-17)

Suggested reading Revelation 7:9-17

When we first moved to Ingleton, Mrs. R. an elderly widow---was our neighbour. She'd not had an easy life, knowing times of poverty and personal tragedy. I used to take her shopping on a Monday morning and if she had coal for the fire and food for the table, she was content.

A few months after our arrival, Mrs. R. celebrated her eightieth birthday with a family party in her home. It was a happy gathering, as she celebrated the occasion with children and grandchildren. In total, there must have been almost thirty people crowding into her terraced house.

Sometime later, we were being shown photographs of the event and imagine our embarrassment when on the official family photograph, our four-year old daughter was pictured prominently. We had no idea that she had even gone next door. Joanna used to 'pop' in to see Mrs. R. and so, thankfully, there was no objection to her being on the family photograph.

Joanna was welcomed onto the family photograph but as believers a far greater privilege has been extended to us. We have been adopted into the family of God and are 'heirs of God and co-heirs with Christ'. As the only begotten Son, Jesus is sure to receive the Father's full inheritance. And, our inheritance is just as certain because we are 'co-heirs with Christ'. We are part of that 'great multitude that no one could count' (Revelation 7:9) who have been changed from being slaves to being the royal heirs of an eternal kingdom. How great, how amazing is our status in Christ.

Since God had a Son of his own, and such a son, how wonderful God's love in adopting us! We needed a Father but He did not need sons

(Thomas Watson)

14 April

> 'And we know that in all things God works for the good of those who love him, who have been called, according to his purpose'. (Romans 8:28)

Suggested reading 2 Corinthians 12:1-10

As a boy, whenever I had a heavy cold or flu symptoms, my mother would bring out Fennings Fever Mixture. The very sight of the bottle was almost sufficient to convince me that I was feeling better. It had a most bitter taste and even now, the very thought of it is almost enough to set my teeth on end.

Years afterwards, I discovered that before I took the mixture, mother sweetened it with sugar to make it more palatable. What it must have tasted like without the sugar does not bear thinking about.

But why did my mother put me through this 'torture'? There was only one reason. She loved me and knew that ultimately it would be for my benefit.

God often helps and provides for us in unexpected ways but while some providences are happy and enjoyable, others can be dark and bitter. And yet, we can depend upon our Father in heaven to sweeten such providences with evidence of His love and mercy.

Paul had a 'thorn in the flesh' and he found it so distressing that three times he pleaded with the Lord for it to be taken away. The thorn, however, was not removed and Paul later rejoiced that it was so. Through the thorn he proved that God's grace was sufficient and that when weak, it was then that he was strong.

May the Lord enable us to accept providences, be they sweet or bitter.

Happy the man who sees God employed in all the good and ill that chequers life.

(William Cowper)

15 April

> 'Always be prepared to give an answer to everyone who asks you to give the reason for the hope that you have. But do this with gentleness and respect'. (1 Peter3:15)

Suggested reading Colossians 4:2-6

On a door-to-door visiting, I came across a middle-aged man who made it very clear he was not pleased to see me. He began by telling me he was an atheist and that science had disproved God.

It was difficult to get a word in as he seemed angry with God and hostile towards me. I have never been able to understand why some atheists are angry with Someone who, they say does not exist. I have no such feelings towards Father Christmas, the Man in the Moon or the Tooth Fairy.

Eventually, he quietened down and during the next hour, we had a sensible conversation. Indeed, we parted on reasonable terms, agreeing to continue the debate by e-mail. This we did for several weeks and though I do not pretend he was converted, nevertheless I was encouraged by a comment he made at the end of an e-mail. 'I am beginning to warm towards you---this is very worrying'.

I took this comment as a compliment but also as a rebuke, for I am sure there have been times when I have been too aggressive and argumentative with the unconverted. Even if I won the argument, I lost the person. Paul says, 'Be wise in the way you act towards outsiders; make the most of every opportunity. Let your conversation be always full of grace, seasoned with salt'. (Colossians 4:5-6) Peter says, 'Always be prepared to give an answer---but do this with gentleness and respect'.

We need to be constantly reminded that 'how we say it' is just as important as 'what we say'. May we ever 'speak the truth in love'. (Ephesians 4:15)

When you speak, remember God is one of your listeners.

(Anon)

16 April

'The gospel concerning the glory of the blessed God'.
(1Timothy 1:11)

Suggested reading.1 Timothy 1:12-17

Christians once widely distributed The Challenge --- an evangelistic paper ---- and we had a friend who rarely left his home without a copy. One evening, I was standing just behind him at the chip shop, when he handed a Challenge newspaper to the man taking the order. Not appreciating what the paper was, he was about to wrap the fish and chips in it, when my friend intervened and explained that he wanted him to read the paper.

Several years ago, one summer Sunday afternoon, I was giving out gospel leaflets on Morecambe promenade. One of the leaflets was entitled 'Four things God wants you to know' and was an excellent summary of the Christian gospel. I handed the leaflet to a young man, who then took great delight in standing right in front of me and tearing the leaflet into a multitude of pieces.

The gospel is good news, and yet sadly, it is often treated as it was inadvertently treated by the man in the chip shop or by the young man on the promenade. It is viewed either with hostility or as being less important than yesterday's newspaper.

But the gospel is glorious----no newspaper can tell me how I can be forgiven, be reconciled to God or have an eternal home in heaven. Tragically, in ignoring or vehemently opposing the gospel, people are rejecting their only means of salvation.

There is nothing attractive about the gospel to the natural man: the only man who finds the gospel attractive is the man who is convicted of sin.

(Oswald Chambers)

17 April

> 'But God said to him, "You fool! This very night your life will be demanded from you. Then who will get what you have prepared for yourself"?

Suggested reading Ecclesiastes 3:1-15

My grandfather was born on this day in 1880 and he spent his life as a signalman on the railway. This meant he was meticulous when it came to telling the time. 'What time is it, Grandad'? ' It is eight and a half minutes past ten' would be his precise reply.

'That is the six twenty from Lancaster---he's three minutes late'. Time was important to Grandad and not for him a wristwatch but the pocket watch and chain, which was favoured by most men of his generation.

At the age of eighty-eight, Grandad was taken into hospital and a few days before he died, he handed his faithful pocket watch to his son. 'Take this', he said, 'I won't be needing it anymore'. He knew that for him, time was almost over and eternity was about to begin, but having trusted Jesus Christ as his Saviour, he knew that his eternity would be with Christ in heaven.

In human hearts, there is a God-given awareness that there is "something more than this transient world". "He has set eternity in the hearts of men,"(Ecclesiastes 3:11). If Christ does not return beforehand, then we all have to die. But death is not the end; it is the prelude to eternity and, for the believer, an eternity that will be spent with Christ in heaven. As we commit our souls to Christ, so we are in safe hands for time and eternity.

There is nothing more certain than death, nothing more uncertain than the time of dying. I will therefore be prepared at all times for that which may come at any time.

(Anon)

18 April

'If someone forces you to go one mile, go with him two miles' (Matthew 5:41)

Suggested reading: 2 Kings 6:8-23

Our son, Andrew, was born on a Saturday morning and as I visited Pat that evening, I told her it would be Monday before I saw her again, as I was preaching the next day at Hellifield in North Yorkshire.

I took the morning service, had lunch and then to my surprise, my host said, "We are now going to see Pat and the baby". Morecambe was an hour's run from Hellifield, but Brian put me in his car and keeping---I hope---within the speed limits, we raced to the Queen Victoria Hospital.

A surprise for me but an even greater surprise for Pat, as we were able to spend this unexpected time together. It was then full speed back to Hellifield, in order to take the evening service.

If Brian had taken me to a hospital, twenty minutes away, that would have been appreciated but a hospital, an hour away---he was going the 'second mile'.

Any Roman soldier could compel a Jewish civilian to carry his baggage for one Roman mile. This was not an easy task and may have been resented by many but Jesus gives his followers the principle of the 'second mile', as a means by which they could be distinctive from the culture of the day.

To go 'beyond the call of duty' is a powerful witness, especially in a society where the tendency is always to put your own needs before the needs of others.

Love never asks, 'How much must I do'? But 'how much can I do'?

(Frederick Agar)

19 April

> 'Jesus said, "Let the little children come to me, and do not hinder them, for the kingdom of heaven belongs to such as these". (Matthew 19:14)

Suggested reading Psalm 78: 1-8,

When we moved to Ingleton in 1979, the Wednesday Special children's meeting was well established and Pat and I were to be involved until our retirement in 2009. It was always interesting to interact with the children and the meetings could be both enjoyable and challenging.

On being asked 'what is an idol'? One youngster replied 'someone who will not work'. By contrast, one January evening, we were plunged into darkness, when a girl went to the back of the church and switched off all the lights.

I was, therefore, able to sympathise when a helper came to me, somewhat distressed because she had lost her temper with an unruly child. The irony was the theme for the meeting had been 'the fruit of the Spirit'.

There had not been much patience, kindness, gentleness, self-control evident in her demeanour that night but nevertheless an indication of just how challenging children can be. Her remorse was genuine and I am sure this 'lapse' was never ever repeated.

Let us pray for Christian parents and children's workers as they seek to teach and train boys and girls in the ways of the Lord.

Let us not fool ourselves---without Christianity, without Christian education, without the principles of Christ inculcated into young life, we are simply rearing pagans.

(Peter Marshall)

20 April

'Surely goodness and love will follow me all the days of my life, and I will dwell in the house of the Lord for ever'. (Psalm 23:6)

Suggested reading Genesis 50: 15-21

My brother travelled up from Wigan to take our ladies meeting in Ingleton and, as his custom was, he arrived in good time for a meal. That evening also happened to be the night of our annual children's party, and Pat had been busy all morning making sandwiches, buns, biscuits etc. When it was time for the meeting, Pat put the food in the boot of Jim's car, as it was a means of getting them down to church.

Jim took the meeting, stayed behind for a drink and then shot off back to Wigan with all the food still in the boot of his car. I got a frantic phone call from Pat and I set off in hot pursuit. After seven or eight miles, I saw Jim's car in the distance and, with headlights flashing, I raced up behind him.

Now, when Jim saw this speeding car with its headlights flashing, his first thought was, 'Oh no, an unmarked police car---what speed was I doing when I went through that village'? Of course, it wasn't a police car at all, it was me and I was on an errand of mercy. I was there to save the children's party and to save my brother the embarrassment of arriving in Wigan with a boot full of food.

It might sometimes seem that we are being pursued by trials and troubles, but at the end of the journey the believer will be able to testify with David that rather than being pursued by trials and troubles, he has instead been followed by the goodness and love of God. Our shepherd---the Lord Jesus---leads his sheep and his two sheepdogs---Goodness and Love---they follow to guard and to keep us. We are guided and protected as we head to the house of the Lord.

Times are bad; God is good.

(Richard Sibbes)

21 April

> Day after day every priest stands and performs his religious duties; again and again he offers the same sacrifices, which can never take away sins. But when this priest had offered for all time one sacrifice for sins, he sat down at the right hand of God' (Hebrews 10:12)

Suggested reading Hebrews 9:23-28

Homework done, the book would be handed into the teacher, in order to be marked. There was often a measure of apprehension when the book was returned, as there was one word which we never wanted to see and that was the word REPEAT. But, if the work was not up to standard, it had to be repeated.

Dare I say it, but my wife is almost hyperactive and consequently, it is difficult to get her to sit down in the evening. There are so many things that still need to be done. Her work is not finished and, therefore, she cannot sit down.

God raised Jesus from the dead because his atoning death at Calvary was a perfect work, a finished work, an unrepeatable work. And, having been raised from the dead, Jesus was received into heaven and sat down at the right hand of God'. He sat down because his redeeming work was done.

What a contrast to the Old Testament priests. They never sat down. They always stood as they had to offer again and again the same sacrifices----sacrifices that could never take away sins. (Hebrews 10:11). As believers, we rest and rejoice in a finished work.

Nothing needs to be added to Christ's finished work, and nothing can be added to Christ's finished work.

(Francis Schaeffer)

22 April

> 'Even the very hairs of your head are all numbered'. (Matthew 10.30)

Suggested reading Jeremiah 1:4-10

After my barber retired, I persuaded Pat to be my hairdresser, and for the next twenty years, I think she did remarkably well. However, Pat was never satisfied with her 'cutting' and eventually persuaded me to make an appointment with a 'proper' hairdresser.

Unfortunately, my first venture was not altogether a success, and I emerged looking more like a 'skinhead' than a 'Beatle'. My pleas for Pat to revive her hairdressing skills fell on deaf ears, and eventually, I went to the barber shop in my own village. This time, I was delighted with the outcome, as a most pleasant lady gave me just the trim I required.

Covid restrictions were in operation, and so before I could be dealt with, there was the sanitising and cleaning procedure. I do not know who had been in the chair before me, but I was quite amazed by the amount of hair swept up. Perhaps he, too, had gone from being a ' Beatle' to a skinhead.

If I had been asked how many hairs had been swept up, I could not have hazarded a guess. I understand the average human head has 1,000,000 hairs and we lose fifty to a hundred hairs every day, but those stats do not help me in numbering either the hairs on my head or the head of anyone else.

Such is the omniscience of God that he knows not only the number of hairs on my head but on the heads of everyone. When I watch certain quiz shows on television, I marvel at some contestant's breadth of knowledge. But their knowledge is minimal in the extreme when compared to omniscience---the knowledge of all things. We can only say with the Psalmist David, 'such knowledge is too wonderful for me, too lofty for me to obtain'. (Psalm 139:6)

God does not learn things; He knows them from the beginning.

(R.C. Sproul)

23 April

> 'No one can serve two masters. Either he will hate the one and love the other, or he will be devoted to one and

despise the other. You cannot serve both God and Money' (Matthew 6:24)

Suggested reading Luke 9:57-62

In 1990, I had the privilege of meeting Chris Balderstone when he visited a friend in Ingleton. If you are not interested in sport, then the name will not mean much to you but Chris was both a professional footballer and an international England cricketer.

On 15 September 1975, Chris made history by taking part in a County Championship cricket match and a Football League game on the same day. Having played cricket for Leicestershire during the day, he changed into his football kit to play for Doncaster Rovers in an evening match, thirty miles away.

History will never be repeated as it would not be possible now to get both a professional football and a professional cricket contract. Each sport requires a total commitment on the part of its professionals.

It is not possible to give total allegiance to God and to something else. Jesus specifically mentions money, knowing it is so easy for material wealth to become a god and to 'master' us. It was money that led Judas Iscariot to deliver Jesus into the hands of the enemy and it was material possessions that caused the Rich Young Ruler to reject the Saviour. They hoped they could serve two masters but one master will always come out 'on top'.

If we love God, we must do so with an 'undivided heart' placing everything---money, time, talents etc. ---at his disposal. In serving him, we shall find that we are serving the very best of Masters.

I have this day been before God and have given myself---all that I have and am---to God; so that I am in no respect my own, I have given myself clean away.

(Jonathan Edwards)

24 April

> 'Let us not give up meeting together, as some are in the habit of doing' (Hebrews 10:25)

Suggested reading Luke 4: 14-22

My daughter enjoyed school but was not over enthusiastic when it came to PE and games. She was often looking for excuses and the opportunity to take advantage of her occasional asthma attacks. This was particularly so as she got older and when, uncannily, her wheezing always seemed to be worse on a Friday morning. However, she could only be excused if a parental letter was taken to the school.

One Friday—Joanna wanting to miss games---I wrote the PE teacher a letter, which I later learned had been pinned to the staff noticeboard. 'Dear Madam. Please can Joanna be excused games today, as she is anticipating an asthma attack around 10.45 this morning'. I think the staff knew precisely what I was trying to say.

During my thirty years as a pastor, I met a few believers, thankfully not many, who suffered from what I called 'Sundayitis'. They were always well enough to do what they wanted on other days, but strangely they were afflicted by tiredness or illness on a Sunday. I hope I am not being judgemental but perhaps there are times when we all need to ask the question, 'Are there times when things prevent me from going to church that would not stop me from going anywhere else? An honest self-examination can be a necessary exercise.

An avoidable absence from church is infallible evidence of spiritual decay.

(Frances Ridley Havergal)

25 April

> 'you turned to God from idols to serve the living and true God'. (1 Thess. 1:9)

Suggested reading: Isaiah 44:9-20

Most days I take my daughter's dog, Desmond, for a morning walk and it is often an interesting experience. I chat with other dog owners but tend to get to know the name of the dog rather than the owner. I was recently introduced to Edward and Dorothy who were a brother and sister, and to Dave the dachshund who was wearing a bow tie.

One morning, walking past a secluded bungalow, I noticed a dog in the window. It was still there when, a few days later, I walked the same route. On the third occasion, seeing the dog in the self-same position, I had to reluctantly concede, that it was not a live animal at all but an ornamental dog.

It looked like a dog but in truth, it was a dead inanimate object.

So, it is with all the gods of this world, be it the god of pleasure, the god of materialism, the god of fame and popularity. They promise much but because they are dead gods, they can never meet our deepest needs. 'You shall have no other gods before Me' is the first commandment--- wise are those who obey, foolish those who choose to disobey.

Man in his rebellion against the Creator remains incurably religious, and he seeks to satisfy this instinct by making his own deities. He much prefers these lifeless puppets to the one true living God, because they allow him to pull all the strings.

(Geoffrey B. Wilson)

26 April

> 'But go, tell his disciples and Peter, "He is going ahead of you into Galilee. There you will see him, just as he told you". (Mark 16:7)

Suggested reading Joshua 1:1-9

As a child in the 1950s, shopping with mother was a very different experience to what it is today. There were no supermarkets and so it was a trek from shop to shop with the highlight being a weekly visit to the indoor or open-air market.

I was reminded of this when a friend recalled a conversation his daughter had with her young child. She was telling the infant, he had no need to be afraid, as Jesus, although we cannot see him, is always with us and wherever we go, Jesus is already there. 'O, I know', said the child, 'He always there to open the door when we go to the supermarket'.

Another change from the 1950s---then we did not have automatic doors!

The child's application of the truth might have been faulty but he had understood the gist of it. Jesus is present with believers at all times. This is true even when perhaps because of sin or sickness or sorrow, we do not feel his presence.

Jesus promised, 'Surely, I am with you always, to the very end of the age'. (Matthew 28:20) Right until He comes again, there will never be even a day or an hour when the Lord Jesus is not present with his followers. Moses 'persevered because he saw him who is invisible'. (Hebrews 11:27) We must do the same. Jesus cannot be seen by mortal eyes but with the eye of faith we see that he is always near.

Yet though I have not seen and still
Must rest in faith alone,
I love you dearest Lord and will
Unseen but not unknown.

(Roy Palmer)

27 April

> 'Demas, because he loved this world has deserted me'. (2 Timothy 4:10)

Suggested reading 1 John 2:15-19

Pat and I had only been courting a short time when she invited me to her home for a meal. Expecting a light meal, I had already eaten a substantial amount before going to Pat's home. To my embarrassment, I soon discovered that 'tea' was in fact, a three-course meal. Wanting to create a good impression with my future mother-in-law, I did full justice to the meal and ate all that was put in front of me.

That same evening, we had been invited to the home of a retired couple in the church. My stomach felt 'heavy', but even more uncomfortable when the lady of the house brought in the supper. Sausage rolls, sandwiches, scones, cakes, and biscuits were set before us, and knowing the trouble the lady had taken, I felt I just had to eat.

Later that evening, I walked Pat home, gave her a goodnight kiss, and then rushed round the corner to be as sick as a dog. Food is good and enjoyable to eat but the danger comes---as I found that night---when you abuse it. I suffered because of my over-indulgence.

There are many things in this world which can bring pleasure to the believer. Work, art, music, sport, and hobbies are all things we can rightly enjoy but the danger comes when we overindulge and abuse these things. There are believers who are 'weak and sickly' because work or a hobby has become almost an idol and spiritual exercises have been pushed out. We are in the world but how important it is that we use the world but do not abuse it.

An idol may be defined as any person or thing that has usurped in the heart the place of pre-eminence that belongs to the Lord.

(Arthur Wallis)

28 April

>'You, the righteous God, who probes minds and hearts'.
>(Psalm 7:9)

Suggested reading 1 Samuel 16:1-13

It was May Day, and we went with our grandchildren and Desmond the dog to Ilkley Carnival. Seeing there was a dog show, I entered Desmond and our granddaughter in the 'Best Junior Handler' category. Sadly, the Boston terrier was not at all co-operative, and so, not unexpectedly, they were unplaced.

Later that month, it was the Otley Show and despite his Ilkley performance, I felt Desmond should have a second chance. He could not go in the 'Dog with the waggiest tail' category, as he does not have one, so I entered him for the 'dog with the most appealing eyes'. There were over twenty entrants but much to our surprise and joy, he came fourth and won a green rosette.

Ilkley Carnival was a test of his behaviour and Desmond was found wanting, whereas the Otley Show judged his appearance and he was prize-worthy.

Judging by 'outward appearance' Samuel would have anointed Eliab to be the next king but the Lord 'looking at the heart', chose his youngest brother, David. Humans, as well as dogs, are often judged by their outward appearance; their physique or mental ability can make them highly prized by others. But, 'the Lord does not look at the things people look at'. God probes minds and hearts'. That means, though we can deceive others, and others can deceive us, no one is able to deceive God. He is not taken in by outward appearance, God examines the heart

We can tell how men look, but He can tell what men are.

(Matthew Henry)

29 April

'This only have I found: God made man upright but men have gone in search of many schemes'. (Ecclesiastes 7:29)

Suggested reading Genesis 1:26-31

With Morecambe being a seaside resort, many happy hours were spent, as a teenager in the 1960s, on the fairground. The ghost train, the helter-skelter, the bumper cars all had their attractions.

Other rides were, however, more challenging. The dive bomber consisted of twin cars mounted on a vertical arm with the cars spinning on their own axis. I only ever once went on the dive bomber and being thankful to survive the horrendous experience, I vowed never to put myself through it again.

Indoors, there were the amusement machines where youngsters dreamt of 'making money' but dreams never became a reality. There was, also, the hall of mirrors, which I found fascinating, because in the mirror I was either very tall and slim or very small and fat. It was me but my image was distorted.

Men and women are made in the image of God, but because of the sin of Adam and Eve, it is now a distorted image. Whenever humans are loving and kind and sacrificial, then something of God is still to be seen in them but we are not what God originally intended us to be. The image is distorted because we are all sinful, fallen creatures.

Amazingly, Jesus came into this world so to save us and change us, that we might 'be conformed to the likeness of God's Son'. (Romans 8:29) Through faith in Christ, the image, though distorted, can be restored.

We human beings have both a unique dignity as creatures made in the image of God and a unique depravity as sinners under his judgement.

(John R. Stott}

30 April

> '----when we were God's enemies, we were reconciled to him through the death of his Son' (Romans 5:10)

Suggested reading Revelation 5:9-14

People are invited to the Royal Garden Party at Buckingham Palace because of who they are and what they have achieved. Pat was kindly nominated because of her services to children in Ingleton.

In the grounds of Buckingham Palace, Pat and I mixed with mayors, ambassadors, politicians, bishops and with others who were being honoured because of their service to the community.

Each one was appearing in the presence of the Queen because of what they had done. It was a reward for their efforts.

How different it will be in heaven. Not one of us will be there because of what we have done---we will only be there because of what Jesus has done. It is only through his sacrificial death that anyone will be worthy to appear in the presence of God.

In heaven, all praise, honour and glory are given to Christ, the Lamb of God (Rev. 5: 12-13) because ---'you were slain and with your blood you purchased men for God from every tribe and language and people and nation' (Rev. 5:9) Heaven is not gained by what we have done for God but rather, through what God has done for us in Jesus Christ.

He died that we might be forgiven,
He died to make us good.
That we might go at last to heaven,
Saved by his precious blood.

(Cecil Frances Alexander)

BIBLE READINGS MAY

1 May

> 'I even found an altar with this inscription: TO AN UKNOWN GOD. Now what you worship as something unknown I am going to proclaim to you' (Acts 17:23)

Suggested reading Romans 1:18-23

My daughter in-law teaches at a school in Singapore and as part of her extra-curricular duties, she was allocated to coach an U7s girl's football team.

At her first session, Sarah told the girls to go and collect a football but the response of one girl was not too encouraging. 'Miss', she asked, 'what is a football'? The girl was not being facetious. She did not know what a football was.

It seems that Sarah has much work to do. If this girl is ever to understand or become proficient at the 'beautiful' game.

The Singaporean youngster was ignorant about football but multitudes of young people, today, are ignorant about God and the Christian faith. In general, children do not go to Sunday School and in most schools, the Bible is never taught. We cannot say that young people have rejected the faith because in many cases they have never been taught the faith.

It is not always easy for Christian workers to get access to children and young people but every generation needs to know the basics of the Christian faith. Because, without that knowledge, there is nothing for the Spirit of God to work upon.

Will you pray, today, for Sunday School workers, for Christian school teachers and for Christian societies who still have access to our schools? There is so much work to be done.

Grace cannot reign where ignorance reigns.

(Thomas Watson)

2 May

> 'See to it that no one misses the grace of God and that no bitter root grows up to cause trouble and defile many' (Hebrews 12:15)

Suggested reading Matthew 5:27-30

Our terraced house in Ingleton had a small front garden, which was only exposed to the sun for a few hours in the morning. Consequently, it was never easy to grow things and so Pat decided to turn it into a wildflower garden.

One morning, there was a knock on the door and standing there was our neighbour. 'I've just pulled this up. Japanese knotweed. It will take your garden over'. Pat was not too impressed by this neighbourly interference but perhaps the man was doing us a favour. Japanese knotweed can grow at an alarming rate, soon overtaking a garden and causing potential damage to tarmac and to properties.

Our neighbour had taken decisive action but it may have been necessary to stop more serious problems in the future.

Sin is nothing to 'play' with, and little sins can very soon grow and become impossible to master. Jesus, in the Sermon on the Mount, emphasised that sin needs drastic action. He did so by the use of vivid language; gouging out eyes and cutting off hands. Jesus was not suggesting that we mutilate our bodies but, recognising the power and effect of sin, he was encouraging us to take decisive and appropriate action. Far better to be safe than to be sorry.

The most deadly sins do not 'leap' upon us; they 'creep' upon us.

(Stephen Olford)

3 May

> 'Dear friends, now we are children of God, and what we will be has not yet been made known. But we know that when he appears, we shall be like him, for we shall see him as he is'. (1 John 3:2)

Suggested reading Ephesians 5 22-33

I knew I must be getting older when, for my birthday, my family bought me a one -thousand -piece jigsaw. It was entitled 'Grandad's Attic', and on the box there was a heart-warming picture of a grandfather and grandson playing with a train set in the attic. Having grandsons and a lifelong interest in trains, it seemed to be the ideal present.

I have, however, to confess that I struggled with the jigsaw. Perhaps I did not have the patience for a one- thousand- piece jigsaw and as I tried to get the pieces to fit together, I sometimes looked with incredulity at the picture on the box. What I had before me bore so little resemblance to the picture on the box.

In the Bible---on the box---it says that the church of Christ will be 'a radiant church without stain or wrinkle or any other blemish but holy and blameless'. In the Bible ---on the box---it says, 'we shall be like him'. But, when I see the church and my own heart, I sometimes wonder 'is it possible'? What I see now bears so little resemblance to what is on the box.

But do not despair. God has promised that His Word will be fulfilled, His church will be glorious, His people will be perfect. One day, what is on the box will most surely come to pass. The 'jigsaw' will be complete.

We shall never come to the perfect man till we come to the perfect world.

(Matthew Henry)

4 May

> 'Enoch, the seventh from Adam, prophesied----"See the Lord is coming with thousand, thousand saints attending"'. (Jude 14)

Suggested reading 1 Thessalonians 4:13-18

I have in my possession a photograph which rarely sees the light of day. It is the 1954 crowning of the Bare Methodist Sunday School queen, with attendants and page boys. The two-page boys with silk shirts and short back and sides haircuts are me and my six-year-old twin brother. Not a photograph I rush to share with family and friends.

However, I have another similar photograph, which tells an altogether different story. It is 1984 and my daughter, Joanna, is in the retinue, as the Ingleton Gala queen is crowned. A special occasion for her and for me---so special that we delayed until evening our holiday departure for Scotland. And, a photograph I am happy to show to anyone.

When the Lord Jesus returns to this earth, he will be accompanied by believers---they will be part of his retinue. Today, with Him, we are often despised and rejected but how different it will be when Jesus comes again. We will have a status and honour which we never had on earth. On that day there will be no embarrassment for the believer---just pure unadulterated joy.

Amazingly, this truth was prophesied by Enoch, the seventh from Adam. Almost at the beginning of time, God through Enoch foretold what would happen at the end of time.

Lo! He comes with clouds descending,
Once for favoured sinners slain;
Thousand, thousand saints attending
Swell the triumph of His train;
Hallelujah!
God appears on earth to reign.

(John Cennick and Charles Wesley)

5 May

> 'for prophecy never had its origin in the human will, but prophets, though human, spoke from God as they were carried along by the Holy Spirit. (2 Peter 1:21)

Suggested reading Micah 5:1-5

There are two Ingletons---Ingleton (North Yorkshire) where I lived for forty years and Ingleton (County Durham). Prior to the introduction of postcodes, it was not unusual for post meant for Durham to be delivered to North Yorkshire.

One morning, I received a phone call from a man wishing to get married at St. John's church in Ingleton. I was puzzled on two fronts as I am not a vicar and there is no St. John's church in Ingleton.

However, things became a little clearer as the conversation proceeded and I realised that the man had got the wrong Ingleton. It was not the church in Ingleton, North Yorkshire but rather the one in County Durham for which he was seeking.

Years later a MP had to apologise to her constituents for confusing the two villages. Opening the village show in Ingleton, County Durham, she described the beautiful waterfalls and the deep caves for which the village was famous. Unfortunately, her researchers had failed her and she was, in fact, speaking about Ingleton, North Yorkshire---seventy miles away!

There were two Bethlehems in Israel, in Bible times, and that is why Micah, in his prophecy is quite specific. Jesus was to be born in Bethlehem, Ephrata not in Bethlehem of Zebulun. There is nothing vague or ambiguous about Biblical prophecy---what is foretold has and always will be fulfilled, right down to the smallest detail. Powerful proof that 'prophets, though human, spoke from God, as they were carried along by the Holy Spirit'. The Bible is the Word of God.

Because we believe the Scriptures to be the Word of God and we believe does not lie, we begin by accepting all its statements, including those which are historical, as true, rather than suspending judgment about them until they are proved to be true.

(David Samuel)

6 May

> 'When he comes, he will convict the world of guilt in regard to sin and righteousness and judgment'. (John 16:8)

Suggested reading Matthew20:1-16)

Ted was a retired farmer who tragically, as a young man, had witnessed the death of his wife in childbirth. Any faith Ted might have had was shattered, and feeling an intense anger and bitterness towards God, 'he went out and committed every sin in the book'. (Ted's own words)

Ted moved to a cottage in Ingleton and at the invitation of his neighbours, he began to attend church on Sunday evenings. As he did so, he found his own bitterness and anger starting to melt away, and this was to culminate in a night that Ted would never forget.

It was the concluding meeting of our Harvest Mission and the preacher chose as his text 'the harvest is passed, the summer is ended and we are not saved' (Jeremiah 8:20) There was a palpable sense of the Lord's presence and Ted was so affected that for three days, he could neither eat or sleep.

In a distressed condition, he called at my home on the Wednesday afternoon, overwhelmed by a sense of guilt and shame. I had the joy of leading Ted to Christ and later at our church prayer meeting, he testified to his new found faith. Converted at the age of seventy -two---'the eleventh hour' (Matthew 20:6) --- Ted was baptised and for the next twelve years, he was a most faithful member of the church.

Jesus said the Spirit would 'convict' and never before or since have I seen anyone under such conviction of sin. This conviction varies from person to person but without it there can be no true conversion. We need to see something of the holiness of God and feel the loathsomeness of our sin before Christ and his death can become personal and precious to us.

Christ is not sweet till sin is made bitter to us.

(John Flavel)

7 May

'The prayer of a righteous man is powerful and effective'. (James 5:16)

Suggested reading Acts 12:1-12)

In the days when most homes only had coal fires, there was a need for wood as well as coal. Chopping sticks was almost a hobby to my grandfather and I suspect he found it a pleasurable exercise. He enjoyed working with wood and my first train was built by him, with the wheels being made out of bobbins. Later, not being able to afford a cricket bat, he shaped one for me and with it, I scored a host of runs in 'test matches' against my brother.

On one occasion, I went into 'Granddad's hut' and he was not chopping wood or shaping it, he was doing something equally important: he was sharpening his axe. And how necessary that was, if sticks were to be chopped and made ready for the fire.

It is good when a church is active, preaching and evangelising---reaching men and women, boys and girls with the good news of Jesus Christ. Churches must be evangelistic churches, but something else is essential. How vital it is to seek the Lord and to plead with Him for His blessing upon our endeavours. That is why we can never underestimate the importance of personal and communal prayer. Otherwise, we are trying to chop sticks with a blunt axe.

If we ever forget our basic charter----'My house is a house of prayer'---we might as well shut the church doors.

(James S. Stewart)

8 May

'One thing I do know. I was blind but now I see' (John 9:25)

Suggested reading Mark 8:22-26

For a number of years, my grandmother was almost blind, and this placed a strain upon her and also other members of the family. As a boy, I tried to help by reading to her the morning newspaper, but this was not without its difficulties, as Grandma was also very deaf. Consequently, one had to 'shout' the news and even then, Grandma could not always hear what was being said.

It was, therefore, a significant day when Grandma agreed to have a cataract operation. What today is a procedure accomplished in minutes was a far riskier operation in the 1950s and 1960s. The patient was in hospital for several days and after the operation had to lie immobile in a darkened room. When the bandages were eventually removed, they had to be replaced by thick glasses.

Grandma's sight was not in any way fully restored but nevertheless, what a difference. She now had some sight and as well as walking unaided, she could, with the help of a magnifying glass, read newspapers and magazines by herself.

As believers our eyes have been opened---we, too, can testify 'I was blind but now I see'----and yet our 'spiritual vision' is not yet perfect. There are verses in the Bible we do not understand and providences we cannot make sense of. We see people 'like trees walking' (Mark 8:24) or as Paul puts it 'a poor reflection in a mirror'. That is how it is now and will be until we get to heaven, for it is:

Then I shall see and hear and know
All I desired and wished below.
And every power find sweet employ
In that eternal world of joy.

(Isaac Watts)

9 May

> Abraham said: 'I have been so bold as to speak to the Lord, though I am nothing but dust and ashes' (Genesis 18:27)

Suggested reading Psalm 47

The recent passing of the Queen and the Duke of Edinburgh reminds me of my one small claim to fame---the day the Duke spoke to me and I spoke to the Duke. It was a scorching May afternoon and I was escorting Pat, when she had been invited to a Royal Garden Party at Buckingham Palace.

Now I would not want anyone to think it was a deep and significant conversation because that was far from being the case. As he strolled by, the Duke turned to me and asked 'Have you got your sun cream on'? I responded by saying, 'No, but I should have'. That was the sum of our conversation---- no more than twelve words between us----and yet, years afterwards, I still recall the 'conversation' with pride and satisfaction.

I was thrilled and honoured to be in the presence of the Duke of Edinburgh and to engage, albeit, in the briefest of conversations. But that is a pale reflection of how we should all feel whenever we come into the presence of God. Is it not truly amazing that through his Word, the Creator of the Universe speaks to us and through prayer we can speak with the Lord God Almighty? True, God is our Father and our Friend but He is still 'a consuming fire' (Hebrews 12:29) Let us marvel and rejoice, therefore, at communion with God and approach him yes, with boldness and confidence but also with reverence and awe.

True worship is a blend of godly fear and trembling with joy that we are accepted in the Beloved.

(Errol Hulse)

10 May

> 'The virgin will be with child and will give birth to a son, and they will call him Immanuel---which means, "God with us". (Matthew 1:23)

Suggested reading Mark 3:31-35

For many years, making cards has been Pat's hobby----birthday cards, Christmas cards, cards for all occasions with the proceeds going to support a number of different Christian charities.

It is increasingly difficult to buy a Christmas card with a nativity theme and so one year, most of the cards we sent had been made by Pat. There were a variety of cards but on each she put the words 'Immanuel---God with us'.

To our amusement, one Christmas Eve, we received a card through the post addressed to 'John, Pat, Aaron and Immanuel'. The sender must have thought there had been an addition to our family.

I suppose a child could be called 'Immanuel' but the only true Immanuel is Jesus---the Son of God. And yet, through faith in Christ, God can be with us, just as he was with Mary and Joseph, two thousand years ago.

Jesus said, 'Whoever does God's will is my brother and sister and mother' (Mark 3; 35) And the writer to the Hebrews says, 'Both the one who makes men holy and those who are made holy are of the same family. So, Jesus is not ashamed to call them brothers' (Hebrew 2:11)

Quite amazing but if we are believers, Jesus is our brother. We are in the same family----'Immanuel' is indeed 'with us'.

Adoption, as the term clearly implies, is an act of transfer from an alien family into the family of God himself. This is surely the apex of grace and privilege

(John Murray)

11 May

> 'Nevertheless, God's solid foundation stands firm, sealed with this inscription: "The Lord knows those who are his". (2 Tomothy 2:19)

Suggested reading Matthew 13: 24-30 and 36-43

Every Sunday morning when I preach at a certain church, a husband and wife are sat together in the congregation. When I announce the Scripture reading, the man takes a Bible out of his pocket and follows what is being read. And then, throughout the sermon, whenever a verse is referred to, in either the Old or the New Testament, he diligently turns to the verses.

I was amazed, therefore, when talking to his wife to be informed that her husband is not a believer. For over thirty-years, he has been attending church on a Sunday morning, studiously following all that is said but has never come to personal faith in Christ. His wife is understandably concerned about him, still praying that the day will come when he is brought to repentance and to personal faith.

The professing, visible church is made up of wheat and weeds-----believers and unbelievers. They can be sitting next to each other in the same congregation. And, it is not always possible for us to discern the difference. Jesus speaks of this in the parable of the wheat and the tares. '----while you are pulling the weeds, you may root up the wheat with them. Let both grow together until the harvest'. (Matthew 13:29-30)

Jesus then goes on to explain about the harvest. 'The harvest is the end of the age, and the harvesters are the angels'. (Matthew 13:39) At the end of the age, Jesus will return and the angels will separate the wheat from the weeds. The angels---not men-- are the reapers because they know all who have truly repented. (Luke 15:10) There is then a different destination for the wheat and the weeds with believers going to heaven and the unrepentant going to hell.

Repentance and personal faith are all-important, as it determines our eternal destination

To believe in heaven but not in hell is to declare that there were times when Jesus was telling the truth and times when he was lying.

(John Blanchard)

12 May

> 'Dear friends, now we are children of God, and what we will be has not yet been made known. But we know that when he appears, we shall be like him, for we shall see him as he is' (1 John 3:2)

Suggested reading Romans 8:18-30

In the 1970s, each week I handed the 'dole' out to an unknown, unemployed, penniless young woman. As she stood, waiting for her money, in no way was she different or distinctive from anyone else in the queue.

However, not many years later, she was a famous comedy actress with her own shows on the stage and television. She went on to win numerous accolades and was honoured by being awarded both the OBE and the CBE. When she died, a statue was erected to her in her home town.

What a transformation.

However, it falls into insignificance when we consider the transformation awaiting the child of God. Now our bodies are subject to disease and death but one day we will have a body 'like his glorious body' (Philippians 3:21) Now we still sin but in heaven there will be no sin 'for the old order of things has passed away' (Revelation 21:4) Now we are unknown, despised, even persecuted but when Jesus comes again 'the righteous will shine like the sun in the kingdom of their father'. (Matthew 13:43)

What a transformation---way beyond our imagining.

There are three things which the true Christian desires in respect to sin; justification that it might not condemn; sanctification, that it might not reign; and glorification that it may not be.

(Richard Cecil)

13 May

> 'After the Lord Jesus had spoken to them, he was taken up into heaven and he sat at the right hand of God' (Mark 1619)

Suggested reading Acts 1:1-11

April 27 1974 was at the time Morecambe Football Club's finest hour. It was the FA Trophy Final at Wembley Stadium and they beat Dartford by two goals to one.

The FA trophy was a national competition introduced in 1969 for semi-professional clubs and to win the trophy was an outstanding achievement, witnessed by a crowd of 19,000.

I happened to be in Morecambe town centre when the players arrived back in the resort. They rode on an open-top bus, displaying the trophy, and as they did so, thousands sang, applauded and cheered. The conquering heroes were welcomed home.

It is a mundane illustration, but gives a slight insight into what happened on Ascension Day. On Easter Day, Jesus triumphed over sin, death, Satan and hell. He defeated the enemy. That was Easter Day but forty days later Jesus returned home and the whole of heaven turned out to greet him. Angels, archangels, cherubims, seraphims and thousands of his saints acknowledged and acclaimed his triumph. In the words of the hymnwriter:

Hark, those bursts of acclamation!
Hark, those loud triumphant cords!
Jesus takes the highest station:
O what joy the sight affords!
Crown Him! Crown Him1
King of Kings and Lord of Lords!

(Thomas Kelly)

14 May

'You shall have no other gods before me'. (Exodus 20:3)

Suggested reading: Ezekiel 14: 1-8

From supporting Morecambe FC for many years to writing articles for magazines, football is a hobby which has brought me hours of enjoyment.

2024 was the year of the European Football Championship and yet, without I hope sounding unpatriotic, I was not too disappointed when England failed to win the trophy. The reason being that, for many, football has replaced Christianity and become an idol.

The stadium is their church, the stands their pews, the team their god, the manager their saviour, some player their messiah. The referee is the devil and instead of hymns and songs, they have their chants and anthems. Therefore, though England got to the final, I fear we would have witnessed idolatry if they had actually won the trophy.

Human beings are religious beings. We were made to worship and if we do not worship the one true God, then we will create our own deities. But they are false gods and because they are false, they are bound to fail and to disappoint. The gods of pleasure and of materialism---they promise much but they can never meet the deepest need of the human heart. That is why I was not too disappointed when England failed to win the Euros.

Satan doesn't care what we worship, as long as we don't worship God,

(D.L. Moody)

15 May

> 'Blessed are the poor in spirit, for theirs is the kingdom of heaven'. (Matthew 5:3)

1 Corinthians 16:1-4

In Methodism, church officers were called stewards----circuit stewards, society stewards, chapel stewards and poor stewards. As a boy, I misunderstood what was meant by a poor steward. I used to think that such an officer either had no money or was not very good at the job.

Of course, it meant neither of these things. At the communion service, there was always an offering for the poor and these were the church officers who administered that fund.

Being a poor steward never had the same status as being a circuit or a society steward and appropriately the office was often filled by those who were genuinely 'poor in spirit'.

When we meet at the Lord's table, we remember One who 'though he was rich, yet for your sake, he became poor'. (2 Corinthians 8:9). It was fitting, therefore, to express our thankfulness by being generous to others.

Is not every believer called upon to be a 'poor steward'? To be characterised by a spirit of humility and to have a continual concern for the poor and for all who are not as fortunate as we are.

We are to give to the poor out of pity. Not to be seen and applauded, much less to get influence over them; but out of pure sympathy and compassion we must give them help.

(Charles H. Spurgeon)

16 May

> 'Without the shedding of blood there is no forgiveness'
> (Hebrews 9:22)

Suggested reading Matthew 27:45-50

Aaron, our multi-handicapped son, was in Manchester Children's Hospital for major surgery. It was for him a high-risk operation and we were understandably anxious as we accompanied Aaron to the doors of the operating theatre. But why would loving parents ever subject their child to the pain of the surgeon's knife? There is only one explanation. It was necessary because there was no alternative.

Aaron, due to his disability, suffered from a condition which caused the contents of his stomach regularly to leak back into his oesophagus. This resulted in severe heartburn and the constant threat of pneumonia. The only possible remedy was the operation he was now facing. It was necessary because there was no alternative.

Why did God subject his Son---the apple of his eye---to the agony and humiliation of the cross? There is only one answer. It was necessary---

there was no other alternative. God could not overlook our sin. To do so might have been loving but it would not have been just. Justice demanded that sin be punished and paid for. Calvary---where God's love and justice met---was the only remedy for sin.

'God demonstrates his own love for us in this: while we were still sinners, Christ died for us'. (Romans 5:8)

In the cross, sin is cursed and cancelled. In the cross grace is victorious and available.

(G. Campbell Morgan)

17 May

'We do not know what we ought to pray for, but the Spirit himself intercedes for us with groans that words cannot express'. (Romans 8:26)

Suggested reading 1 Kings 8:12-21

For the first ten years as a preacher, I did not have my own transport and was dependant either on public transport or the kindness of family and friends. One summer Sunday, I decided to cycle from Heysham to an afternoon service being held in a farmhouse near Carnforth. I soon discovered that, though I was a young man, fourteen miles on a gearless bike in scorching hot weather was not a good idea.

I had left myself short of time, hills appeared where I am sure they had never been before, and what I expected to be a leisurely ride turned out to be more demanding than any stage of the Tour of France. I arrived a minute before the service was due to start and though I managed to announce the first hymn, I was so exhausted and out of breath, there was no way I could possibly sing it.

My desire was to praise the Lord but out of weakness, I could not do it.

It is a comfort to the believer that the Lord 'knows how we are formed, he remembers that we are dust'. (Psalm 103:14) There are times when we want to pray but because of illness or circumstances or ignorance, either we cannot pray or we do not know how to pray. It is then that 'the Spirit himself intercedes for us with groans that words cannot express'. David could not fulfil his desire to build the Temple but God graciously commended him because the desire to do so had been in his heart. (1 Kings 8:18)

If it is your desire to worship, to pray, to witness, to be involved in Christian work and yet circumstances mean it is not possible---do not be discouraged. The Lord knows and we will be rewarded not just for what we do did but also for what we wanted to do.

Actions speak louder than words, but with God, motives speak louder than either.

(Arthur Neil)

18 May

> 'These people honour me with their lips, but their hearts are far from me'. (Matthew 15:8)

Suggested reading Psalm 84

From being a boy, football has been one of my hobbies and I cannot begin to calculate how many matches I must have seen. Sadly, it is not an interest shared by my wife and in over fifty years, we have only been to one or two games together. Pat finds football boring and uninteresting.

How come then that on a Saturday morning at 9.30, she is to be found on a touchline, watching a game of football? What has brought about the change? Well, this is a girl's under-12 match and not only is our granddaughter playing but our grandson is the referee. Pat has a personal interest in what is taking place and I have almost to restrain her as she gets caught up in the excitement. Especially when Elodie scores but the goal is disallowed for offside---by her brother!

Does this not illustrate what was once the attitude of many of us to the church and to Christianity? We were bored and not interested. What made the difference? Well, we came to have a personal interest in the One who is at the heart of Christianity. There came a time when we came to see, yes----Christ had died for sinners but more than that, he had died for me. He had borne my sin, my guilt, my punishment. It became personal and now we were eager to learn more about him and to worship him in church. With the Psalmist 'I rejoiced with those who said to me, "Let us go to the house of the Lord". (Psalm 122:1) in Jesus

Worship is giving to the Lord the glory that is due in response to what he has revealed to us and done for us in Jesus Christ his Son'.

(Oswald B. Milligan)

19 May

'Elijah was a human being, even as we are' (James 5:17)

Suggested reading 2 Corinthians 1:3-11

Having broken my wrist, I sat one morning in a café in Bradford, feeling somewhat sorry for myself. An elderly lady, sitting at the next table, asked me what I had done. When I told her, she said, 'Five years ago, I did the same. I fell and broke my wrist. But give it time, be patient. Do the physio, and you will find the pain goes and your hand will get back to normal'.

My spirits immediately lifted. This lady had suffered what I was suffering, and therefore, I could identify with her and she could empathise with me. The wrist was still broken and painful but I left the café feeling so much better than I had when entering it.

The Bible is an honest book for, in it, we see both the triumphs and the failures of the saints. And whilst we do not rejoice in the weaknesses of a Jacob, David or Peter, we are comforted in knowing they were all human beings 'even as we are' . They faced the same trials and temptations as we do, because we are all engaged in the same spiritual battle. 'We are surrounded by a great cloud of witnesses' (Hebrews 12:1) and just as they depended on divine resources, so too can we in our fight with the world, the flesh and the devil.

Empathy is your pain in my heart.

(Halford E. Luccock)

20 May

> 'When tempted, no one should say "God is tempting me". For God cannot be tempted by evil, nor does he tempt anyone; but each is tempted when, by his own evil desire, he is dragged away and enticed'. (James 1:13-14)

Suggested reading Joshua 7:16-21

Our three youngest grandchildren have lived in Singapore for most of their childhood and whilst there are many things they enjoy---especially the climate---there are certain things they do miss. That is why, on a recent Christmas visit, they were thrilled when it snowed---not something they had ever seen in Singapore.

However, this summer---being in the UK---Reuben had a strange wish; he wanted to be stung by a nettle! Something we go out of our way to avoid, he wanted to experience because, in Singapore, he has never come across a stinging nettle. We took him on a number of country walks but I never heard of his wish being granted.

It seems strange that anyone should want to be stung by a nettle and yet how often, especially young people---even though they know they will be stung---are still allured and tempted by particular sins. For example, it is well known that drink, drugs, sexual immorality etc. have been the ruination of many but young people are still drawn to them.

Adam added to his sin by trying to throw the blame upon God---'the woman you put here with me----she gave me some fruit from the tree and I ate it' (Genesis 3:12) James emphasises, 'when tempted no-one should say "God is tempting me". For God cannot be tempted by evil, nor does he tempt anyone'. We must not blame God, neither must we hold the devil responsible. The temptation may come from him but it only becomes sin when we acquiesce to his suggestion. Ultimately, it is our 'own evil desire' which causes us to sin.

Temptation is the tempter looking through the keyhole into the room where you are living; sin is your drawing back the bolt and making it possible for him to enter.

(J. Wilbur Chapman)

21 May

'I will not sacrifice to the Lord my God burnt offerings that cost me nothing'.

(2 Samuel 24:24)

Suggested reading 1 Corinthians 9:14-23

I had been taking a midweek Bible study and at the end of the meeting, I was given an envelope which, on the front, thanked me for my ministry. I put it in my pocket and opened it later when I got home. Inside the envelope---despite an intensive search---I found nothing. Pat kindly commented, "perhaps that is what your Bible study was worth".

A few weeks later, I had a phone call from an anxious treasurer who was having difficulty balancing the books. Before he went into detail, I was able to tell him that I was the answer to his 'problem'. Though embarrassed he was relieved and since then, we have often laughed about the incident.

There is, however, a serious challenge in this humorous incident. Does our worship, our giving, our service cost us anything or are we just content to offer to the Lord that which makes no demands upon us? The Apostle Paul, if necessary, was prepared to forego remuneration (1 Corinthians 9:14-15), sleep, food, drink, clothing, every home comfort (2 Corinthians 11:27) for the sake of the gospel.

Am I prepared to sacrifice money, time, and energy for the sake of others and for the extension of the kingdom of Christ?

If Jesus Christ be God and died for me, then no sacrifice can be too great for me to make for him.

(C.T. Studd)

22 May

> 'I tell you, now is the time of God's favour, now is the day of salvation'. (2 Corinthians 6:2)

Suggested reading Luke 14:15-24

In the 1970s, I regularly went to Blackpool, when the illuminations were on, to engage in open-air evangelism. Saturday afternoon was spent on the promenade but after a teatime snack, we made our way to the Brunswick Working Men's Club.

This was a popular venue and vast numbers queued waiting for the doors to open. The crowd was generally good humoured and several of us took it in turns to distribute leaflets and to preach the gospel.

Every week, there were those who failed to gain admission: some because they did not have the right documentation but others for another reason. The club reached its seating capacity and a steward would then come to the front of the queue and raise the sign 'FULL'. Many who had been waiting for up to an hour had to walk away sad and disappointed.

Universalism teaches that everyone will get to heaven but that is contrary to what Jesus taught. We need the correct documentation because 'small is the gate and narrow the road that leads to life, and only a few find it'. (Matthew 7:14) It is essential that we repent and trust Jesus as Saviour, because only those who do so will gain access to heaven.

That is a solemn truth but the good news is---heaven is not yet full. When Jesus comes again it will be but until He returns, there is still room. How vital it is that we do not delay in making our commitment to Christ, for we never know when the day of grace will end and the day of judgement begin.

God has promised forgiveness to your repentance but he has not promised tomorrow to your procrastination.

(G. B. Cheever)

23 May

> 'My dear children, I write this to you so that you will not sin. But if anybody does sin, we have one who speaks to the Father in our defence---Jesus Christ the Righteous One'. (1 John 2:1)

Suggested reading Luke 22:31-38

One of the joys of being a child in the 1950s was going to the circus----the big top, the master of ceremonies, the clowns, the animals. But, above all, I enjoyed the trapeze artists and tightrope walkers. How brave they were, as they exercised their skills way beyond the admiring audience.

However, the majority of them had a safety net, and whilst this, in no way, lessened my admiration for them, it did mean that if anything went wrong, there was something in place to stop them crashing to the floor.

I am sure the circus artists did not perform thinking they could be careless, as the net would always be there to protect them. I am sure that was not their attitude at all. No, they were determined not to slip or fall but if they did, then the safety net was a provision to ensure that their fall was not final or fatal.

The believer does not want sin. In his heart there is the determination not to sin, and yet there are times when he slips and falls into sin. How wonderful that, in His grace and mercy, the Lord has made provision for such times. 'If anybody does sin, we have an advocate with the Father---Jesus Christ, the Righteous One. He is the atoning sacrifice for our sins'. (1 John 2:1-2) 'If we confess our sins, he is faithful and just and will forgive us our sins and purify us from all unrighteousness'. (1 John 1:9)

We do still slip and fall into sin but because of this provision, our fall is not final or fatal. Thank God for the safety net---but let us be careful not to abuse it. The provision is not for those who want to sin but rather for those whose desire it is, not to sin.

If Christ had not ascended, he could not have interceded, as he now does in heaven for us. And do but take away Christ's intercession and you starve the hope of the saints.

(John Flavel)

24 May

> ' the Counsellor, the Holy Spirit, whom the Father will send in my name, will teach you all things and will remind you of everything I have said to you'. (John 14:26)

Suggested reading: Acts 5:1-11

The doorbell rings and there are two strangers standing on the doorstep. Almost inevitably, it is a visit from the Jehovah Witnesses and whilst I am sad to see them peddling heresy from door to door, nevertheless I treat them with courtesy and respect.

There are, of course, things we can agree on---people are ignorant of the Bible and as a nation, we have abandoned God. But, there are major doctrines denied by the JWs, which means their teaching is heretical.

On this occasion, consistent with JW teaching, I am told that the Holy Spirit is a force, a power and not a Person. I respond by asking 'How can the Holy Spirit be a Comforter if he is not a person'? The answer is quite ingenious: 'A hot water bottle can comfort you and that is not a Person'.

Full marks for ingenuity but not a satisfactory answer. I reply, 'true---but can a hot bottle teach you? Can a hot water bottle lead you into all truth'? Here the analogy obviously breaks down.

The Holy Spirit is a Person—the third Person of the Trinity, the third Person of the Godhead. In Acts 5:3, Peter says to Ananias 'you have lied to the Holy Spirit' but goes on to say in Acts 5:4, 'you have not lied to men but to God'. Proof indeed that the Holy Spirit is God. Not an impersonal force but our Guide, our Teacher, our Counsellor and our Comforter.

The doctrine of the Trinity is the differentiating doctrine of the Christian faith.

(D. Martyn Lloyd---Jones)

25 May

> 'I will build my church and the gates of Hades will not overcome it', (Matthew 16:18)

Suggested reading Revelation 2:1-7

On holiday in Wales, we crossed the border into Shropshire to visit the market town of Oswestry. Coming out of a car park, there was a large church ahead, with a banner displayed outside of the building. From a distance, I thought the banner said 'Sunday Message' and momentarily, I was encouraged.

However, to my dismay on getting closer, I discovered the words were not 'Sunday Message' but rather 'Sunday Massage'. Far from being a place of worship, the redundant church was now a health and fitness centre. Another indication that to many, the body is far more important than the soul.

Churches will close, 'lampstands' can be removed, the visible church can become weaker and weaker. The reasons are various---changes in population, churches not preaching the gospel, secularism grabbing a nation. The reasons are various but it can be depressing to see the number of redundant churches in villages, towns and cities.

However, the true, invisible church made up of all who have repented and trusted Christ as Saviour—that church can never become weaker. Every second it gets stronger, as believers are added to the church on earth by conversion and added by death to the church in heaven. It is the one true church, with two different branches---one on earth and the other in heaven.

Christ Jesus will build His church and ultimately it will be made up of 'a great multitude that no one could count'. (Revelation 7:9) Praise God!

The church shall survive the world and be in bliss when that is in ruins.

(Matthew Henry)

26 May

> 'We all, like sheep, have gone astray, each of us has turned to our own way'. (Isaiah 53:6)

Suggested reading Luke 15:1-9)

Having moved, in August, to our new home in Burley in Wharfedale, we bought a book of local walks and on a beautiful autumn morning, set off down the delightfully named Staircase Lane in Bramhope. We kept on moving or otherwise, we might have become engrossed picking blackberries or gathering conkers. Eventually, our walk took us into the picturesque Chevin Forest, where many of the trees were shedding their leaves.

We were greatly enjoying the walk but soon discovered how easy it is to go astray. Not at all sure where we were, we vacated the forest and seeing a café across the road, we relished our bread and soup. On leaving, we told a young man where we wanted to be and he told us to 'turn left and to keep on walking'. The trek took us down a very steep hill, and we were both thankful that we were going downhill and not uphill.

We continued walking but nothing seemed familiar and so we sought advice from a man getting into a utility van. His response was far from encouraging. 'You are going in the wrong direction. You are miles from where you want to be'. He must have seen how crestfallen we were, but taking pity on us, he said, 'Get into the van'. This we did, and he kindly dropped us off just half a mile from my vehicle. Pat and I were so grateful, not just because we were leg weary, but also because we were in time to pick up our grandchildren from school.

We have all gone 'our own way' and have diverted from the 'straight and narrow way'. This means that, in our foolishness and rebellion, we have all wandered far away from God. In order to rescue us, Jesus did far more than our kind friend, Jesus took the initiative---seeking us and dying for us on the cross of Calvary. Have we expressed our gratitude and thankfulness to Him?

> God had only one Son and he made him an evangelist.
>
> (R.C. Lucas)

27 May

> 'For Christ's love compels us, because we are convinced that one died for all, and therefore all died'. (2 Corinthians 5:14)

Suggested reading 1 John 4:7-21

Having started secondary school, we went for our first physics lesson with a teacher who had a fearsome reputation. His initial task was to write down our names and within minutes we saw his 'fearsome reputation' was well earned.

'Name'? He asked.
'Michael Price' was the reply
'I cannot hear you'.
'Michael Price'---in a slightly raised voice.
I cannot hear you.
'Michael Price'---in a more confident voice
'I still cannot hear you'.
'Michael Price'---now in a voice that the deaf could hear.
'Outside'

Poor Michael had incurred the wrath of Mr. P and was dismissed from the class for ten minutes. Mr. P. had begun as he meant to go on and for the next two years, in one way or another, we were all to suffer at his hands. I got the distinct impression that, though he knew and liked his subject, Mr. P. did not like children---an unfortunate characteristic in any teacher!

There is a challenge here to every pastor, preacher, evangelist, children's worker and indeed, to every believer. Do we love men and women, boys and girls? This is the hallmark of the Christian. 'Everyone who loves has been born of God and knows God. Whoever does not love does not know God, because God is love'. (1 John 4:7-8) We must know and love the Bible---that is essential—but we must also know and love people.

A man may be a good doctor without loving his patients; a good lawyer without loving his clients; a good geologist without loving science; but he cannot be a good Christian without love.

(D.L. Moody)

28 May

> 'Endure hardship with us like a good soldier of Jesus Christ'.
> (2 Timothy 2:3)

Suggested reading Ephesians 6:10-20

From being a child, many of my Saturday afternoons have been spent watching either football or cricket matches. I have always found this a relaxing experience but one Saturday, it had unexpected consequences.

It was the tea break at Lancaster Cricket Club, which borders the River Lune and I climbed an embankment to get a better view of the river. Coming down, I stumbled and in so doing, tore some tendons in my shoulder. This meant a visit to A and E, resulting in my arm being put in a sling.

This was to prove both amusing and embarrassing when, the next morning, I entered the pulpit with my arm in a sling and continued my series from Ephesians 6, on Christian warfare! I had to convince the congregation I had not dressed up to be a 'visual aid'.

Life for the believer is not a picnic or a cricket match but a battle, as we fight the world, the flesh and the devil. Because of the death and resurrection of Jesus, the war is won, victory is assured but we still have many battles to face. Paul is speaking from experience when he tells Timothy to 'endure hardship with us as a good soldier of Jesus Christ'. Trials and troubles, suffering and pain are an inevitable part of Christian discipleship and they have to be 'endured'.

There are times when discipleship is enjoyable but there are other times when it calls for endurance. At such times we need to follow the example of our Captain and Commander 'who for the joy set before him endured the cross'. (Hebrews 12:2)) Christ endured and he has provided us with all the spiritual armour that is necessary 'so that when the evil day comes, you may be able to stand your ground' (Ephesians 6:13)

The Christian life is not a playground; it is a battleground

(Warren Wiersbe)

29 May

> 'Therefore, if anyone is in Christ, he is a new creation; the old has gone, the new has come' (2 Corinthians 5:17)

Suggested reading Colossians 3:5-14

A young man began to attend our church who, prior to his conversion, had been a hippy. He still dressed as a hippy and had some 'way out' clothing but this made no difference and he was warmly welcomed into the fellowship of the church.

Some months later, there was a remarkable change in his attire. He now wore a shirt and tie, and even bought a suit. What a change! The old gear had gone and new gear had been put on. But why?

Well, he had started going out with a young lady from the church. Now, he had a new affection, a new relationship, and this could be seen---even in his wardrobe.

Paul uses this very picture in Colossians 3. As believers, who have come to faith in Jesus Christ, we too have a new affection, a new relationship and this should be seen in our spiritual wardrobe. We have to rid ourselves of 'anger, rage, malice, slander, filthy language' (Colossians 3:8) and clothe ourselves with 'compassion, kindness, humility, gentleness, patience' (Colossians 3:12)

How is your spiritual wardrobe? Are there old attitudes we need to get rid of and new things we need to put on?

'Putting on Christ' is not one among many jobs a Christian has to do; and it is not a sort of special exercise for the top class. It is the whole of Christianity.

(C.S. Lewis)

30 May

> 'God chose the foolish things of the world to shame the wise; God chose the weak things of the world to shame the strong'. (1 Corinthians 1:27)

Suggested reading John 14:1-7

Travelling the A65 between Skipton and Kendal, one is attracted to a giant poster in a farmer's field, on which, a Bible text is prominently displayed. 'Jesus answered, "I am the way and the truth and the life. No one comes to the Father except through me'. (John 14:6) It is thrilling to think of the many motorists who are confronted every day by those words of Jesus.

But why are they there? Well, I know the farmer and as a Christian, he wishes to share the gospel with the passing motorists. And yet, that is not the fundamental reason those words are on display. The real reason is that the disciple, Thomas, gripped by doubt and fear, said to Jesus, 'Lord, we don't know where you are going, so how can we know the way'? (John 14:5)

It is impossible to estimate how many have been converted and are in the kingdom of heaven through the words of Jesus in John 14:6, but we only have John 14:6 because of the question asked by a confused and anxious disciple in John 14:5.

This is the providence of God, taking the question of a weak disciple and causing it to be used in a way Thomas could never have imagined for the eternal benefit of multitudes.

What an encouragement to every frail, doubting believer. We all have weaknesses and shortcomings but despite that, God can use us to build his church and fulfil his purposes. Such is his amazing providence he can so transform our deficiencies that they become a means of blessing to others.

The men that have moved the world for God have done what they have done not because they were strong but because they were weak, and their weakness was transfigured by grace into an instrument in the hands of God for blessing.

(James Philip)

31 May

> 'Rejoice and be glad, because great is your reward in heaven'. (Matthew 5:12)

Suggested reading Matthew 6:1-7

Pat and I had taken a Ladies meeting at a church in the Yorkshire Dales and as we left, I was handed an envelope. On the front it said 'John--- with many thanks'.

I usually do not open such an envelope until I get home, but on this occasion, having to wait whilst Pat' popped into a shop', I did open it and my eyes almost 'popped' out of my head. For, inside the envelope, there was a cheque for £831.54. I knew the ladies had appreciated our ministry but surely not to that extent!

I then noticed that the cheque was made out to a John but it wasn't me---it was another John. Apparently a 'John' who had done work for the church and this was the payment for his services. I had been handed the wrong envelope and was only too happy to give it back.

Sometimes, in material ways, we are rewarded on earth, as believers express their appreciation but the greater rewards are not as tangible. The reward of knowing that we are engaged in the Lord's work and that others have benefitted spiritually through our witness and ministry. This is something that can never be measured in monetary terms.

There are rewards on earth but Jesus promised the greater reward will be in heaven. Our works, our obedience, our sacrifice----these are not the means by which we gain heaven for we are 'saved by grace through faith' but they are the things which determine our reward in heaven. Although, we cannot altogether understand it, Jesus taught there will be 'lesser' and 'greater' rewards in heaven.

In heaven to be even the least is a great thing, for all will be great.

(Thomas a Kempis)

BIBLE READINGS JUNE

1 June

> 'Satan, himself masquerades as an angel of light. It is not surprising, then, if his servants also masquerade as servants of righteousness' (2 Corinthians 11:14-15)

Suggested reading Matthew 16: 21-28

The first radio programme I can ever recall hearing was the 1950s comedy, 'Educating Archie'. It was hugely popular and surprisingly so because it was a ventriloquist act on the radio. To me, as a boy, Archie Andrews was a real person, not a dummy being operated by Peter Brough.

Up to fifteen million listeners tuned in each week to the Light Programme and the Archie Andrews fan club had two hundred and fifty thousand members. It was also possible to buy Archie Andrews lollipops, soap, comics and annuals.

Legendary BBC broadcaster, Alistair Cooke once said 'I prefer radio to TV because the pictures are better' and this perhaps explains the popularity of Educating Archie.

As a ventriloquist speaks through a dummy, so Satan speaks through men and women. This in no way negates personal responsibility but nevertheless, they are being motivated by the devil. That is why when Peter said he would never allow Jesus to go to the cross, his Master said 'Get behind me, Satan'. (Matthew 16:23) Jesus recognised who was speaking.

This was something I sought to remember when preaching in the open air and faced with obscenity and blasphemy. However, appalled and outraged I felt, I needed to tell myself they were only 'carrying out their father's desire' (John 8:44) I trust this caused me to be forthright but, at the same time, compassionate.

A man who is not a Christian is Satan's prisoner. Satan has him where he wants him.

(J.I. Packer)

2 June

> 'The evil deeds of the wicked ensnare them; the cords of their sins hold them fast'. (Proverbs 5:22)

Suggested reading John 8:31-41

How often today we hear swearing and blasphemy even from the mouths of young children. They are to be pitied rather than blamed, as I suspect they are just repeating what they have heard in their homes. Sadly, what begins in childhood can become an unbreakable habit in adulthood.

On one occasion, doing street evangelism, I came across such a young man, whose language was vile and blasphemous. When I commented on this, his reply was, 'You can't swear; you daren't'---I can; I am free to swear'.

I responded by saying, 'Yes, you are free to swear, but are you free not to swear'? Our subsequent conversation was both sad and informative. Swearing was such a part of this young man's normal vocabulary that despite his obvious irritation, the vile words continued to come. Yes, he had the freedom to swear but no freedom not to swear.

Many boast of freedom, even when they are in bondage to habits and desires they do not have the power to break. True freedom is not the right to do as we please; it is the liberty to do as we ought, and that freedom is to be found in Christ. Jesus said, 'If the Son sets you free, you will be free indeed'. (John 8:36)

The only freedom that man ever has, is when he becomes a slave to Jesus Christ'.

(R. C. Sproul)

3 June

> 'No-one can come to me unless the Father who sent me draws him'. (John 6:44)

Suggested reading John 12:20-33

A boy and a girl, both known to me, were in the same class at school but the girl had no time for the boy. Indeed, she said some very derogatory things about him. And yet, twelve years after school, this same boy and girl got married.

I was at their wedding but I don't recall the girl being dragged down the aisle against her wishes. On the contrary, when the minister asked, 'Do you have this man to be your lawful husband?' She said 'I do.' There was no compulsion; it was her own voluntary decision. What had happened between school and this moment? The man had courted and wooed the girl, until she now wanted to be his wife.

No-one ever becomes a Christian who does not want to be a Christian. No-one is ever dragged against their wishes into the kingdom of heaven. No Jesus said 'I, when I am lifted up from the earth, will draw all people to myself'. His cross draws reluctant sinners to Himself. Jesus makes men and women willing to trust Him, because they are drawn by His love for them.

This is the power of the gospel. Hard hearts are melted and proud hearts are humbled, as Jesus, the heavenly Bridegroom woos his prospective bride.

The distinguishing mark of a Christian is his confidence in the love of Christ, and the yielding of his affections to Christ in return.

(Charles H. Spurgeon)

4 June

> 'There is a way that seems right to a man but in the end, it leads to death'. (Proverbs 14:12)

Suggested reading Acts 4:1-12

Shortly after having moved house, it was dark and returning home one evening, I turned confidently into what I thought was the driveway of our new home. Somehow, things seemed rather unfamiliar and this was confirmed when the door was opened by a somewhat bemused gentleman. I had not driven into my own driveway but that of my neighbour.

Realising I had gone wrong, I apologised to my neighbour and I had then to reverse before I could negotiate my own driveway. That night I was taught an embarrassing lesson----whilst there were many driveways down Croft Road, only one led to my house.

Many ways to God? Many roads to heaven? That is the mantra of so many, at the present time, but the Bible is quite explicit. Jesus said, 'I am the way--no one comes to the Father, except through me' (John 14:6) There is only one way to our heavenly home and that is through faith in Jesus Christ. To some, other ways might seem attractive, even logical but they are destined to end in death and disappointment. It is only the 'narrow road that leads to life' (Matthew 7:14)

If we are on the wrong road, we need to turn around---to repent---and to trust in 'The Way'. Jesus is the only one who can reconcile us to God and ultimately, bring us to heaven.

There are as many paths to Christ as there are feet to tread them, but there is only one way to God.

(A. Lindsay Glegg)

5 June

> 'Grow in the grace and knowledge of our Lord and Saviour Jesus Christ'

(2 Peter 3:18)

Suggested reading Acts 2:42-47

Covid restrictions meant we had more time to devote to our garden, which became a source of great pleasure. There were frequent trips to the garden centre to buy plants, and as I read the instructions, I was again reminded of how healthy growth was not automatic.

Hostas----moist soil in partial shade
Clematis----well-drained soil and a sunny sheltered position.
Hydrangea---prefers moist, well-drained soil
Lilac---fertile, well-drained soil in full sun.

The plants might survive in other conditions, but each has its own particular requirements for thriving.

As believers, our great desire is to become more and more like Jesus, but sanctification is not automatic. Just as a plant needs the right conditions, the same is true for a Christian and those conditions are set out in the Bible.

We need to be taught from the Scriptures. We need the fellowship of the Lord's people and a regular reminder of the death of our Saviour. We need to spend time in prayer. These are the means the Lord has provided if we are to grow in our likeness to Him.

Are we availing ourselves of the means? Are we fulfilling the conditions?

God will do everything that we cannot do in order that we may live, but will do nothing that we can do in order that we may grow.

(Anon)

6 June

> 'No-one knows about that day or hour, not even the angels in heaven, nor the Son but only the Father' (Matthew 24:36)

Suggested reading Romans 8:18-27

Picking my children, up at railway stations pinpointed two truths concerning the return of Christ. On the first occasion, on arriving at the station, I checked the information monitor and it had the words I was wanting to see. 'ON TIME'.

The same is true of the Second Coming of Christ. Sometimes, when we see the wickedness in the world, we might feel that it has been delayed, but according to the Divine timetable, known only to the Godhead, it is ON TIME.

On the second occasion, on the platform waiting to meet my son, the train pulled in and hundreds seemed to disembark from the carriages. I was on tiptoe, straining my neck, until I saw Andrew walking towards me.

In Romans 8, Paul says that is what creation is doing right now; she is on tiptoe, straining her neck, looking out for the return of Christ. Creation, as she waits for her deliverance, groans with earthquakes, volcanic eruptions, floods and droughts. She groans knowing that her ultimate redemption and deliverance does not lie with Greenpeace or Friends of the Earth but rather with the coming again of Jesus Christ. 'Creation itself will be liberated from its bondage to decay and brought into the glorious freedom of the children of God'. (Romans 8:21) With the Apostle Peter, 'we are looking forward to a new heaven and a new earth'. (2 Peter3:13)

The only remedy for all this mass of misery is the return of our Lord Jesus Christ. Why do we not plead for it every time we hear the clock strike?

(Anthony Ashley Cooper)

7 June

> 'I rejoiced with those who said to me, "Let us go to the house of the Lord". (Psalm 122:1)

Suggested reading Hebrews 10:19-25

Aaron, our multi-handicapped son, was very ill in hospital, and throughout the Saturday night, he was lovingly nursed by a young Indian lady. This was much appreciated by Pat, who found the nurse comforting and reassuring.

As she went off duty at eight o'clock the next morning, Pat said 'Are you going home to bed'?

'No', she responded, 'I'm going to church'.
'Which church is that'? Asked Pat.
'Parr St. Evangelical Church in Kendal', the nurse said.

Amazingly, this was the church that, after my retirement, Pat and I had recently started to attend, but due to Rupal's shifts and my preaching engagements, we had never worshipped at the same time.

After a stressful night, this conversation was a real encouragement to Pat.

Sadly, some excuse themselves from worship for trivial reasons, but how refreshing to meet some for whom worship is so important that no excuse is acceptable. After a demanding and tiring night, Rupal still put worship before anything else.

Every time we meet for worship, we are rehearsing what we shall do throughout eternity. So, is it not strange if we are reluctant to get to the practices----to do on earth what will occupy us in heaven?

I mean it when I say I would rather worship God than do anything else.

(A.W. Tozer)

8 June

> 'Jesus our Lord-----He was delivered over to death for our sins and was raised to life for our justification'. (Romans 4:24-25)

Suggested reading 1 Corinthians 11:23-34

For a couple of years, I had been Vice Chair of Governors at a school for multi-handicapped children. It was a demanding position but made much easier by the competence and expertise of the Chair of Governors. It was, therefore, a great shock when I received a phone call from the headteacher to say that this well-respected man had collapsed and died.

A week later, it was a solemn group of men and women who met for their appointed meeting and poignantly saw an empty chair. I started the meeting by asking the governors to stand for a minute's silence, as we fondly remembered our departed friend. It was a sombre occasion and not without its tears.

When we meet at the Lord's Table, we do not meet to remember a dead friend; we rather meet to remember a Saviour who was dead but is now alive forevermore. This means there is solemnity but also rejoicing because the One we remember though absent in body is present in spirit. And, at His coming, we shall see His physical form again.

Wondrous His love for me
At Calvary
Glorious His victory
At Calvary
Vanquished are death and hell
O, let His praises swell
Ever my tongue shall tell
Of Calvary

(George Perfect)

9 June

> 'Keeping a clear conscience, so that those who speak maliciously against your good behaviour in Christ may be ashamed of their slander. For it is better, if it is God's will to suffer for doing good than for doing evil'. (1 Peter 3:16-17)

Suggested reading John 19:1-16

For many years, my son has had an interest in juggling, unicycling and other circus skills and has taught these arts at a number of after-school clubs. Not surprisingly, he has passed this interest on to his son who is now an accomplished juggler and unicyclist.

Recently, as a family, they travelled from Singapore and visited a school in Vietnam with which they have close contact. During the visit, Andrew and Reuben entertained the students by putting on a circus show, which was very well received.

On returning to Singapore, Andrew and son had to make a dash from the airport, otherwise Reuben would have been late for his trampoline class. His wife, Sarah, was left to deal with customs and she faced an unexpected problem. Going through their luggage, customs came across three menacing looking knives and called the police. Sarah was interrogated but by means of a video on her phone, she was able to show they were 'juggling knives' and not being imported for any sinister purpose. How ironic---the knives that had been used to good effect in Vietnam were now suspected of being potential tools for evil in Singapore.

Sometimes, as believers our good works can be misconstrued and we face unwarranted criticism. It is never easy but Peter wisely reminds us 'it is better, if it is God's will, to suffer for doing good than for doing evil'. And, in so doing, we are following in the footsteps of Jesus who was arrested, tried and crucified, even though as Pilate acknowledged, 'as for me, I find no basis for a charge against Him'. Not just a good man but a perfect man and yet Jesus was put to death because He was misrepresented and his deeds misconstrued.

Prophets of God have usually been on the receiving end of more mud than medals

(Anon)

10 June

> 'The grass withers and the flowers fall but the word of our God endures forever'. (Isaiah 40:8)

Suggested reading Luke21:29-38

When I was thirteen, I received as a Christmas present an Encyclopaedia of Science. The sciences were never my strong subjects and so the encyclopaedia proved to be a great help as I prepared for GCEs in Physics and Chemistry.

However, though I still had the book, it was of little help to my own children when they took their exams in the 1990s, and in the future, it will be of even less help to my grandchildren. Why? Some of the information is now either out of date or irrelevant.

There is only one book which can never be out of date and which will always be relevant and that book is the Bible. The Bible is the word of God and because God is omniscient and unchanging, so too are the Scriptures.

Speaking to the Sadducees, Jesus said, 'But about the resurrection of the dead---have you not read what God said to you, 'I am the God of Abraham, the God of Isaac and the God of Jacob? He is not the God of the dead but of the living'. (Matthew 22:31-32)

Jesus quotes Exodus 3:6---what God had spoken to Moses some fourteen hundred years earlier----but He says to the Sadducees 'have you not read what God said to you'? The word spoken to Moses was still relevant for the Sadducees because God and His Word never change.

The Christian feels that the tooth of time gnaws all books but the Bible. Nineteen centuries of experience have tested it. It has passed through critical fires no other volume has suffered, and its spiritual truth has endured the flames and come out without so much as a smell of burning.

(W.E. Sangster)

11 June

'Fools mock at making amends for sin' (Proverbs 14:9)

Suggested reading 2 Corinthians 5:1-10

School assembly always followed the same pattern---a hymn, Bible reading and prayer, followed by notices for the day. On a Wednesday morning the notices contained the names of those who, that week, were heading for detention. One Wednesday the headmaster decided not only to 'name' the miscreants' but also to 'shame' them by reading out their individual offences. Sadly, not a good idea.

As the charges were read out, instead of the 'hush of disgust' which the head had expected, there were instead 'guffaws of laughter'. For some reason 'spitting at a prefect from an upstairs window' brought forth much merriment. Rarely did the headmaster lose his cool, but he did that morning and abandoning the experiment, he ordered us all to our classrooms.

To many, sin is a 'laughing matter', not to be taken too seriously and certainly nothing to worry about'. This, however, is not how God sees sin. In His eyes, all sin is vile and loathsome and must be judged. On the Day of Judgement there will be no mirth or jollity, just the sober realisation that all our words and actions are known to God. When propositioned by Potiphar's wife, Joseph had the right response, 'how then could I do such a wicked thing and sin against God'? (Genesis 39:9)

As believers, let us never be influenced by the 'spirit of the age' but rather always see sin, as God sees it-----something so abhorrent that it could only be forgiven through the death of Christ on the cross of Calvary.

Sin is so big that it takes a Christ with a cross to measure it.

(Anon)

12 June

> 'Come, let us bow down in worship, let us kneel before the Lord our Maker'. (Psalm 95:6)

Suggested reading Acts 12:1-12

One of my earliest childhood memories is of visiting my grandparent's home. When it was time to leave, Grandad would commend us all to God in prayer. Grandad was an elderly man but we all followed his example, as he got up from his chair and on to his knees.

Posture is not the most important thing in prayer but I learned as a child, that speaking to God was different from speaking to anyone else.

As a young married couple, Pat and I had an elderly widower staying with us on holiday. On the Tuesday evening, he asked to be excused because 7.30 pm on a Tuesday was the time of the prayer meeting at his home church in London. This was long before the days of Zoom but he wished to join with his church family at the Throne of Grace.

Would not our churches be healthier and stronger if more believers had the attitude of that elderly man? How few attend prayer meetings when they are at home, never mind thinking about it when they are away on holiday.

In the Acts 12:12 at the house of Mary, 'many people had gathered and were praying'. What a difference it would make if the same could be said of our churches today.

We shall never see much change for the better in our churches till the prayer meeting occupies a higher place in the esteem of Christians.

(Charles H. Spurgeon)

13 June

> 'He appeared so that he might take away our sins. And in him is no sin' (1 John 3:5)

Suggested reading Luke 18 9-14

In 1964, I was a member of the Morecambe Grammar School chess team, which won the Lancaster and Morecambe Chess League, and this was the first time a school team had been champions. It was a notable achievement, meaning we were better than many adult players in the area.

However, during the year, any grandiose ideas about our ability were severely dented. We had a visit from John Littlewood, an England chess player who, in the course of his career, had played a world champion. He came to play simultaneous chess, which means he took on twenty players at once. If my memory serves me right, he won seventeen matches and drew the other three. So, we were perhaps not quite as good as we thought.

When we compare ourselves to others, we always come off well---feeling we are good as or better than most. Others, however, are not the standard by which we shall be judged. Christ is the standard, and when we compare ourselves to the One who was without sin, we see our true condition. But, how amazing that the One without sin was prepared to die for those full of sin.

Christ was made sin but never a sinner. Sinner means one who is personally affected by sin; Christ's person never was. He never had any fellowship with sin, other than of love and compassion to bear it as our High Priest and Substitute.

(Abraham Kuiper)

14 June

> 'This is how we know what love is: Jesus Christ laid down his life for us'. (1 John 3:16)

Suggested reading Romans 5:1-11

We had been invited to the home of some friends for morning coffee, and Pat decided to buy flowers or a plant for our hostess. We called at the supermarket on route, and Pat chose a freesia plant. The lady at the checkout commented on the freesia. During the conversation, Pat commented that yesterday had been our forty-ninth wedding anniversary and freesia had formed part of her bridal bouquet.

On hearing this, the assistant insisted the plant was now hers, completely free of charge. Pat protested, but the lady let her into a supermarket secret. 'If a customer is being difficult or awkward, a gift can be given to appease them, but I don't do that', said the assistant. 'I give freebies not to unpleasant people but nice ones'. So, a happy Pat came out of the store with the freesia and we were able to tell our friends that the plant was indeed a free gift.

It is always easier to love and be nice to those who are loving and nice to us. The supermarket assistant demonstrated this. But such was the love of God that He gave His Son to die on a cross not for 'nice' people but sinful rebels. There was nothing to attract Him but rather everything to repel Him. Amazing---is it not? God's incomparable love is shown to us in the incomparable death of Christ.

'God so loved that he gave----and the giving----with Calvary at its heart, was not a trickle but a torrent.

(Paul S. Rees)

15 June

> 'No eye has seen, no ear has heard, no mind has conceived what God has prepared for those who love Him'. (1 Corinthians 2:9

Suggested reading 2 Timothy 4:1-8

John was an interesting, if a somewhat eccentric neighbour. Every morning, even when he was in his eighties, he would set off at 5.30 am for his morning walk. He was always accompanied by his walking staff and many a morning, I would be wakened, as he passed by our house, by the sound of the tapping of his stick.

He would often chat with me about his schooldays, his war experiences and his various occupations. During one of our conversations, he made this sad comment. 'Forgive me, John, for always talking about the past, but when you get to my age, you don't have a future'.

Sadly, as their physical and mental capacities decrease, this is how many older people can feel but how different it is foe elderly saints. They know that the best is yet to be. They have a glorious future, a wonderful hope, because they know that their future and their hope are centred in Christ.

Paul could look back with satisfaction---'I have fought the good fight, I have finished the race, I have kept the faith'---but he could also look forward with eager anticipation. 'Now, there is in store for me the crown of righteousness, which the righteous judge, will award to me on that day'.

And Paul adds 'not only to me, but also to all who have longed for his appearing'. All believers have this wonderful hope, this glorious future because their faith is in Christ.

God assures us of a future that is better than all our past.

(J. Charles Stern)

16 June

> '-----judge nothing before the appointed time; wait till the Lord comes. He will bring to light what is hidden in darkness and will expose the motives of men's hearts'. (1 Corinthians 4:5)

Suggested reading John 5: 16-23

For a number of years, I was umpire for Ingleton Cricket Club in the Westmorland Cricket League. I tried to be scrupulously fair but all umpires are human and I certainly made wrong decisions. I remember giving a batsman out caught and the player seemed most unhappy. As he walked back to the pavilion, a number of Ingleton fielders conceded that the batsman had played the ball into the ground before it had been caught. He should not have been given out.

I made the decision in good faith but it was undoubtedly the wrong decision. I later apologised to the batsman, and he graciously accepted that I had made a genuine mistake. That was one error I knew about---how many more did I make that I knew nothing about?

How reassuring that Jesus Christ---no human being---will be our Judge. As man and God, He will be unbiased and being Omniscient, He will be in possession of all the facts. No miscarriages of justice, no need for appeals or retrials---'will not the Judge of all the earth do right?' (Genesis 18:25)

Does this not also mean, we should never 'write anyone off' or judge them in a final sense, as we are not in full possession of all the facts? Therefore, 'judge nothing before the appointed time; wait till the Lord comes'. (1 Corinthians 4:5)

The fact that Jesus will sit upon the throne of judgment will be the consternation of his enemies and the consolation of his people.

(John Murray)

17 June

> 'Clement and the rest of my co-workers, whose names are written in the book of life'. (Philippians 4:3)

Suggested reading Revelation 21:22-27

When we moved to Ingleton, we bought a visitor's book, and initially, we conscientiously asked all callers to No.10 New Village, to sign the book. Regrettably, it was not a practice we maintained, but it is fascinating, forty years later, to read many of the things written.

Nostalgic happy memories come back as we recall friends, pastors, missionaries not just from the UK but Europe, Africa, Asia and Australia. Some we only saw the once, when they were on holiday in Ingleton and some have since gone to their eternal rest. It was a privilege to entertain them and to enjoy their fellowship.

The Lamb's book of life in heaven is not a 'visitor's book but rather the record of all who have repented of sin and trusted Jesus as Saviour. The names of believers from every age and nation are to be found in the book and their names are recorded for all eternity.

Jesus said to his first followers, 'rejoice that your names are written in heaven'. (Luke 10:20) This means that, however discouraging our circumstances might sometimes be, as Christians we can always be a thankful and a joyful people.

When God writes our name in the Lamb's Book of Life, He doesn't do it with an eraser handy, He does it for eternity.

(R.C. Sproul)

18 June

> 'And we, who with unveiled faces all reflect the Lord's glory, are being transformed into his likeness with ever increasing glory, which comes from the Lord, who is the Spirit'. (2 Corinthians 3:18)

Suggested reading Acts 6:8-15

My son, just two years younger, bears a striking resemblance to Pep Guardiola, the Manchester City manager and this has often been remarked upon. When Andrew's children were very young, whenever Pep was on the television or pictured in a magazine, we would ask them 'who's that'? Inevitably, their response would be 'Daddy'.

My grandfather was a Methodist preacher for over 70 years and speaking to a lady, sometime ago, she commented "Your grandfather was such a lovely man, that as a girl whenever he preached at the mission, I thought it was Jesus in the pulpit".

We cannot be sure as to the exact physical appearance of Jesus and even if we were to resemble him physically, that would be nothing to our credit because we cannot determine our outward appearance.

However, it is a different thing altogether to resemble Jesus in character and that should be the desire of every believer. Not that, on earth, we will ever attain the perfection which characterised Jesus but nevertheless that should be our aim. Indeed, the work of the Holy Spirit in a believer's life is to make us more and more like Jesus.

This does not mean we are passive for it is as we see the glory of the Lord in the Word of God, that we are transformed. May we continue to be changed into his likeness, knowing 'that when he appears we shall be like him, for we shall see him as he is'. (1 John 3:2)

From morning to night keep Jesus in your heart, long for nothing, desire nothing, hope for nothing, but to have all that is within you changed into the spirit and temper of the holy Jesus.

(William Law)

19 June

> 'This is my blood of the new covenant, which is poured out for many for the forgiveness of sins'. (Matthew 26:28)

Suggested reading Matthew 3: 1-6 and 13-17

When my children were young, sometimes they would protest if they had to bathe in the same water. 'I'm not going in that. He/she has been in it. I want some clean water'. Invariably, their anguished protests fell on deaf ears and they were bathed in the same water.

Jesus was baptised in the River Jordan and in a sense, it was 'dirty' water because in its waters sinners had confessed a multitude of sins. And yet, Jesus was baptised in that same water because he wished to identify Himself with those He had come to save.

When Aaron came to us, as a ten-week-old baby, we were told that he had been baptised with water from the River Jordan. Whatever we might think about infant baptism, the vital thing is not the water gathered from the Jordan but the blood shed on Calvary. The Bible calls it 'the precious blood of Jesus' (1 Peter 1:19? And it is precious because 'without the shedding of blood there is no forgiveness' (Hebrews 9:22)

Release! Signed in tears, sealed in blood, written on heavenly parchment, recorded in eternal archives. The black ink of the indictment is written all over with the red ink of the cross: 'the blood of Jesus Christ cleanses us from all sin'.

(T. De Witt Talmage)

20 June

> 'Let us not give up meeting together, as some are in the habit of doing, but let us encourage one another----and all the more as you see the Day approaching'. (Hebrews 10:25)

Suggested reading Psalm 96

My mother-in-law attended a Baptist church and one Sunday morning, the lady sat next to her said, 'you don't come at night as well, do you'? My mother-in-law said that she did to which the woman replied, 'I only come in the morning. It's like a dose of medicine. I like to get it over with'.

A young man started to worship with us but his attendance at church was very intermittent. One Sunday, I commented that we had not seen him for a while. 'That's right', he said, 'some Sundays the Spirit tells me to worship God, not in church but out on the hills'.

What a blessing, I thought, that the Spirit does not tell the pastor, the preacher, the Sunday school teacher or the organist to do that: otherwise, the church would not function at all.

The worship of Almighty God is the greatest activity on earth that we can ever engage in. Indeed, it is a foretaste of what we shall be doing in heaven, throughout the eternal ages. How sad and disturbing, therefore, if professing believers have a casual or lackadaisical attitude to worship.

The Psalmist said 'Better is one day in your courts than a thousand elsewhere; I would rather be a doorkeeper in the house of my God than dwell in the tents of the wicked'. (Psalm 84:10) Does my heart echo with an 'Amen' to these words of the psalmist?

I can safely say, on the authority of all that is revealed in the Word of God, that any man or woman on this earth who is bored and turned off by worship, is not ready for heaven.

(A. W. Tozer)

21 June

> 'Esther had kept secret her family background and nationality just as Mordecai had told her to do'. (Esther 2:20)

Suggested reading Luke 22:54-62)

On honeymoon, at a Christian guest house in Llandudno, Pat and I had decided not to reveal that we were newlyweds. However, our cover was blown on the very first morning, as we were sitting at breakfast with an elderly couple.

No problem with the cereals or the full English breakfast; no, the trouble began with the toast and marmalade. As Pat prepared to pass me the butter, I discreetly shook my head. 'Oh', exclaimed Pat, 'I never knew you had toast and marmalade without butter'. I hope the kick under the table did not do too much damage.

The elderly couple were very understanding but from that moment onwards, they knew we were on honeymoon.

I chose to hide my identity as a newlywed, but do I ever conceal my identity as a believer? There might be occasions, as with Esther in Persia, when it is prudent to do so. However, on other occasions, as with Peter, it can be sheer cowardice.

Before he ever denied Jesus, Peter had 'followed at a distance and 'sat down with them'. Then, concealing his identity, he had merged with the crowd. If it means being unpopular or ostracised there is always the temptation to merge with the crowd and not identify as a follower of Jesus. As with Peter, this inevitably leads to pain and sorrow, as we feel the guilt of being ashamed of Jesus.

Jesus, how could I ever be, ashamed of you who died for me?
Ashamed of you, whom angels praise, whose glories shine through endless days?
Ashamed of Jesus, that dear friend, on whom my hopes of heaven depend?
No, when I blush, be this my shame, that I no more revere his name.

Joseph Grigg (1720-68) and Benjamin Francis (1734-99)

22 June

> "I say to you that many will come from the east and the west, and will take their places with Abraham, Isaac and Jacob in the kingdom of heaven.' (Matthew 8:11)

Suggested reading Matthew 17:1-8

I was married in 1972, four years before my twin brother but the week after he got married, his wedding photograph appeared in the local paper. A few days later, I was in Morecambe town centre when a man enthusiastically rushed up to me. Shaking me warmly by the hand, he said, 'Congratulations! I have just seen your photo in the paper'.

I was rather taken aback but not wanting to embarrass the man, I just thanked him and made rather a hasty exit.

'Will we recognise one another in heaven?' Is a question which is often asked but the answer is surely not in doubt. On the Mount of Transfiguration, Moses, Elijah and Peter recognised each other, even though they were separated from each other by hundreds of years.

Jesus spoke of taking 'places with Abraham, Isaac and Jacob in the kingdom of heaven' and the inference is we shall know who we are sitting with. We shall recognise and converse with the patriarchs.

Indeed, because what is imperfect now will be perfect then, there will be no errors of identification in heaven. We shall know each other better than we ever did on earth.

Will we recognise and be reunited with our loved ones? I am often asked this question---and my answer is always a resounding yes. Someday soon, I know, I will be reunited with all those in my family, who are already in heaven---including my wife, Ruth.

(Billy Graham)

23 June

Jesus said, 'If you love me, you will obey what I command'. (John 14:15)

Suggested reading Exodus 20:1-17

Reading an article in a local newspaper, I was disturbed to see the Lord's Name being taken in vain. I contacted the paper and was put through to the young reporter responsible for the article. I expressed my concern and disappointment but she could not understand what I was getting hot under the collar about. To her such language was obviously just an acceptable, everyday expression.

How sad, if a generation has grown up so ignorant of the Ten Commandments that they do not even know when they are being broken.

A harassed and tearful mother was speaking to me about her daughter. 'She says she can prophesy and speak in tongues but, what she cannot do, is help me with any of the housework'.

There are multitudes who are ignorant of the Ten Commandments but as believers, we do not have that excuse. It is not sufficient, however, to know them---we have also to obey them. Whatever gifts the girl may or may not have had, they are never an excuse for not obeying the fifth commandment. We should desire to say with the Psalmist, 'I delight in your commands because I love them'. (Psalm 119:47)

The Ten Commandments are not a set of do's and don'ts, rather for the Christian they are rules for thankful living.

(Samuel J. Kistemaker)

24 June

'I wrote to the church, but Diotrephes who loves to be first, will have nothing to do with us'. (3 John: 9)

Suggested reading Matthew 20:20-28

Desmond, my daughter's dog, is a lovable Boston terrier who I take for a walk most mornings. To say he is spoilt would be an understatement and

I have to admit my share of responsibility. I give him too many treats and when he is with me, he is certainly 'leader of the pack'.

To give Desmond more exercise and to get him used to being with other dogs, my daughter arranged for him to be picked up on Thursdays by a dog walker. Apparently, all went well for the first few weeks, until a new dog was introduced to the group and it was then that the trouble began. Both dogs wished to dominate and to be 'leader of the pack'. The situation became unmanageable and Desmond's weekly jaunt came to an end, when it was recommended that he be excluded from the group.

A desire to dominate not only causes trouble amongst dogs but sadly, amongst believers as well. This was true of Diotrephes in the C1st church. Self-centred and self-seeking, he wanted the pre-eminence and rather than serving others, he expected others to serve him.

The attitude of Diotrephes directly contradicts the teaching and actions of the Lord Jesus. 'You know that the rulers of the Gentiles lord it over them, and their high officials exercise authority over them. Not so with you. Instead, whoever wants to become great among you must be your servant, and whoever wants to be first be your slave---just as the Son of Man did not come to be served, but to serve, and to give his life as a ransom for many'. (Matthew 20:25-28)

May we never have the attitude of Diotrephes---'your attitude should be the same as that of Christ Jesus'. (Philippians 2:5)

Let my name be forgotten, let me be trodden under the feet of all men, if Jesus may thereby be glorified.

(George Whitefield)

25 June

God said, 'Take off your sandals, for the place where you are standing is holy ground'. (Exodus 3:5)

Isaiah 6:1-7

Since moving into our retirement bungalow, Pat has insisted that my shoes or trainers are taken off in the hallway and replaced by a pair of slippers. No dirt or dust may be brought in from the outside, and yet, strangely, this is a requirement confined to me and not to other visitors to our home.

I had hoped that, with the passing of time, this requirement might not be as rigorously enforced but, four years on, there is no indication yet that this will ever be the case. I have to make my daily contribution towards the cleanliness of the premises.

Many faiths, as a sign of reverence, still perform their acts of worship barefooted. Just as men today might remove their hats before attending a place of worship, so there are those who remove their shoes. It is a recognition of God's holiness but also of man's sinfulness.

Whilst we may not physically remove our shoes, we must not miss the spiritual application. God is a holy God and we dare not come into His Presence carelessly or with unconfessed sin in our heart. 'Who may ascend the hill of the Lord? Who may stand in his holy place? He who has clean hands and a pure heart'. (Psalm 24:3-4)

When we see even a glimpse of God's holiness, we will bow in worship.

(R.C. Sproul)

26 June

'the little foxes that ruin the vineyards' (Song of Solomon 11:15)

Suggested reading: 2 Samuel 11:1-21

Having Showered, dressed, and breakfasted, I knew it was considerably later than 4.25, which my watch was showing. The second hand was not moving, the watch had stopped and I presumed it needed a new battery.

I left the watch with a local jeweller and on returning, he had a surprise for me. The watch did not need a new battery. No---the silver nickel plate had fallen off one of the numbers and settled at the base of the watch and was preventing the second hand from moving.

The watch was opened up, the miniscule piece of nickel silver removed and the problem was resolved. Both a cheap and quick solution.

All sin is sin in the sight of God and yet in this world, some sins are considered more serious and have greater penalties. For example: physical adultery more serious than lust, murder more serious than bearing a grudge, stealing more serious than coveting.

But 'little foxes ruin vineyards'. They stop our spiritual progress and as with David, they can lead to greater sin. Therefore, 'little' sins must be 'put to death' (Romans 8:13) before they do even greater damage.

It is a great sin to love a small sin

(Anonymous)

27 June

> 'For there is one God and one mediator between God and mankind, the man Christ Jesus, who gave himself as a ransom for all people'. (1 Timothy 2:5-6)

Suggested reading 2 Corinthians 5; 11-21

We are fortunate to live just a few minutes away from Ilkley Moor; immortalised in the Yorkshire song 'On Ilkley Moor baht' at' (to the uninitiated, 'On Ilkley Moor without a hat) The moorland, with panoramic views, has miles of trails and pathways and is ideal either for long or short walks.

One winter's afternoon, we'd had a pleasant walk on the moor with our grandson and his two sisters and, were journeying home in the car. As we did so, a dispute broke out between the two sisters, resulting in raised voices and tears. Our grandson had seen it all before and, much to our amusement he wryly commented, 'That is why I should always sit in the middle'.

Man was estranged from God because of his sin and rebellion, and consequently a go-between, a middle-man was needed. This need was met by One who was both God and man. Jesus came as the mediator--- not to an office to negotiate, but to a cross in order to deal with the sin that separated us from God.

If we are to be saved and reconciled to God, we must trust in Jesus, because He is the 'one mediator between God and mankind'. There is no other---Jesus is the one and only Saviour.

The cross of Jesus Christ is a two-way street; we have been brought to God and God has been brought to us.

(Donald Grey Barnhouse)

28 June

> 'Faith comes from hearing the message, and the message is heard through the word of Christ'. (Romans 10:17)

Suggested reading Luke 16-19-31

For several years in the 1970s, I went down to Wembley Stadium on Cup Final Day, not to watch the match, but to take part with others in open air witness.

1976 was a memorable year because Southampton, the underdogs, were playing Manchester United, the hot favourites. Southampton were known as 'The saints' and Manchester United as 'The Red Devils, and down Wembley Way, there were numerous banners saying that the 'Saints' were going to beat the 'Sinners' or that the 'red Devils' were going to beat 'The Saints'. This gave us good openings as open-air preachers, and we were able to engage in conversation with many of the supporters.

I talked with a Southampton supporter who admitted he was not too confident. 'I will be a believer', he said, 'if Southampton win---but I don't think it will happen'. Well, to the shock of the football world, it did happen---Southampton won by one goal to nil. But I would be very surprised if the result brought the Southampton supporter to repentance and faith. In the excitement and joy of the occasion, I expect he forgot the promise he had made.

People often claim that if they could see---a miracle or a sign---then, they would come to faith. But this is contrary both to Biblical teaching and experience. Thousands witnessed the miracles of Jesus but where were they when he was crucified? They might have been impressed by what they saw but it did not bring them to faith.

No, 'faith comes from hearing'. (Romans 10:17). The Spirit of God applies the Word of God to our hearts and it is then that we are convinced and converted. How important it is, therefore, that the Gospel is preached and that the Gospel is heard. This is the means, ordained by God, by which faith is engendered in human hearts.

The Word generates faith and regenerates us.

(Joseph Alleine)

29 June

> 'Therefore, since we have been justified through faith, we have peace with God through our Lord Jesus Christ'. (Romans 5:1)

Suggested reading Isaiah 40; 18-26

A friend in the Midlands telephoned to tell me that an oak tree opposite his home had been knocked down to make way for a new housing estate. He was sad to see the old tree destroyed, and yet, there was something that made him feel even sadder.

A group of residents attached a cross to the tree and on it wrote the age of the tree, the date it was knocked down and the words 'rest in peace'. Even more disturbing, at a Harvest Thanksgiving Service, a local church invited neighbours to 'come and mourn for the oak tree and make your peace with nature.

That is New Age teaching---it is not the Christian gospel. The gospel invites us not to make our peace with nature but rather, through the death of Jesus, to make our peace with God.

We are saddened but not altogether surprised when the unconverted 'worship and serve created things rather than the Creator' (Romans 1:25) but it is most alarming when professing Christians sign up to the same agenda. Saving the planet and being at one with nature is the new religion and we must not be deceived or influenced by it. Paul said, 'do not conform any longer to the pattern of this world, but be transformed by the renewing of your mind'. (Romans 12:2)

Posterity will someday laugh at the foolishness of modern materialistic philosophy. The more I study nature, the more I am amazed at the Creator.

(Louis Pasteur)

30 June

> 'Christ Jesus, Who, being in very nature God did not consider equality with God something to be grasped, but made himself nothing, taking the very nature of a servant, being made in human likeness'. (Philippians 2:5-7)

Suggested reading Matthew 16:13-20

Suits were once the order of the day for bankers, solicitors, doctors, accountants, etc. but for some professions, more casual dress now seems to be acceptable. This can especially be so when the weather is hot and sultry.

My sister-in-law was a doctor's receptionist and one summer's day, a young doctor went on a home visit, dressed in a T-shirt, Bermuda shorts and sunglasses. When the elderly patient opened the door, she showed him under the stairs---she thought he had come to read the gas meter.

However, although her appearance suggested otherwise, he was still the doctor.

Lying in a manger? Hungry, thirsty, tired and weeping? Taking a towel, washing and wiping his disciple's feet? Surely, He cannot be God but He is---this is the God/man.

Not surprising that many only saw Jesus as being a man but this is the miracle and the mystery of His Incarnation. Jesus was truly a man but He never ceased to be God. That is why He is the 'mediator between God and mankind' (1 Timothy 2:5) and demands both our worship and obedience.

Jesus did not cease to be the Son of God when he became man. He did not drop his deity, which is an impossible thought. He remained what he was and added what he had not had, namely a human nature, derived out of a woman, a human mother. He became the God-man.

(R.C.H. Lenski)

BIBLE READINGS JULY

1 July

> 'All of us have become like one who is unclean, and all our righteous acts are like filthy rags'. (Isaiah 64:6)

Suggested reading Philippians 3:1-11

The doorbell rings and on a Spring morning, I am greeted by a tramp---not an unusual sight in the 1980s. However, this 'man of the road' comes with an interesting request. Having given him a drink and a snack, he asks whether my wife has any buttons, which she can sew onto his jacket. He explains he is making his way to the Lake District, looking for hotel work, and he wants to be smart and tidy.

Pat finds some buttons and though the 'fragrance' coming from the jacket is somewhat overpowering, she manages to complete the repair job. Minutes later, the man continues his journey, replenished and with new buttons on his jacket. Sadly, his appearance and clothing are such that I cannot imagine the man being acceptable to any prospective employer.

The Bible does not suggest that all our good deeds, our righteous acts are of no value, but they are worthless where acceptance with God is concerned, because they are all tainted by sin. The righteousness of Christ and His death upon the cross are the only grounds for our acceptance with a holy God. Otherwise, our very best deeds are nothing more than putting 'buttons' upon a filthy jacket.

If there be ground for you to trust in your own righteousness, then all that Christ did to purchase salvation, and all that God did to prepare the way for it, is in vain.

(Jonathan Edwards)

2 July

> 'Blessed are the pure in heart, for they will see God'. (Matthew 5:8)

Suggested reading Psalm 24

It was a November morning and with a thick blanket of fog causing low visibility on the road, I had to be careful as we drove to the shops.

Later that morning, I was walking the dog across the fields and I got chatting to a walker from Bradford. 'It's a real pea-souper' he said, and began to relate what his father had told him about Bradford in the 1940s and 1950s.

At that time, houses and mills were coal fired, and the combination of smoke and fog meant that 'pea-soupers' were a regular occurrence. Indeed, his father had told him that the only time you could ever see, across the valley from Bradford, was the first two weeks in August, when the mills were shut down for holidays.

Clean air acts and the introduction of smokeless fuels hopefully means that real 'pea-soupers' are now a thing of the past.

It is because of sin that we are not able to see the true beauty and majesty of God. Our vision of the Almighty is blurred and dimmed by hypocrisy and impurity. In the words of the Apostle Paul, 'now we see only a reflection as in a mirror'. (1 Corinthians 13:12)

The purer, the more sanctified we are now, then all the clearer is our view of God, and yet the 'fog' will never be fully taken away until we get to heaven. Then, 'we shall see face to face' (1 Corinthians 13:12) and it will not be for just a fortnight but rather forever and ever.

There will be no sin in heaven, for those who are in heaven will not have it in them to sin anymore.

(J.I. Packer)

3 July

> 'If anybody is preaching to you a gospel other than what you accepted, let them be under God's curse '. (Galatians 1:9)

Suggested reading Jude 1-4

On our way to a midweek meeting in the Yorkshire Dales, we drew into a petrol station, not for fuel--- but sweets for the journey. Pat duly made the purchase and with time ticking by, opened the car door and got into the passenger seat.

It was a blue car but not a Volkswagen Polo and the driver, whilst a man, was not her husband. Much to the man's surprise and amusement, Pat had returned to the wrong car. Apologising profusely, she got out and made her way to the right vehicle.

There were a number of cars parked at the service station but I suspect only one of them was going to Ripon that night.

On the world's forecourt, there are many faiths, cults and isms but only one will get us to heaven. That faith is Biblical Christianity, centred in the person and work of the Lord Jesus Christ. 'Salvation is found in no one else, for there is no other name under heaven given to mankind by which we must be saved' (Acts 4:12)

We have to be careful for just as the blue car was a similar colour to my Volkswagen, so there are cults which counterfeit the Christian faith. We are saved through repentance and faith in Jesus Christ-----nothing more, nothing less, and nothing else.

Christ is not only the Saviour but the salvation itself.

(Matthew Henry)

4 July

>'For no matter how many promises God has made, they are "Yes" in Christ. And so, through him the "Amen" is spoken by us to the glory of God'. (2 Corinthians 1:20)

Suggested reading Ecclesiastes 5:1-7

Thankful for the success of the Covid vaccinations, Pat went to the local surgery for her booster. The staff were efficient and the deed had soon been done.

As she left the room, the nurse said 'just sit down for fifteen minutes and then you will be able to drive'.

'O, that is wonderful', said Pat, 'I have never been able to drive in my life'.

The nurse was greatly amused and needlessly apologised for her previous inapplicable statement.

Sadly, we sometimes make promises which, knowingly or unknowingly, we are not able to keep. To knowingly do so is to be dishonest but there are promises we fully intend to keep, and yet because of illness or circumstances we are not able to do so.

How different are the promises of God. Because He is holy, all-knowing and all-powerful, every promise He has made has either been fulfilled, is being fulfilled or will be fulfilled.

'For the earth will be filled with the knowledge of the glory of the Lord as the waters cover the sea'. (Habakkuk 2:14)

'He will wipe away every tear from their eyes. There will be no more death or mourning or crying or pain, for the old order of things has passed away'. (Revelation 21:4)

Such promises almost seem 'too good to be true' and they would be if made by man, but they have been made by God and therefore, they will be fulfilled. Rest and rejoice in the sure promises of God.

My future is as bright as the promises of God.

(Adoniram Judson)

5 July

> 'Your word is a lamp for my feet, a light on my path'. (Psalm 119:105)

Suggested reading 1 Samuel 1:8-18

The Bible should never be used as a horoscope---by which I mean we should never just pick a verse out, and use it as a motto for the day. And yet, there have been times when the verse for the day on my Scriptural calendar has remarkably addressed a situation.

One morning, a young lady was in our home in deep distress because it seemed that she and her husband would never have the child for which they longed. My wife and I spoke with her but our words brought her little comfort.

I went up to my study and the text on the calendar that day was the words of Eli, spoken to Hannah, when she was in great distress because of her childlessness.

'Go in peace, and may the God of Israel grant you what you have asked of him'. (1 Samuel 1:17)

I gained an inner certainty that the young woman would conceive and I felt prompted to tell her so. Twelve months later, she joyfully shared the news that she was pregnant, and in due time, she gave birth to twins.

I repeat we have to be careful how we use the daily verse on a Scripture calendar, but I do thank the Lord for those occasions when, in a remarkable way, His word has been 'a lamp for my feet and a light on my path'.

The Bible is not a kind of horoscope by which to tell your fortune but I do not deny God sometimes reveals his particular will by lighting up a verse of Scripture. But this is not his usual method, and it is highly dangerous to follow such supposed guidance without checking and confirming it.

(John R. W. Stott)

6 July

> 'They say to the seers, "See no more visions" and to the prophets, "Give us no more visions of what is right. Tell us pleasant things, prophesy illusions. Leave this way, get off this path, and stop confronting us with the Holy One of Israel". (Isaiah 30:10-11)

Suggested reading Amos 7:10-17

In the 1980s, the MOT was not as stringent or as detailed as today. At that time, I had an old car, and when I took it to a local garage, I was told it had no chance of passing a test. However, a friend informed me that if I took the car to a garage in the next town, it might get the certificate.

Rightly or wrongly, I accepted his advice and went to this 'MOT-friendly' garage. After a quick inspection, I was assured there was no problem, and with a 'bit of welding', the car would pass the test. A time was arranged, the work was done and the certificate was granted.

I was happy because I could not have afforded another car, but in hindsight, I wasn't sure whether it had been a wise move. Was the car safe, or was it a potential danger to me, my family and others? In contrast to the first garage, the second told me what I wanted to hear, but was it telling the truth?

Sometimes people do with the church what I did with the garage. A church tells them they are sinners who can only be saved through trusting in the atoning death of Jesus. They are told something they do not want to hear, so they try another church.

Here things are very different: everyone is a child of God and everyone is going to heaven; there is no need for repentance or saving faith. These pleasant things are what they want to hear, and they readily accept them, even though it is not the truth. And just as I was possibly placing myself in danger with the car, so such people are placing themselves in spiritual peril.

Heresy is picking out what you want to believe and rejecting, or at least ignoring the rest.

(A. W. Tozer)

7 July

> 'The eyes of the Lord are everywhere, keeping watch on the wicked and the good'. (Proverbs 15:3)

Suggested reading Genesis 16:7-16

Saturday morning and having shopped at the supermarket, we pop into the café for a coffee and croissant. As we are enjoying our 'elevenses' I recognise a familiar face---not in the café but on the wall of the café.

It is a photograph of the supermarket's cheese buyer, but Alan is also a deacon at a church, where I frequently preach. The photograph has the Mona Lisa effect---Alan's eyes following us wherever we happen to be.

Later, that day I send an e-mail to Alan, to tell him of our surprise encounter. He responds by expressing the hope that his photograph did not put us off our coffee and croissant.

'The eyes of the Lord are everywhere'. Is there not here both a warning and a comfort? We can be deceived into thinking that certain sins can be hidden from God, but nothing could be farther from the truth. 'Nothing in all creation is hidden from God's sight. Everything is uncovered and laid bare before the eyes of him to whom we must give account'. (Hebrews 4:13) How essential that all sin is repented of and covered by the blood of Jesus.

There is a warning here but for the believer, there is also comfort. Because 'the eyes of the Lord are everywhere', every tear, every heartache, every need is known to Him. Hagar said 'You are the God who sees me' (Genesis 16:13) He sees, He knows all about your personal situation and therefore, He is able to support you and to provide for you in your time of need.

Though the Lord is out of sight, we are not out of his.

(Matthew Henry)

8 July

> 'Do not be surprised at the fiery ordeal that has come on you to test you, as though something strange were happening to you'. (1 Peter 4:12)

Suggested reading Acts 14:19-28

When we moved into our home in Burley in Wharfedale, we decided that the old boiler needed replacing, and we engaged the services of a local heating engineer.

It was a cold, frosty December morning when the man arrived and started on the work in the garage. Pat sympathised that he was having to work in such freezing conditions, but his response was down-to-earth and realistic.

'You cannot be a heating engineer without having to work in cold and damp conditions'.

The heating engineer knew the environment in which he had to work, and was not surprised by cold and damp conditions. As believers, we have to live in a world 'under the control of the evil one'; a world which is hostile to the things of God. Jesus said, 'in this world you will have trouble'. (John 16:33) The Apostle Paul promised, 'everyone who wants to live a godly life in Christ Jesus will be persecuted' (2 Timothy 3:12)

We should, therefore, not be surprised by the hardships, the painful trials and the opposition that so often we have to face. It is all part of our calling and a sign that we are indeed true believers.

Sin has turned the world from a paradise into a thicket; there is no getting through without being scratched.

(Thomas Boston)

9 July

> 'Now Naaman was commander of the army of the king of Aram. He was a great man in the sight of his master and highly regarded because through him, the Lord had given victory to Aram. He was a valiant soldier but he had leprosy'. (2 Kings 5:1)

Suggested reading Romans 3:9-18

For my birthday, our daughter kindly bought Pat and I tickets for 'An Evening with Michael Parkinson'. It was a most informative experience as, in conversation with his son, Michael, he recalled his remarkable journey from a pit village in Yorkshire to being one of our best loved entertainers.

During the evening, extracts were shown on screen from his TV series, and in interviews with Mohammed Ali, George Best and Shane Warne. Michael explained that each was a genius--- perhaps the best or amongst the best there has ever been in their particular sport. He then added something of significance ----'but each had a flaw'.

What was true of those three great sportsmen is sadly true of us all. In many a person, there is much to admire---be it their intellectual capacity, their physical achievements, their creative ability---and yet each has a 'but'. Academic but selfish. Athletic but proud. Artistic but covetous.

We all have a 'but' because 'there is no one righteous, not even one.' (Romans 3:10) We are sinful people and our flaws, our sins are demonstrated in a variety of different ways.

By contrast, Jesus had a 'but' and yet it was altogether different to ours. For he was 'tempted in every way that we are BUT did not sin' (Hebrews 4:15 Good News Translation)

Because of his sinlessness, Jesus is the only one who can forgive us our sins. He can save and cleanse us from our 'buts' and make us fit for heaven.

Man is a good thing spoiled

(Augustine)

10 July

> '---- admitting that they were foreigners and strangers on earth'. (Hebrews 11:13)

Suggested reading John 17:20-26

My brother, after four major operations, had been in hospital or nursing homes for over sixteen months. As he gained strength, we discussed his accommodation options for the future, and there seemed to be four possible alternatives. He could return to his own home, downsize and buy something smaller, go into sheltered accommodation or remain in a nursing home. He was undecided but then unexpectedly, he had a relapse and died shortly afterwards.

This was a shock but Ken was a believer and I now see there was a fifth and better option---the Lord calling him to his heavenly home. A home incomparably better than we can ever experience on earth; a home where the believer experiences the immediate presence of Jesus.

A highly esteemed believer had been called home and the next Sunday, I preached on heaven, emphasising what our brother was now enjoying. After the service, a ninety- year-old man, with a twinkle in his eye, asked, 'Is envy a sin'? At first, I was rather taken aback, until I recognised just what he was saying.

As believers, we do not have a 'death wish', rather with the Apostle Paul, we have a 'Christ wish'. We know where we are going but better still, we know to Whom we are going.

Christ is the centre of attraction in heaven.

(Archibald Alexander)

11 July

> 'In the beginning was the Word, and the Word was with God; and the Word was God. He was with God in the beginning' (John 1:1-2)

Suggested reading John 14:5-14

I am a twin, forty-five minutes younger than my brother. When I was born, it was in the days before scans, so my birth must have shocked my mother, as she did not know she was having twins. We were identical twins, and during our early years, we dressed alike. However, it was good being a twin, as we were never bored, always having an opponent when it came to football, cricket or board games.

The downside to being a twin came as we got older. Because we were identical twins, some assumed our views on everything must be identical. True, we thought the same about many things, but there were issues where our views were very different. As twins, we were close but not that close, and it was sometimes frustrating having to establish one's own identity.

Twins might be close, but they can never know the intimacy and oneness which God the Father and God the Son enjoyed. Because Jesus had the nature of His Father, He also had the mind of His Father, enabling Him to speak the words and do the works of Almighty God. From eternity, Jesus had known this intimacy with His Father, but it was broken when 'he himself bore our sins in his body on the tree.' (1 Peter 2:24) This is what our sin did to Jesus---no wonder He cried out in agony 'My God, my God, why have you forsaken me"? (Matthew 27:46)

The characteristics of God Almighty are mirrored for us in Jesus Christ. Therefore, if we want to know what God is like, we must study Jesus Christ.

(Oswald Chambers)

12 July

> 'Come, all you who are thirsty, come to the waters; and you who have no money, come buy and eat! Come, buy wine and milk without money and without cost'. (Isaiah 55:1)

Suggested reading Romans 6:19-23

Since childhood, I have watched football matches, but in my early days, money was tight and I could not even afford to watch my local non-league team, Morecambe. But that did not mean I never got to see The Shrimps. On a Saturday afternoon, their matches kicked off at 3 pm, but the gates opened at half-time, and children got in free.

My routine was to first watch the Morecambe Grammar School Old Boys football team, which kicked off at 2 pm, where there was no charge, before crossing to Christie Park for the second half of Morecambe's match. True, I did not see the whole game, but forty-five minutes was better than nothing

'There is no such thing as a free lunch'. This is generally true---you do not get something for nothing. Thankful as I was for free half-time admission, it still meant I did not get to see all of the match.

Such, however, is the grace of God that, in the gospel, there is something far more wonderful than anything that could ever be purchased with money. Forgiveness of sin, peace with God, the indwelling presence of Christ, an eternal home in heaven---these are just some of the benefits which are ours in Christ, and we do not have to pay a thing.

We do not have to pay a thing but someone else did, because none of these things come cheaply. They were paid for by the precious blood of Jesus, which He shed on Calvary's cross. We cannot earn, or in any way, pay for our salvation but we receive it as a free gift when we turn from sin and put our faith in Jesus.

There can be no thought of 'cheap' forgiveness when we remember that our redemption cost God the life of his beloved Son.

(Geoffrey B. Wilson)

13 July

> 'Out of the same mouth come praise and cursing. My brothers and sisters, this should not be'. (James 3:10)

Suggested reading Luke 6:37-42

It was Remembrance Sunday and suddenly the solemnity of the occasion was broken by a deafening noise. A man in the gallery had left his seat, stamped down the stairs, and slammed both an inner door and outer door of the church. Apparently, the man was a pacifist and had taken great exception to the minister saying it was 'a glorious thing to die in war'.

Irrespective of the rights or wrongs of what the minister was saying, it seemed a strange way for a pacifist to make his protest. I would have expected a 'man of peace' to have registered his objection in a less aggressive and a gentler way.

After I had preached at a Sunday evening service, we all participated in the Lord's Supper. Within minutes an 'unholy' sound was coming from a side room, as church officers, with raised voices tore into one another. Having just 'examined ourselves' in the presence of the Lord, such behaviour was surely inconsistent and hypocritical.

At times, we all stand accused of hypocrisy and inconsistency, and the Bible is right: 'this should not be'. Whenever I am tempted to lie or gossip, to be bitter or jealous, to belittle or humiliate another person, may I remember the words of James. 'This should not be'. May I be saved from looking 'at the speck of sawdust in my brother's eye' whilst 'failing to see the plank in my own eye'? (Luke 6:42)

If the world despises a hypocrite, what must they think of him in heaven?

(Josh Billings)

14 July

> 'Let no debt remain outstanding, except the continuing debt to love one another, for whoever loves others has fulfilled the law'. (Romans 13:8)

Suggested reading Luke 19:1-10

Pat had helped at Mums and Tots, and picking her up from church, we went to a local supermarket for our midday meal. It was very quiet and having ordered, we took our seats in the restaurant. Twenty minutes, thirty minutes, forty minutes later----still no sign of any food. Apparently, a member of staff had walked out, causing turmoil in the kitchen.

After 50 minutes, the meal did arrive, and with it a profound apology and the reimbursement of our money. I must say that the chips and chicken pie had never tasted better---either because I was so hungry or because the meal had not cost me anything!

A frustrating experience but all credit to the supermarket for their response. Their apology was accompanied by action.

Zaccheus, having been forgiven by Jesus, showed the reality of his salvation by making restitution. 'If I have cheated anybody out of anything, I will pay back four times the amount'. (Luke 19:8) His restitution did not save him but it was proof indeed that 'salvation had come to his house' (Luke 19:9

This should be the response of every new convert and every true believer. To seek forgiveness from those we have offended and if possible, to make restitution for any wrongs we might have done.

In so doing, we show the reality of our conversion and our gratitude to the Lord by word and by action.

Real repentance produces confession and forsaking of sin, reconciliation and restitution, separation from the world, submission to the Lordship of Christ and filling of the Holy Spirit.

(Vince Havner)

15 July

> 'I am the Lord, your God, who takes hold of your right hand and says to you. Do not fear; I will help you' (Isaiah 41:13)

Suggested reading John 10:22-42

When I walked with my young grandchildren through fields, they held my hand but if we were walking by the side of a busy road, then I held their hand.

How reassuring to know that, in our trials and troubles, we are not holding the Lord's hand, rather it is the Lord who is holding our hand.

We are prone to wander and to go astray but we are safe and secure in His grip.

My wife is an experienced backseat driver--'You are going too fast. You are too near the car in front. I wish you would slow down'. Sadly, I am not always too enamoured by her comments.

There is, however, some good advice I do need to heed: 'I wish you would keep both hands on the wheel'. A bad habit which I suspect many drivers are guilty of, putting themselves and others at unnecessary risk.

Jesus tells us in John 10 that, as believers, we are in his hand but also in the hand of his Father. Both hands are upon us; therefore, we are doubly secure, and therefore nothing and no one can snatch us or separate us from the Godhead.

The reason no Christian can be snatched out of the Father's hand is that it was the Father who placed him there.

(John Blanchard)

16 July

> "I tell you, whoever hears my word and believes him who sent me has eternal life and will not be judged but has crossed over from death to life'. (John 5:24)

Suggested reading Ephesians 2:1-10

We met Mr. Moxham and his wife when we had been on honeymoon in Llandudno, and, after his wife died, he came to stay with us in Morecambe. We continued to exchange Christmas cards until we moved to Ingleton in 1979, but then the cards from Mr. Moxham stopped. Being an elderly man, we presumed that he had either died or was now in care.

In 1982, I was in my study, when, walking past the window was—Mr. Moxham. I was quite taken aback and immediately telephoned Pat who had gone to see a friend. I thought it might be too much of a shock if she was to see a 'dead' man walking.

Later that day, we met up with Mr. Moxham and he came to our midweek meeting. It transpired that he knew we had moved from Morecambe to Ingleton but he had mislaid our new address.

Dead men don't walk, and so if a person has a desire for worship, for prayer, for Bible study, that is a sure sign they have been raised from spiritual death, and have found new life in Jesus. Dead men don't walk, and that is why we all need to experience the new birth before we can walk with God.

Becoming a Christian is not making a new start in life; it is receiving a new life to start with.

(John Blanchard)

17 July

> 'God's household, which is the church of the living God, the pillar and foundation of the truth'. (1 Timothy 3:15)

Suggested reading Amos 8:1-12

Pat and I were on holiday and as we explored the area, we were dismayed at the number of redundant churches. In almost every town and village, buildings which had once echoed to the praises of God, were now warehouses or shops or homes.

Our spirits were not lifted when, on buying a local newspaper, we read in the property section an article entitled 'Praying for a home'. Estate agents were quite excited at the number of churches and chapels now on the market, and how, at a reasonable cost, they could be converted into 'fantastic' family homes. I am afraid we could not share their enthusiasm. When churches close, God is not worshipped, the gospel is not preached, and the moral and spiritual decline of a nation intensifies.

At the time of Amos, there was 'a famine of hearing the words of the Lord' and this indicated that God was displeased with the nation. The closing of churches ----even those being converted into 'fantastic' family homes---is not something to be celebrated but rather something to mourn. Deceit and falsehood can only increase when 'the church of the living God, the pillar and foundation of the truth', is forsaken and abandoned. May God have mercy upon our nation.

To forsake Christ for the world is to leave a treasure for a trifle, eternity for a moment, reality for a shadow, all things for nothing.

(William Jenkyn)

18 July

> 'Ascribe to the Lord the glory due his name; bring an offering and come into his courts. Worship the Lord in the splendour of his holiness; tremble before him, all the earth'. (Psalm 96:8-9)

Suggested reading John 4:19-26

Yesterday I recalled, with sadness, the number of redundant churches which are now houses or shops or warehouses. Thankfully, there are buildings which have moved in the other direction.

The church building, in which I pastored for thirty years, had previously been a car showroom and before that, the Co-op. But then, proving the faithfulness of God, a small group of believers had been able to purchase the property and convert it into a place of worship.

It was the Lord's provision and a most adequate building, and yet there were some in the village who hesitated to come to a service because, in their eyes, it was not a 'proper' church building.

This was an issue Jesus deals with in John Ch.4. There were Jews and Samaritans who felt the most important thing was the place where God was worshipped. For the Jews, it was Jerusalem and for the Samaritans, Mount Gerizim. Jesus refutes this erroneous thinking and tells the Samaritan woman. 'A time is coming and has now come when the true worshippers will worship the Father in the Spirit and truth, for they are the kind of worshippers the Father seeks'. (John 4:23)

May we never be so preoccupied with the place that we fail to worship the Person. May our worship of the Lord be in spirit and truth.

God made us to be worshippers. That was the purpose of God in bringing us into the world.

(A.W. Tozer)

19 July

'Remembering the words the Lord Jesus himself said: "it is more blessed to give than to receive" (Acts 20:35)

Suggested reading 2 Corinthians 9:1-7

As a pastor, with a wife and two children, money was never too plentiful but we knew that the Lord who had called us would always provide for us. There were occasions when needs were met in a remarkable way, but usually, they were met through the generosity of the Lord's people.

For several years, a few days before Christmas, an envelope was put through our door containing a monetary gift. This meant there were 'extras' we now enjoyed at Christmas which, otherwise, we could not have afforded. Even though we were never able to personally thank the anonymous giver, we could thank the Lord for prompting one of his children to be so generous.

The Bible has much to say about giving. Paul reminds the Corinthian believers that 'God loves a cheerful giver' (2 Corinthians 9:7) whilst Jesus, in the Sermon on the Mount, commends the anonymous giver. 'When you give to the needy, do not let your left hand know what your right hand is doing'. (Matthew 6:3)

'It is more blessed to give than to receive' (Acts 20:35) 'Your Father who sees what is done in secret will reward you' (Matthew 6:4) There is the promise of blessings now and rewards in the future for cheerful, anonymous givers. My generous, unknown friend is numbered in that category.

When a man gives, the world still asks, 'What does he give'? Christ asks, 'How does he give'?

(Andrew Murray)

20 July

> 'See I have engraved you on the palms of my hands'. (Isaiah 49:16)

Suggested reading Acts 9:10-19

My wife and I were asked to visit Marcus in hospital as, due to Covid, his wife was having to isolate. It was, therefore, necessary to telephone the ward and arrange a time to visit. The nurse was very nice but there was a problem: the ward had a Mr Geoffrey but not a Mr. Marcus. Patient confidentially meant she could not give us any information about Mr. Geoffrey, and it looked as though we had reached an impasse.

However, when we gave the name and address of Mr. Marcus's next of kin and they matched the details of Mr. Geoffrey's next of kin, we were given a 2 pm appointment. How strange the hospital knew him as Geoffrey but not Marcus, whilst we knew him as Marcus and not Geoffrey. Thankfully we were able to visit Mr. Geoffrey/Marcus and spend time with him.

I thought I knew Marcus well, and in some ways I did. Yet I did not even know his first name. How different if one is a child of God. He knows us by name, which means He knows us individually and intimately.

In Acts 9, the Lord knew both the names and addresses of Judas and Saul. As believers, all our names are engraved on the palms of his hands----they cannot be removed, and therefore, we can never be forgotten or forsaken.

My name is graven on His hands,
My name is written on His heart;
I know, that while in heaven He stands,
No tongue can bid me thence depart.

(Charitie Lees De Chenez)

21 July

'His enemy came and sowed weeds among the wheat'. (Matthew 13:25)

Suggested reading 1 John 4:1-6

Mrs. E. was elderly and becoming rather forgetful but in her home she always had an array of lovely flowers. One day, as I admired her floral display, she sheepishly told me that she had an embarrassing confession to make. She had been watering some flowers, only to later discover, they were not real but artificial,

An understandable mistake, as increasingly artificial flowers do look like the real thing. To add to the confusion, Pat and I were recently sat at a table, where the flowers were real but the greenery artificial. It was only by touch that we were able to discern the difference.

Cults and sects can be both subtle and convincing and that is why many are seduced by them. What they are saying is either so near the truth or mixed with the truth, it is mistaken for the truth. False teachers, like artificial flowers, are not real---they propagate 'fake' news, not the good news of the gospel.

How we need discernment and the illumination of the spirit, if we are to be kept from falsehood and error.

The most dangerous of all false doctrine is the one seasoned with a little truth.

(Anon)

22 July

> 'The God of peace will soon crush Satan under your feet'.
> (Romans 16:20)

Suggested reading Genesis 3:8-19

It was the lunch hour when the relative peace of the office was broken by the shouting and cursing of a drunken man. It was not an altogether unknown experience as men, having over imbibed at the pub, sometimes went to the Jobcentre/Benefits Office, to try to recoup their losses. This man was especially obnoxious, and when he began to threaten the staff, we had no alternative but to send for the police.

In the office, there was a joiner, apparently minding his own business, repairing a faulty window. As the swearing and threats continued, this workman climbed down from his ladder, walked across the floor and planted a right uppercut on the chin of the drunken man. He fell as if poleaxed. The joiner, without saying a word, climbed his ladder and continued his work. Apparently, in his younger days, he had been a champion boxer in the navy.

When the police eventually arrived, they just assumed that the man had slumped to the floor, and getting him to his feet, they dragged him out of the office. The man they took out was certainly quieter and more subdued than the man who had come in.

Satan is a powerful foe, still causing havoc and distress, but we must never forget that he is a defeated foe. He is not as powerful as once he was, because on the cross, Jesus bruised his head. Therefore, whilst we do not underestimate his power, neither do we overestimate it. Jesus is the Victor and Satan's fate is certain.

Our arch-enemy is to be cast into hell---and it will only take one angel to bind him.

(A.Lindsay Glegg)

23 July

> 'Jesus appointed twelve---that they might be with him'. (Mark 3:14)

Suggested reading Psalm 73:23-28

I suffer from white coat syndrome which means my blood pressure is raised due to the stress of being in a clinic. That is not to say my blood pressure is not higher than it should be, but it tends to be raised in the presence of the doctor. Hence the term white coat syndrome, which refers to the white coat which was traditionally worn by doctors.

For this reason, I have my own monitor at home and provide my surgery with the readings from time to time. In the presence of the GP, my blood pressure rises and I was encouraged when a doctor told me her blood pressure is never taken at work but always in the quietness of her own home.

If I want my love for the Lord Jesus to increase, I must spend time in his presence and remind myself, throughout the day that He has promised never to leave me nor forsake me. When I fail to pray, read the Bible, go to church or become too immersed in the world, it is then my love for Jesus grows cold. The closer I keep to the Great Physician, the more my love for Him increases.

Jesus said, "few things are needed----or indeed only one. Mary has chosen what is better, and it will not be taken away from her". (Luke10:42)

To be much like Christ, be much with Christ.

(Anon)

24 July

> ' -----they insistently demanded that he (Jesus) be crucified, and their shouts prevailed. So, Pilate decided to grant their demand. He released the man who had been thrown into prison for insurrection and murder-----and surrendered Jesus to their will'. (Luke 23:23-25)

Suggested reading John 16:7-15

For a time, in the Department of Employment, it was one of my responsibilities to try to obtain work for released prisoners. This was never easy, as many employers were understandably apprehensive about those who had served a prison sentence.

One Saturday evening, I was giving out gospel leaflets and a group of rowdy men were about to hassle me, when one of them intervened. 'Leave him alone, when I came out of prison, he helped me to get work as a painter'. No credit to me but full credit to the employer who gave the man his work opportunity.

In preaching the gospel, we are asking men and women to trust One who was arrested, tried, found guilty and sentenced to death. And yet, how wonderful it is, that millions have done just that---trusted in Christ for their eternal salvation.

This is the work of the Holy Spirit, convicting of sin but also convincing us, as to the righteousness of Christ. (John16:9-10) We trust in Him, assured that Christ is the only One, ever without sin (Hebrews 4:15). Pontius Pilate knew Christ to be innocent but condemned Him to be crucified---the believer knows Christ to be sinless and has trusted Christ for eternal salvation.

While always in contact with sin, Christ continued sinless, for the infection never spread to him.

(G. Smeaton)

25 July

> 'You will fill me with joy in your presence, with eternal pleasures at your right hand'. (Psalm 16:11)

Suggested reading Luke 23: 39-43

I met Miss W. on door-to-door visitation. She loved the Lord but as an elderly believer she was isolated and somewhat eccentric. I called regularly at her home and one January afternoon, found her in a distressed condition. Her house was cold, she was not feeling well and she pleaded with me to get her into a home. I called her doctor who confirmed that Miss W. was under-nourished and in need of extra care.

There was a small nursing home, run by Christians, just three miles away and having negotiated with the owners, I arranged to take Miss W. that evening. She stayed for three weeks and returned home in a much better physical state, having been well-fed and cared for.

I was, therefore, not prepared for her response when, a few days later, I called to see her.

'Never put me in that home again', she scolded.
'Why', I asked 'what was the problem'?

'There was a television in the home', she remarked, 'and I have never ever watched television'.

I thought she might have been more appreciative of my efforts and the kindness she had received at the home but that was all forgotten because of the television.

No home on earth---though pleasant and comfortable---can ever be perfect. 'Fulness of joy' and 'eternal pleasures' are reserved for our home in heaven. Jesus said, 'I go to prepare a place for you'. (John 14:3). Heaven will be perfect because it is prepared by One who is himself, perfect.

Heaven will mean the realization of all the things for which man was made and the satisfaction of all the outreaching of his heart.

(Ernest F. Kevan)

26 July

'I gave you milk, not solid food, for you were not ready for it. Indeed, you are still not ready'. (1 Corinthians 3:2)

Suggested reading Job 23:1-12

I once worked with a young woman who had anorexia nervosa. It was tragic to see her go from being an outgoing, bubbly character to one who was often weak and depressed.

Sadly, there is such a thing as spiritual anorexia nervosa. Believers lose their appetite, they cannot stomach the Word of God, and how soon they become weak, depressed and discouraged.

Preaching at a church one Sunday evening, I saw a man in the congregation that I recognised from years ago.

'I didn't know Jack attended here', I commented to a deacon.
'Jack attends any church where there is cake and biscuits afterwards' replied the deacon.

Jack went where the food was, and in the spiritual realm, it is important that we do the same. We need to regularly attend those churches where souls are fed through the faithful exposition of the Word of God. This is how we 'grow in the grace and knowledge of our Lord and Saviour Jesus Christ'. (2 Peter 3:18)

The Bible calls itself food. The value of food is not in the discussion it arouses but in the nourishment it imparts.

(Will H. Houghton)

27 July

'Jesus----began teaching the people in their synagogue, and they were amazed. "Where did this man get this wisdom and these miraculous powers"? They asked. ------And they took offence at him. ' (Matthew 13:54 and 57)

Suggested reading Matthew 22:15-22

Any Questions has always been one of my favourite radio programmes, and I have been listening to it now for over sixty years. The presenters have changed---Freddie Grisewood, John Timpson, David Jacobs, and Jonathan Dimbleby---but the format is largely unchanged from when the programme was first aired in 1948.

I have been at two live broadcasts---one, on a wild December night, at Queen Elizabeth School, Kirkby Lonsdale, and the other on a balmy spring evening, at Ripley St. Thomas School, Lancaster. On the panel at QES in the early 90s was a young unknown lady named Nicola Sturgeon; whilst in Lancaster, one of the panellists was Theresa May.

Almost without exception, the panellists have been intelligent, educated people, yet I have heard sensible and foolish answers. They have sadly proved that 'knowledge is not wisdom'.

During his ministry, Jesus was asked many questions---some of which were 'trick' questions, as the Pharisees and others tried to trap Him. Sometimes Jesus did not give a direct answer but responded to a question with a question. This was not a politician being devious but the Son of God being wise. Wisdom can only be obtained from God, and whilst politicians and others often possess much knowledge, it has to be said they often lack wisdom.

If you lack knowledge, go to school. If you lack wisdom, get on your knees! Knowledge is not wisdom. Wisdom is the proper use of knowledge.

(Vance Havner)

28 July

> 'All of you, clothe yourself with humility towards one another, because "God opposes the proud but shows favour to the humble". (1 Peter 5:5)

Suggested reading: John 13:1-17

No dishwashers in the 1950s or 1960s and so 'washing up' was a daily chore in every household. As young boys, it was never a task that my brother and I warmed to but nevertheless a task which, from time to time, we were expected to perform.

The contentious issue was, who was going to wash and who was going to dry? And for some reason, washing the dishes always seemed to be the preferred option. Consequently, 'whose turn is it to wash and whose turn is it to dry'?' often became a source of disagreement.

In New Testament times, feet exposed to sand and dust soon became dirty, uncomfortable and needed to be washed. This was a menial task, undertaken by servants, but Jesus did not leave or delegate this task to His disciples. He discharged it Himself---no question as to who would do the washing or who would do the drying'

Jesus, even though He was God Incarnate, did both, and in so doing set before us the example of humble service. 'Christ Jesus: who being in very nature God, did not consider equality with God something to be used to his own advantage; rather he made himself nothing by taking the very nature of a servant, being made in human likeness'. (Philippians 2:6-7)

Am I prepared to do the menial task, or are there some things I consider to be 'beneath me'? Having trusted Jesus as my Saviour, I must then follow Him as my example.

No man has ever humbled himself so greatly; and no man has ever been more exalted as a result.

(John Blanchard)

29 July

> 'All have sinned and fall short of the glory of God. ' (Romans 3:23)

John 1:1-13

One summer, as a student, I worked for a well-known retail store. My duties chiefly consisted of bringing goods from the warehouse onto the shop floor, and on busy occasions, helping in the cafeteria. However, one morning, I was asked to do something quite different.

Apparently, the sales figures were disappointing, targets were not being met and the manager was feeling the pressure. Consequently, I was asked to trawl through back copies of the local paper and underline any article which indicated that visitor numbers were down and money was tight.

Such articles were not plenteous, but there were some and these were passed to the manager. In reporting to head office, he would use these reports as mitigating evidence for disappointing retail figures.

God has set a standard, a target for us all---perfection; the faultless keeping of His commands. That target has not and cannot be met by any human being---we have all fallen short of the standard set by God. Some try to excuse themselves by pleading mitigating circumstances, but that does not change the situation.

We are all sinners who have missed the target and therefore, we all need a Saviour. And that Saviour can only be the One who met the target by perfectly keeping all the commandments of God. The One who could say 'I always do what pleases him' (John 8:29) That One can only be the Lord Jesus Christ who died for sinners upon the cross of Calvary.

It is a lovely sight to see a man treading earth and no mire clinging to his feet; and breathing our polluted air without infection's taint.

(Henry Law)

30 July

> 'He knows how we are formed; he remembers that we are dust'. (Psalm 103:14)

Suggested reading Mark 14:32-42

I often found afternoon services in country chapels a challenge, as farmers battled with drowsiness. In some ways, this was understandable as, an early start, fresh air, a Sunday lunch, a warm chapel, were all factors in inducing sleep. Added to which at lambing and hay time, most farmers were already tired and exhausted.

However, on one occasion, I did fear for the safety of a middle-aged farmer. He was sound asleep but leaning so much to one side, there was a real danger he might end up on the floor. Thankfully, this did not happen but I was a little surprised when, later at the door, he thanked me for my message. I was almost tempted to ask which of the three points he had found to be most helpful.

I never judge anyone who is drowsy in a service for I do not know their individual circumstances. They might not be well, just come off a night shift or having broken nights caring for babies or a sick relative. Only the Lord, besides knowing our spiritual state, knows our physical and emotional condition.

However, if there is no good reason for drowsiness, then 'sleeping in church' is an insult to God, discourteous to the preacher and of spiritual danger to the soul. The Word of God could have convicted and saved a person or encouraged and guided a believer, but through drowsiness, it was not heard or acted upon.

As Eutychus discovered: sleeping in church was dangerous in the C1st and it can still be so today.

Christian, seek not yet repose;
Cast thy dreams of ease away;
Thou art in the midst of foes;
Watch and pray.

(Charlotte Elliott)

31 July

> 'He chose to give us birth through the word of truth, that we might be a kind of first-fruits of all he created'. (James 1:18)

Suggested reading Luke 5:1-11

Meeting a friend I had not seen for a long time, he was soon telling me how he had been on a 'voyage of self-discovery'. This pilgrimage had taken him to South America, and he was most enthusiastic about the many positive things he had learned about himself.

He had written a journal that he invited me to read and whilst it had obviously been, for him, a memorable experience, I cannot say I was over impressed by his findings. It seemed too self-congratulatory to be realistic.

Such voyages are becoming ever more popular, as people travel to far-away places, in order to 'find themselves'.

I, too, have been on a voyage of discovery but my journey did not take me to foreign lands; it took me to the Bible. And what I discovered about myself was neither flattering nor encouraging. I discovered that, in the sight of God, I was sinful, selfish, rebellious and I desperately needed a saviour. It was a humbling but a necessary experience for, in the goodness of God, it brought me to Jesus.

It is almost a paradox but we need to 'find' that we are 'lost' before Jesus is able to save us.

I was lost but Jesus found me
Found the sheep that went astray
Threw His loving arms around me
Drew me back into His way.

(Francis H. Rowley)

BIBLE READINGS AUGUST

1 August

> 'Endure hardship as discipline; God is treating you as his children. For what children are not disciplined by their father'? (Hebrews 12:7)

Suggested reading 2 Timothy 2:1-7

N. had noticeably put on weight and when his blood pressure reading was unhealthily high, he sensibly decided to do something about it.

Some months later, I met N. and scarcely recognised him. He was neat and trim, and carrying no excess weight at all.

'Is it down to diet and exercise'? I asked.
N. answered me in one word. 'Discipline'.

He was right. No doubt the weight loss was due to diet and exercise but without discipline, there will be no diet or increased exercise.

Nothing in the physical or spiritual realm can be achieved without discipline, and it is better to be self-disciplined than to be disciplined by the Lord. In self-discipline, good habits, such as prayer, Bible study, public worship, strengthen our faith and help us to make spiritual progress.

If we fail in personal discipline, the Lord Himself may have to discipline us but this is never punishment. It is rather our Heavenly Father---out of his love and concern---- teaching and training us, in order that we might become good soldiers and better disciples.

In my own personal and pastoral experience, I have never known a man or a woman who came to spiritual maturity except through discipline.

(Donald S. Whitney)

2 August

> 'My Father's house has many rooms; if that were not so, would I have told you that I am going there to prepare a place for you'? (John 14:2)

Suggested reading: Psalm 16

In 1979, Pat and I moved from Morecambe into a terraced house in Ingleton, and this was to be our home for the next twenty-five years. We were happy there but the increasing needs of our handicapped son, meant that a larger house was necessary. Manoeuvring Aaron's wheelchair from one room to another had become almost impossible. Consequently, in 2005, we moved into a house which had been specially adapted for him and this made his care so much easier.

Indoors, walls had been knocked down, doors widened, a ramp and overhead hoists installed, and outside---- a landscaped sensory garden. The property had been purchased by a Trust but it was always known as Aaron's house because it fully met his needs.

Speaking of heaven, Jesus could have said to His disciples, 'I am going there to prepare a place' but he added 'for you'. He made it personal and that is significant because heaven will meet and satisfy all our needs. Every longing and desire will be met because prepared by Christ, our eternal home will be as perfect as Christ, Himself.

Heaven---where the redeemed will find all their heart's desire; joy with their Lord, joy with his people, joy in the ending of all frustration and distress, joy in the supplying of all wants. What was said to the child----"If you want sweets and hamsters in heaven, they will be there"---was not an evasion but a witness to the truth that in heaven no felt needs or longings go unsatisfied.

(James Packer)

3 August

'For the accuser of our brothers and sisters, who accuses them before our God, day and night, has been hurled down'. (Revelation 12:10

Suggested reading 1 John 2:1-6

As a boy, many a summer Saturday afternoon was spent scoring for Morecambe Grammar School Old Boys cricket team. This meant a number of picturesque and interesting cricket grounds being visited. One of these was at Lancaster Moor Hospital, whose facilities included an Art Deco cricket pavilion.

LMH was an old psychiatric hospital and sadly some of the patients had been there for many, many years. A number attended the cricket matches and they were invariably friendly and childlike in spirit. Consequently, they got away with things which would not have been acceptable elsewhere.

When a player was dismissed without scoring, they would place a picture of a duck on the scoreboard and say 'quack, quack, quack'. This was amusing to everyone, except the poor batsman who, having been dismissed for nothing, then had a reminder of his failure, as he returned to the pavilion. 'Insult to injury' comes to mind.

When believers fail, knowing they have let their Lord down, they are often overtaken by sorrow and guilt. This is then made worse by Satan--'the accuser'-who tells them they are not Christians, God will never forgive them, they are just hypocrites. Satan adds 'insult to injury'.

We need to remind ourselves 'there is no truth in him. When he lies, he speaks his native language, for he is a liar and the father of lies'. (John 8:44) The truth is to be found in 1 John 2:1 and it is glorious: 'If anybody does sin, we have an advocate with the Father---Jesus Christ, the Righteous One.

Yes, we do still sin but we are not banished because the Lord Jesus counters every argument of Satan. He speaks on our behalf. Praise be to His Name.

Before the throne of God above
I have a strong, a perfect plea.
A great High Priest whose name is love,
Who ever lives and pleads for me.

(Charitie Lees de Chenze)

4 August

'Let the message of Christ dwell among you richly as you teach and admonish one another with all wisdom through psalms, hymns, and songs from the Spirit, singing to God with gratitude in your hearts'. (Colossians 3:16)

Suggested reading Acts 10:23-33

Pat has a friend who telephones her from time to time, and I always know when this particular lady is on the phone. Pat sits in her chair, and for most of the time, she is silent. This, for Pat, is rather unusual, but she is quiet because she cannot get a word in. It is her friend who is doing all the talking. The phone call is not really a dialogue but more of a monologue. It is not a true conversation because there is no balance between speaking and listening.

I remember an elderly lady once confessing that she had, in fact, dozed off whilst listening to a phone call. That has never happened to Pat, but it is a possibility if you are having to listen but not speak.

Worship is a dialogue between God and man. Therefore, it is not good if three-quarters of a service is given over to music and singing, but only a quarter to the reading and teaching of God's Word. This means that man is doing too much speaking and God is not being given time to speak to us. There must be the proper balance.

Man speaking to God and God speaking to man are both essential aspects of worship. God delights to hear the praises and the prayers of his people, and yet, surely it is more important that we listen to God than that God listens to us.

Speak, Lord in the stillness,
Speak Your Word to me;
Help me now to listen
In expectancy.

(Emily May Crawford)

5 August

'Not looking to your own interests, but each of you to the interests of the others' (Philippians 2:4)

Suggested reading Philippians 2: 5-11

I have always enjoyed singing and for a time, I was a member of a male voice choir. We were a close-knit group and our choir practices were always happy occasions, with much humour and banter.

The marriage of one of our members broke up and he subsequently moved away from the area. Discussing this with the organiser of the choir, I commented how sad this was.

'Yes, it is', he agreed, 'we were already short of tenors'.

Not quite the response I had been anticipating. The setback to the choir being nothing to what the man and his family must have been experiencing.

It has been rightly said that 'the most common disease in the world is 'I' trouble' and conversion does not eradicate the condition. Jesus said, 'whoever wants to be my disciple must deny themselves and take up their cross daily and follow me'. (Luke 9:23). Without daily denial and crucifixion, self will always raise its ugly head.

This does not mean we have to ignore self, but rather that we should put the needs of others before ours. In so doing, we are following the example set by the Lord Jesus.

There was a day when I died to George Muller; his opinions and preferences, taste and will: died to the world, its approval or censure;

died to the approval or blame even of my brethren or friends; and since then, I have striven only to show myself approved unto God.

(George Mueller)

6 August

'Do not forget to do good and to share with others, for with such sacrifices God is pleased' (Hebrews13:16)

Suggested reading 1 Corinthians 16:15-24

After a service, conscious of their failures and inadequacies, many preachers feel the need for encouragement. At one church, this need was met by an elderly lady in her nineties. However, talking to her one day, I discovered her encouragement was not just confined to the preacher

She told me how she had always taken a special interest in children and young people. She sent cards on their birthdays, and wrote to them when they took exams, went off to university, were baptised or became church members.

And she said, 'the wonderful thing is this: those I tried to encourage are now encouraging me. They write to me. They send me cards or call to see me'. Those she had encouraged were now encouraging her. What a worthwhile ministry---the ministry of encouragement

There is so much in society to discourage us that, more than ever, we need the ministry of encouragement. People are anxious, lonely and hurting, and a friendly word or gesture can make all the difference. Paul said. 'I was glad when Stephanus. Fortunatus and Achaicus arrived---for they refreshed my spirit and yours also. Such men deserve recognition'.

(1 Corinthians 16:17-18) Paul---the great Apostle----needed encouragement and he commended the three men who refreshed him.

Can I be a Barnabas, a Stephanas, a Fortunatus or an Achaicus? Can I encourage someone today?

God has a secret method by which he recompenses his saints: he sees to it that they become the prime beneficiaries of their own benefactions.

(I.D.E.Thomas)

7 August

'Be kind and compassionate to one another, forgiving each other, just as in Christ God forgave you'. (Ephesians 4:32)

Suggested reading Galatians 5:22-26

Our multi-handicapped son loved being outdoors and so, when the weather was favourable, Aaron often accompanied me to football and cricket matches. He could not see much or understand what was going on, but his smile confirmed that it was an enjoyable experience for him.

One Saturday afternoon, we went to watch Kirk Deighton Rangers v Robin Hood Athletic in the West Yorkshire League---I recommend such fixtures which I now consider to be far preferable to watching often overpriced professional matches

Prior to the kick off, the referee came straight over to Aaron and confided that he had a five-year-old multi-handicapped son. He welled up as he told me that it was a twenty-four-hour commitment, and he and his wife had not had a night out together since the child was born.

Referees are often a target of abuse from players, managers and spectators, but does anyone ever pause to think what their personal circumstances might be.

As believers, our kindness is grounded in the great kindness of God in sending his Son to be our Saviour, and is modelled on the earthly ministry and sacrificial death of Christ. Kindness is one of the fruits of the Spirit (Galatians 5:22) and is demonstrated as we care for others and seek to bear their burdens.

In a world that can often be unkind and uncaring, this is a sure way in which we can be distinctive and different from others.

Be kind; everyone you meet is fighting a hard battle.

(Ian MacLaren)

8 August

'Our citizenship is in heaven'. (Philippians 3:20)

Suggested reading Genesis 12:1-10

In the 1970s, when I worked in the Department of Employment, some claimants were registered as 'NFA'---no fixed address. If they were fortunate, they would perhaps have a few days in a hostel, followed by a few days in bed and breakfast accommodation. If they were not so fortunate, it might be sleeping on a park bench or on the beach under the pier.

Such claimants were required to daily attend the office, as this was the only way they could be contacted if work became available. NFA was not an enviable position to be in.

As believers, we need to remind ourselves that we are pilgrims in this world---here we have no permanent address. And yet, we are not NFA because we are citizens of heaven, with our permanent home in the City of God.

How important, therefore, that we do not become too attached to the possessions and pleasures of this world. And, as ambassadors of Christ, our standards, too, must be different because ultimately, we are accountable to the God of heaven.

This world is not our home; it is not our natural habitat and this should be demonstrated in our day to day living.

If I find anyone who is settled down too snugly into this world, I am made to doubt whether he's ever truly been born again'.

(A.W.Tozer)

9 August

'In those days Israel had no king; everyone did as he saw fit'. (Judges 21:25)

Suggested reading Matthew 5:17-20

I had arranged to pick up a friend in North Leeds at 12pm, and was making good progress until I joined a queue of stationary traffic in Guiseley. At first, I assumed it must be roadworks but when an ambulance and police car sped by, I feared it might be an accident. Neither proved to be the case but rather a traffic light failure at a busy road junction.

I expect many of us have moaned about being delayed by red lights, but the truth is they help the flow of traffic and avoid chaotic queues. Without them, we are faced with a real safety hazard, and most of us, I suspect, are not sufficiently acquainted with the Highway Code, to know precisely the right action to take.

Eventually I negotiated the junction but it was 12.15 pm when I pulled up outside the home of my friend. All in all, a frustrating and confusing journey.

The ten commandments are God's traffic lights, telling society what we should and should not do. Sadly, as we sometimes ignorantly think we would be better off without the traffic lights, so society has concluded it would be better off without the Ten Commandments.

The tragic results of the commandments being abandoned are now all too evident. Society is ever more confused and chaotic, and this was inevitable because, as without traffic lights, we are exposed to physical danger, so without the Ten Commandments, we are exposed to moral and spiritual danger.

God knew what He was doing when He gave the commandments---how utterly foolish of humans to think that they know better.

God forbids sin, not to stop us enjoying ourselves, but to prevent us destroying ourselves.

(John Blanchard)

10 August

> 'The disciples were called Christians first at Antioch'. (Acts 11:26)

Suggested reading Acts 4:13-22

My headteacher at secondary school set great store on academic achievement but his greater concern was for moral excellence. I remember numerous occasions when all the boys had to stay behind after morning assembly, whilst he expressed his disdain for bad behaviour. Consequently, many of us respected him, not just as our headteacher but also as a father figure.

He had a saying which he repeated over and over again, especially when sport teams were travelling away to take part in competitions. 'Wherever you go, you take the good name of Morecambe Grammar School with you'. We wore the blazer and the tie. We were ambassadors for the school and this was more important than any sporting success.

As believers, wherever we go, we take the good Name of Jesus Christ with us---we are his witnesses/his ambassadors. Therefore, to some extent, what people think of Jesus will be determined by what they see in us.

The disciples did not call themselves Christians----this name was given to them by the people of Antioch. It may have been a term of endearment or a term of derision, but it was given because they were evidently the followers of Christ.

Do people know that I am a Christian----not because I say so---but because my daily conversation and conduct speaks to them of Jesus? Can they see something of him in me?

A Christian's life should be nothing but a visible representation of Christ.

(Thomas Brooks)

11 August

> 'For "you were like sheep going astray" but now you have returned to the Shepherd and Overseer of your souls'. (1 Peter 2:25)

Suggested reading: Psalm 119:169-176

I have always been an early riser and rightly or wrongly, I attribute this to my days as a paperboy, with their 6 am starts. Perhaps I am biased but I have always considered 'the crack of dawn' to be the best time of the day.

Consequently, during my ministry in a North Yorkshire village, it became my custom, to have a 'quiet time', early in the morning. And, rather than resorting to my study, I usually took to the open fields and here communed with the Lord.

One wintry morning, as I walked through a field, I was caught in a sudden snowstorm. It was not too easy to see ahead but soon I was conscious of a herd of sheep running towards me. They were bleating, obviously thinking I was the farmer, coming to feed them.

They could not have been more mistaken, for though I had a packet of Werther's Originals in my pocket, I had nothing with which to feed or satisfy hungry sheep.

What a picture of humanity. Jesus spoke of men and women as being 'like sheep without a shepherd' (Matthew 9:36) and it is an apt description. They run hither and thither, seeking for meaning and fulfilment: so often turning to people or pleasures that can never meet their spiritual need.

Jesus is the good shepherd---the one who said 'I have come that they may have life and have it to the full'. It is in him and him alone that our deepest need can be met. We only stop 'going astray' when we 'return to the Shepherd and Overseer of our souls'.

Now none but Christ can satisfy,
None other Name for me!
There's love and life and lasting joy,
Lord Jesus found in Thee

(Anonymous)

12 August

> 'It is not the healthy who need a doctor, but the sick----I have not come to call the righteous but sinners'. (Matthew 9:12-13)

Suggested reading Romans 10:1-13

As seven-year-olds, my mother took my brother and me to the doctor with sore throats and rashes. He examined us both and concluded, 'I suspect scarlet fever. You need to be isolated. There will be an ambulance within the hour'. We went home tearful and pleading with our mother, but isolation it had to be, and we were soon being transported to Beaumont Hospital in Lancaster.

My memories of the experience are vague, but I remember we could only see visitors through a glass pane; they were not allowed to come to our beds. However, after three days, we got wonderful and unexpected news: Jim and I had not got scarlet fever and we were allowed to return home.

As a treat, I was bought a red bus matchbox toy, which I still have to this day. What a pity I did not keep the box!

Jesus called Matthew, a tax collector, to follow Him and the Pharisees were appalled that Jesus could ever be interested in such a man. Jesus, however, had come to save the sick (sinners), not those who thought they were healthy (without sin). And this is why Matthew responded to the call, whilst the Pharisees rejected it.

Thankfully, I did not have scarlet fever, and in that sense, being healthy, I did not need the hospital or the doctor. But tragically, many are like the Pharisees, denying that they are sinners when the Bible says 'there is no-one righteous, not even one' (Romans 3:10) and 'all have sinned and fall short of the glory of God' (Romans 3:23). Such ones never come to Christ, because though they are sick, they think they are healthy.

The greatest fault is to be conscious of none.

(Thomas Carlyle)

13 August

'The God who made the world and everything in it is the Lord of heaven and earth and does not live in temples built by human hands' (Acts 17:24)

Suggested reading.1 Kings 8:22-30

In recent years, I have been thankful for my sat/nav, which has enabled me to locate churches much more easily. However, there was an occasion when I faced an unexpected problem.

One Sunday afternoon, I went to preach at a village chapel, I had never preached at before. I knew the village and consequently found the building without any difficulty. However, when I looked inside, it was somewhat disconcerting to find half the roof was missing and the building was empty.

I then noticed a group of ladies walking together and I followed them to the village hall, where the service was indeed being held. Apparently urgent repairs were being undertaken at the church, but no one had thought to inform me that the church would be out of use for several weeks.

Paul was speaking to the Athenians who believed that their multiplicity of gods lived in the various temples they had built. The Apostle was at pains to emphasise that, by contrast, the one true God---eternal, transcendent, omniscient---can never be confined to any building made with hands. He inhabits eternity, He is 'the Lord of heaven and earth', and whilst He delights to meet with His people, when they assemble in His Name---He does not need a roof over His head.

Sometimes, the God we worship is too small. We need to see Him for who He truly is---the Lord God Almighty---for only then, will our worship be worthy of Him.

Jesus, where e'r Thy people meet. There they behold Thy mercy seat.

Where'er they seek Thee, Thou art found. And every place is hallowed ground.

For Thou, within no walls confined. Inhabitest the humble mind.

Such ever bring Thee where they come. And going, take Thee to their home.

(William Cowper)

14 August

> 'Whoever wants to be my disciple must deny themselves and take up their cross and follow me'. (Mark 8:34)

Suggested reading Luke 14:25-35

A young couple, with two young children, were wonderfully converted from the world. They had no Christian background but they thrived on the word and their spiritual progress was remarkable.

One Sunday, twelve months after their conversion, they were not at church either morning or evening. It was in the days before mobile phones, and so after the evening service, I drove to their home.

Here I was met by two disheartened believers who were facing family problems and pressures at work. The man looked me in the eye and said 'I never knew it would be like this'.

If he 'never knew', this was not the fault of Jesus, because again and again, He stressed the hardships and pressures of discipleship. Jesus never 'pulled the wool over anyone's eyes'. He always told it as it was.

Perhaps there are times when we are almost dishonest in our presentation of the gospel. In our eagerness to gain converts, we fail to mention the rigours and sacrifices of discipleship. Jesus never did. Indeed, in Luke 14, He challenges 'large crowds' (v25) to 'estimate the cost' (v28) before becoming 'my disciple' (v33). Jesus never tried to win converts by false pretences---neither must we.

Salvation is free but discipleship costs everything we have.

(Billy Graham)

15 August

'Jesus said, "I praise you, Father, Lord of heaven and earth, because you have hidden these things from the wise and learned, and revealed them to little children Yes, Father, for this is what you were pleased to do". (Matthew 11:25-26)

Suggested reading 1 Corinthians 2:6-16

One of the joys of being an itinerant preacher is the generous hospitality and warm fellowship which Pat and I have had with fellow believers. The Sunday roasts we have relished have, I am sure, been superior to many served in hotels and restaurants. At some homes, I have been thankful for the offer of a bed—an afternoon nap refreshing me for the evening service.

Hospitality has also given opportunity for joys and concerns to be shared. On one occasion, preaching at a village chapel, an elderly couple shared with me how disturbed they were by certain things their minister was saying from the pulpit.

'Do you ever question what he says'? I asked.
'Oh no', they replied, 'we can't do that. He's educated---we are not'.

Commendable that they respected their minister but nevertheless sad they felt unable to challenge him.

Paul said 'The person without the Spirit does not accept the things that come from the Spirit of God but considers them foolishness, and cannot understand them because they are discerned only through the Spirit'. (1

Corinthians 2:14). Men and women can have all manner of qualifications but if they are not born again of the Spirit of God, they will never understand spiritual truths. We do not decry education, but we are all in darkness until the light of the gospel breaks in upon us. Only then do Biblical truths become precious and understandable.

The human intellect, even in its fallen state, is an awesome work of God, but it lies in darkness until it has been illuminated by the Holy Spirit.

(A.W. Tozer)

16 August

'A gentle answer turns away wrath, but a harsh word stirs up anger'. (Proverbs 15:1)

Suggested reading Romans 12:9-21

On holiday, one April evening, I went to a football match at Wiggington Grasshoppers, in the York and District League, and here I met a most interesting character. He was the assistant referee and even though seventy-eight years of age, still very alert and agile.

At half-time, he gave me a polo mint and we had a fascinating conversation. He had been a referee for over fifty years, and in his younger days, as a Football League referee, had appeared on Match of the Day. Remarkably in a career of over 3,200, he had only ever sent four players off.

What was his secret? The polo mint.

'Whenever a player rushed up to me', he said, 'complaining about a decision, I used to smile, ask them to cool down and offer them a polo mint. More often than not, it seemed to do the trick'.

Perhaps today, if referees had polo mints in their pockets, they would not need as many yellow and red cards!

The veteran referee was, in fact, enunciating a Biblical principle. Refuse to fight fire with fire. Gentleness can extinguish a fire or, at least, give no more fuel to the fire. A calm, polite response can take a great deal of tension out of potentially volatile situations.

'Forbearance, kindness, gentleness, self-control' (Galatians 5:22) are the fruit of the spirit, and as believers, may they be seen in us, when we are faced with disagreement and division.

Gentle words fall lightly, but they have great weight.

(Derick Bingham)

17 August

'If the Son sets you free, you will be free indeed'. (John 8:36)

Suggested reading John 1:29-39

An ornithophobic has a fear of birds, and although I do not quite fall into that category, nevertheless I do panic when a bird flies into the house. Hot summer days and open windows are an invitation to our feathered friends. And this I discovered when, on entering my study, I came face to face with a startled blackbird. In truth, I was probably more startled than the blackbird.

The bird flew downstairs, whilst I secreted myself in the study and shouted for Pat to take charge. She immediately opened the front door but the frightened bird was not for moving in that direction. Instead, at first, it headed for the bathroom and bedroom windows, where it was in danger of stunning itself. Several minutes were to pass before, eventually finding the door, the bird flew away to freedom. Panic over for bird and for me

Jesus Christ is the door to eternal freedom---freedom from the punishment, the power and ultimately the presence of sin. Sadly, in their search for freedom, many spend years 'banging their heads against a brick wall' without ever coming to Christ.

But He is the way---the only way to freedom. He is the door---the only door to God and to heaven. 'Salvation is found in no one else, for there is no other name under heaven, given to mankind by which we must be saved'. (Acts 4:12)

We find freedom when we find God; we lose it when we lose him.

(Paul Sherer)

18 August

> 'So we fix our eyes not on what is seen, but on what is unseen, since what is seen is temporary, but what is unseen is eternal'. (2 Corinthians 4:18)

Suggested reading 1 Peter 1:1-9

Pat decided she wanted an air fryer for her birthday, and so one was selected from a catalogue and ordered. Within days, it arrived and when unpacked, was placed on the dining room table, whilst Pat eagerly read the attached instructions. Our mouths watered as we anticipated chicken and salmon meals to come

However, calamity was just around the corner. Picking up the air fryer to position it in the kitchen, Pat dropped our newly acquired gadget---it fell and great was the fall of it. Sadly, within a couple of hours of being delivered, the air-fryer was broken, unusable and destined for the recycling centre.

Salt Ayre tip is a household waste recycling centre on the outskirts of Lancaster and Morecambe. Whenever I visited the site, I was reminded that 'what is seen is temporary' (2 Corinthians 4:18), because ready for disposal were fridges, washing machines, cookers, dishwashers, televisions, computers etc. Once they had all been prized and cherished, but now, they were broken, rusted and unwanted.

How important that we distinguish between 'what is seen ' and 'what is unseen'. It may be very tempting to concentrate on material things and yet these are all temporary. It is the 'unseen' which is eternal---the human soul, heaven, God Himself---and yet often, scant regard is given to the spiritual world.

This is why Jesus asked the question, 'What good is it for someone to gain the whole world, yet forfeit his soul'? (Mark 8:36)

We treat sensible and present things as realities, and future and eternal things as fables: whereas the reverse should be our habit.

(Richard Cecil)

19 August

'Jesus said- "Go into all the world and preach the gospel to all creation". (Mark 16:15)

Suggested reading Acts 8:1-8

My mother always fed the birds and it is a tradition that I have happily continued. I now use bird feeders, buying copious amounts of seed, whilst mother always fed the birds with bread.

This was the method used when, one day, I went out to feed the birds with my two-year-old grandson. We both had a piece of bread in our hands, and breaking the bread into small pieces, I put it on the bird table.

I seemed to be doing all the work and turning round, I soon discovered why---my grandson was eating the bread himself. This was certainly not the intended purpose of the exercise.

Sometimes, as believers and churches---are we not guilty of doing the same? Instead of obeying the command of Christ, and sharing the gospel with others, we rather keep it to ourselves. This was not true of the early church, even when 'scattered' because of persecution. 'Those who had been scattered preached the word wherever they went'. (Acts 8:4)

They had a commission from Jesus and were so excited by the gospel, they could not help but share it with others. We have the same commission---may we also have the same zeal and enthusiasm.

Too many Christians are stuffing themselves with gospel blessings while millions have never had a taste.

(Vance Havner)

20 August

'Blessed are the poor in spirit, for theirs is the kingdom of heaven'. (Matthew 5:3)

Suggested reading: Matthew 11:25-30

Eddie attended the church where Pat and I worshipped when we were first married. He was a simple soul, with special needs and we were never quite sure just how much of the gospel Eddie understood.

Two or three weeks before he died, Eddie was taken into a local hospice and was visited by his pastor.

'In a few days time, I'm going home', said Eddie.
'Are you sure', said his pastor, 'you are not very well'?
'Oh', replied Eddie, 'I'm going home to heaven'.
And then he said something which thrilled all our hearts.
'You see, pastor, Jesus died to get me ready for heaven and He has gone to heaven to get it ready for me'.

How wonderful. Eddie might not have known much theology but he knew enough to get him to heaven. He knew 'things---hidden from the wise and learned but 'revealed to little children'. (Matthew 11:25)

Have we Eddie's simple but confident faith in Jesus?

Jesus loves me, he who died.
Heaven's gate to open wide.
He will Wash away my sin.
Let his little child come in.

(Anna Bartlett Warner)

21 August

> 'Simon, Simon, Satan has asked to sift all of you as wheat. But I have prayed for you, Simon that your faith may not fail. And when you have turned back, strengthen your brothers'. (Luke 22:31-32)

Suggested reading Matthew 4:1-11

After a busy Sunday, Pat and I decided to relax by taking Desmond, our daughter's dog, for a Monday morning walk. It was a cold but bright January day, and it was good to be out in the fresh air.

I had Desmond on a lead, but suddenly something caught his eye and he darted in front of Pat. With no time to take evasive action, Pat tripped over his lead, banging her head on the ground and breaking her glasses.

We sought medical advice, knowing that a bang on the head can be serious, but thankfully, there were no repercussions, except for bruised arms and legs, and a 'shiner' of a black eye.

Naturally, this brought the usual jocular comments from family and friends, but most accepted our version of events!

Satan is ever out to 'trip up' the believer, and at times, he does, causing us pain, remorse and disappointment. We do stumble, despite the restraining hand of God and the prayers of Christ, and yet we do not altogether fall. Our faith may falter, but it does not fail, and that will be true until we reach heaven and are, then, forever outside the reach of Satan.

Though Christians be not kept altogether from falling, yet they are kept from falling altogether.

(William Secker)

22 August

> 'He (Jesus) began to teach them that the Son of Man must suffer many things and be rejected by the elders, the chief priests and teachers of the law, and that he must be killed and after three days rise again. He spoke plainly about this. (Mark 8:31-32)

Suggested reading Matthew 28:1-15

As a child, our daughter had numerous pets---hamsters, gerbils, guinea pigs---which brought her great happiness. The downside was the grief she experienced whenever one of the animals died.

One morning she had gone to school, when I noticed that a recently bought gerbil was not breathing. We had a burial, and then I went to the pet shop in Settle and bought an almost identical gerbil.

On her return from school, we waited with bated breath but thankfully, Joanna did not detect it was a different gerbil and a 'time of mourning' was prevented. It was many, many years later before I made her aware of our deceit.

I hope my deceit was for justifiable reasons, but concerning the resurrection of Jesus, the disciples were not guilty of any kind of deceit. It was the elders, chief priests and soldiers who invented a story that the disciples had stolen the body of Jesus. However, the Gospel writer makes it clear that this story was an invention, a concoction on the part of some who, while knowing Jesus had risen from the dead, had no desire to face the truth.

Even more tragic, there are those who would accuse Jesus, Himself, of deceit. They deny His physical resurrection saying, without a shred of evidence, 'He only swooned on the cross', or 'He had a twin brother who impersonated Him'.

Such myths can easily be refuted, but they make Jesus out to be a liar, a deceiver, because He said, He would rise and had risen, from the dead. Let not the cynics accuse Christ, and in so doing, undermine the wonder of the resurrection, which is the bedrock of the Christian faith. 'He committed no sin, and no deceit was found in his mouth' (1 Peter2:22)

In an age of unbounding unbelief and scepticism, we shall find that the resurrection of Christ will bear any weight that we can lay upon it.

(J. C. Ryle)

23 August

> 'John saw Jesus coming towards him and said, "Look, the Lamb of God who takes away the sin of the world". (John 1:29)

Suggested reading John 4:39-42

Linton Falls is a beauty spot on the River Wharfe, near to Grassington, in North Yorkshire. On a spring-like Valentine Day morning, Pat and I decided to take a walk by the river.

Linton Falls is clearly signposted and soon we are on the footbridge, photographing the waterfalls. Due to a dryish few weeks, the falls are not as spectacular as sometimes but nevertheless, still an impressive sight.

We do the short circular walk and the limited rainfall means that it is safe to use the stepping stones which cross the river. A lovely walk frequented by walkers and dogs, and with it being half-term, there are a number of parents and children.

I mention the signpost and stepping stones because they are a visual aid of what the believer ought to be. As with John the Baptist, we are signposts to point others to Jesus. A signpost does not draw attention to itself and that should be just as true of us, as it was of John the Baptist, who said, 'He must become greater; I must become less'. (John 3:30)

We are to be signposts but also stepping stones as we seek to encourage one another on the pilgrim pathway. There are many dangers and pitfalls to be negotiated, and we are called to support those who are weak and troubled. Was not Ananias the stepping stone by which Paul---as a new convert---was accepted by the disciples in Damascus? (Acts 9:19)

Then let us ever bare
The blessed end in view
And join with mutual care
To fight our battle through
And kindly help each other on
Till all receive the starry crown

(Charles Wesley)

24 August

> "For my thoughts are not your thoughts, neither are your ways my ways", declares the Lord. "As the heavens are higher than the earth, so are my ways higher than your ways and my thoughts than your thoughts". (Isaiah 55:8-9)

Suggested reading Romans 11:33-36

As a young and inexperienced pastor, I used to visit an elderly lady every Thursday afternoon. It was not something 'set in stone' but I soon came to see it was not a good idea.

One Thursday, I was unable to visit her in the afternoon but decided to call after tea. It was a January evening, with snow on the ground, so I put my wellingtons on and walked to her home. I rang the doorbell and the reception I got was frostier than the night air.

She had expected me in the afternoon and she was obviously displeased that I had not come. The lady thought she knew my timetable and was disappointed because I had not adhered to it.

God is sovereign, but sometimes we think we know his timetable and we get upset when he does not act how and when we think he should. At all times, we have to bow to His sovereignty, recognising that 'His thoughts are not our thoughts and His ways are not our ways'. Ultimately, God knows best and therefore, even when we cannot understand His dealings with us, we continue to trust in Him. This is what it means to 'walk by faith and not by sight'.

The man who measures things by the circumstances of the hour is filled with fear: the man who sees Jehovah enthroned and governing has no panic.

(G. Campbell Morgan)

25 August

'Whoever conceals their sins does not prosper, but the one who confesses and renounces them finds mercy'. (Proverbs 28:13)

Suggested reading Luke 12:1-12

One morning, in the Jobcentre, I interviewed a man who had not worked for a number of years and was apparently making no effort to find work. As we discussed his situation, he said he had a confession to make.

Leaning across the table, he explained he did not really want work and his reasoning was quite ingenious. 'If I don't take a job', he said, 'it means there is a job for someone who does want one'. For a moment, I was speechless---not quite the logic one was expecting from a man in receipt of welfare benefits.

I think he was basically lazy, but in his warped thinking, he was turning a vice into a philanthropic virtue.

How often we try to excuse our sin or to put a gloss on it. My anger was justifiable. My bitterness was understandable. I wasn't gossiping---I was just imparting information. I wasn't being covetous---with more money, I can help worthy causes.

There may be times when we deceive ourselves but we can never deceive God. 'Nothing in all creation is hidden from God's sight. Everything is uncovered and laid bare before the eyes of him to whom we must give account'. (Hebrews 4:13)

Sin must be confessed not concealed--- it is then that we experience the mercy of God and know the blessedness of sin forgiven.

When man uncovers his sin, God covers it. When man cloaks, God strips bare. When man confesses, God pardons.

(Augustine)

26 August

'The secret things belong to the Lord our God, but the things revealed belong to us and to our children for ever, that we may follow all the words of this law'. (Deuteronomy 29:29)

Suggested reading Matthew 25:1-13

It was 1986 when a card appeared in a shop window in Ingleton. A man had moved into the village and wished to meet with anyone who was interested in the Second Coming of Christ. I telephoned the man and arranged to call at his home one evening.

Shortly after arriving, he produced a book on the Second Coming, which he had written himself. It was quite a volume, containing charts and calculations, and stretching to over two hundred pages. The book reached its climax in the closing pages, where we were informed that Jesus would return in 1984.

Despite already being two years out of date, the man was not at all perturbed. He explained that with the passing of time, certain calendars had changed, but he was still confident that he would be right to within a few tears.

How foolish! Not even the angels in heaven know the time of the Lord's return. It has been hidden from them, just as it has been hidden from us. Indeed, as a man on earth, it was concealed even from Jesus, Himself.

We must not attempt to reveal what God has been pleased to conceal. Jesus said to His disciples, 'It is not for you to know the times or dates the Father has set by his own authority'. Our focus must be upon the certainty of His coming, rather than on the timing of His coming.

Precisely because we cannot predict the moment, we must be ready at all moments.

(C.S. Lewis)

27 August

'What does the Lord require of you? To act justly and to love mercy and to walk humbly with your God'. (Micah 6:8)

Suggested reading Genesis 5:18-24

As a young boy, my grandparents came every Wednesday to see us. They did not live many miles away but nevertheless, it involved two bus journeys. When they got off the bus in Morecambe, they then had a half-mile walk to our home.

There were many times we thought that Grandad must have come on his own because he would come round the corner and there was no sight of Grandma. But then, supported by her walking stick, Grandma would appear---arriving at our home, several minutes after Grandad.

They had been married for over sixty years and yet, on those occasions, their walk was not as close as one might have expected.

You may have been walking with the Lord for a few or for many years, but is your walk with Him as close as it might be? Or have you drifted, wandered away? Have other things come between you and God?

As believers we are called to walk with God; not to walk just above the standards of the world. It is not easy but possible because Enoch did it in a world just as, or even more depraved than ours. And this is what he is commended for in the Bible, not for being a preacher or a prophet. Enoch had this testimony he 'walked with God'.

Take away everything I have, but do not take away the sweetness of walking and talking with the King of glory.

(John Stam)

28 August

> "Very truly, I tell you, you will see heaven open, and the angels of God ascending and descending on the Son of Man". (John 1:51)

Suggested reading Genesis 28:10-17

Holidaying in East Yorkshire, we decided to spend a day in Lincoln. Prior to 1981, it would have been a longish car ride, but in that year, the Humber Bridge was opened, cutting many miles off the journey.

Once the world's longest single-span suspension bridge, it runs for almost a mile and a half from Hessle to Barton on Humber. There is a toll booth for motorists but free access for cyclists and walkers.

One of our passengers feels a little nervous as we drive on to the bridge but all in all, it is an exhilarating experience, and within minutes, we have crossed the river Humber and are in Lincolnshire.

Two areas of England that were once cut off by geography are now joined together----the bridge having brought industrial, commercial and tourist benefits.

A far greater expanse was covered when Jesus died upon the cross of Calvary. He bridged the chasm between heaven and earth: the gulf between God and man.

All who repent and trust in Christ are reconciled to God and are bound for heaven. A fee has to be paid in order to cross the Humber Bridge, and a fee had to be paid before anyone could be reconciled to God and go to heaven. It was a fee that we could never have paid, but through the amazing grace of God, it has been paid for us by the atoning death of Jesus.

As to the holy patriarch
That wondrous gift was given
So seems my Saviour's cross to me
A ladder up to heaven.

(Elizabeth C. D. Clephane)

29 August

'Demetrius is well spoken of by everyone---and even by the truth itself. We also speak well of him, and you know that our testimony is true'. (3 John 12)

Suggested reading Daniel 6:1-5

As a village pastor, I was frequently asked to provide a character reference. More often than not, knowing the integrity of the person, this was something I was more than happy to do. Only on rare occasions did it prove to be a challenge.

A homeless young man, whom I scarcely knew, after he had been evicted from his council flat, for damaging the property, gave my name as a reference to a housing association.

This was when wisdom was needed. My sympathy for the 'sofa surfing' young man had to be balanced against my responsibility to the housing association. I can only hope that what I wrote was fair to both parties.

Daniel in the Old Testament and Demetrius in the New Testament, though not flawless, had excellent character references. But only Jesus had the perfect reference because His reference was from God. 'A voice from heaven said, "This is my Son, whom I love; with Him I am well pleased". (Matthew 3:17)

To have a good testimony before men is important, but at the end of our days, to be approved by God is even more important. 'Well done, good and faithful servant'. (Matthew 25:21) is the reference we should desire beyond all others.

Reputation is what men think you are; character is what God knows you are.

(Anonymous)

30 August

> 'For just as through the disobedience of the one man, the many were made sinners, so also through the obedience of the one man, the many will be made righteous' (Romans 5:19)

Suggested reading Genesis 3: 14-19

As Aaron, our multi-handicapped son, got older, we had a bedroom/bathroom extension built onto the house. This greatly helped in our care of him, but it did mean that whilst he slept downstairs, we slept upstairs. However, a baby monitor in his bedroom allayed our fears.

Early one morning, we were awakened by his cry. Jumping out of bed, I dashed to the top of the stairs---and I can remember nothing else. Apparently, I fell down the stairs and knocked myself out.

Pat telephoned 999, and my next recollection is looking into the eyes of a paramedic and being asked various questions. Besides feeling a little groggy, I suffered no ill effects and did not require any further treatment.

My 'fall' was relatively minor and had no lasting consequences, but I was still thankful for the speedy intervention of the paramedics. Tragically, Adam's fall in the Garden of Eden---his rebellion and disobedience of God's command- -was serious, and it had eternal consequences for him and the whole of mankind. Sin, separation from God, death and judgement are all the results of Adam's 'fall'. Genesis chapter 3 is the explanation for all the woes of the human race.

That is the bad news, but 'gospel 'means good news and it is centred in Christ. He---the Great Physician—came from heaven to earth and died upon a cross, so that sinners might be forgiven, reconciled to God and have an eternal home in heaven.

Pat sent for the paramedics, but God, in his grace 'sent his Son to be the Saviour of the world'. (1 John 4:14), and 'while we were still sinners, Christ died for us' (Romans 5:8) Are we thankful? Are we repentant? Are we trusting Jesus?

We are a bad lot, we sons of Adam.

(A.W.Tozer)

31 August

> 'But I pray to you, O Lord, in the time of your favour; in your great love, O God, answer me with your sure salvation'. (Psalm 69:13)

Suggested reading Luke 1:5-17

My grandfather was a man of prayer and he never came to our house or we to his, without 'a word of prayer' before departing. Even, as an old man, he would get down on his knees and commend us to the Lord.

Granddad died at the age of eighty-eight, and no doubt, from the day of my birth, he prayed for my conversion. This, however, was something he never lived to see, as I was converted some six months after his passing.

Does this mean that all the prayers he offered for me, over the years, were a waste of breath? Not at all. Our prayers are filed in heaven and at the acceptable time, God takes down the file and He answers our prayer.

The angel said to Zacharias, 'Your prayer has been heard. Your wife Elizabeth will bear you a son'. (Luke 1:13) As 'Elizabeth was not able to conceive; and they were both very old' (Luke 1:7), I suspect this was a prayer which they had offered, many years before. But now, in heaven, God was taking down the file and the prayer was being answered.

Believer, pray on! We never know when that heartfelt request will be answered, but it will always be at a time acceptable to God.

Teach us, O Lord, the discipline of patience, for to wait is often harder than to work.

(Peter Marshall)

BIBLE READINGS SEPTEMBER

1 September

> 'Jesus answered, "I am the way and the truth and the life". (John 14:6)

Suggested reading Revelation 1:1-8

When our children were young and money was tight, we saw an advert in the paper: 'Kids travel free on the train'. Convincing myself that the children were as keen as I am on train travel, we eagerly saved the necessary coupons and looked forward to 'the train taking the strain'.

Unfortunately, the offer was not quite what it seemed, as it transpired that you could not use a Family Railcard or book cheap day returns with this 'special offer'. We kept our promise to the children but ended up saving nothing on the journey.

It is obviously wise to always read the small print, whether taking out insurance, opening a bank account, entering a competition or collecting coupons. 'If something seems too good to be true, in all probability, it is too good to be true'.

With Jesus, there is no small print. He not only speaks the Truth, He is the Truth. Nothing He ever said is 'too good to be true' because he never made a promise that he could not keep.

His enemies may have cynically said, "Teacher, we know that you are a man of integrity---- you teach the way of God in accordance with the truth" (Mark 12:14) but nevertheless, on that occasion, they were speaking the truth.

The Apostle John calls Jesus 'the faithful witness' (Revelation 1:5) and so he is; we can fully rest on everything that he ever said. And, though at times we might fail miserably, we must seek to be as truthful as Jesus was.

Fallen human nature has neither grace nor truth in it, but the human nature of Christ was full of grace and truth.

(W.E. Best)

2 September

'But he was pierced for our transgressions, he was crushed for our iniquities; the punishment that brought us peace was on him, and by his wounds we are healed' (Isaiah 53:5)

Suggested reading Matthew 27:15-26

One Saturday morning I was in Liverpool, as later in the day I was speaking at a Bible Convention in the area. In order to relax, accompanied by Aaron, I went to watch Everton Football Club U18s.

Although it was an Everton fixture, amongst the spectators, I recognised the ex-Liverpool Football Club player, David Fairclough. David was affectionately known as 'Super Sub' for, though a talented goal-scorer, he rarely started matches for Liverpool, but frequently came on as a substitute and made an immediate impact.

David kindly agreed to have a photograph taken with Aaron.

Jesus was crucified between two thieves but the middle tree should have been occupied by Barabbas. He was 'a well-known prisoner'

(Matthew 27:16) but when the cowardly Pilate offered the crowd a choice, they shouted for Jesus to be crucified. Thus, it was that Jesus took the place of Barabbas---he became his substitute.

However, Jesus was far more than just the substitute for Barabbas. Taking our sin, our guilt, our punishment, Jesus became the substitute for all who repent and trust in Him. In the words of the Apostle Peter, 'He himself bore our sins in his body on the cross'. (1 Peter2:24)

Bearing shame and scoffing rude,
In my place condemned He stood;
Sealed my pardon with His blood;
Hallelujah! What a Saviour

(Philip Paul Bliss)

3 September

'Do not repay evil with evil or insult with insult. On the contrary, repay evil with blessing, because to this you were called so that you may inherit a blessing'. (1 Peter 3:9)

Suggested reading Matthew 5:38-48

W. C. Field said 'never work with children or animals'. I do not know about animals, but I have often worked with children and known both good and difficult times.

One wintry evening, for reasons known only to herself, a girl ran to the back of the church, switched off all the lights and we were plunged into darkness. Such an event was only good in the sense that it tested my sanctification.

I have, however, other much happier memories. On asking a group of children 'what is an idol'? A girl replied 'someone who will not work'.

We wondered if our teaching had fallen on 'stony ground' after the testimony of one boy. 'At school, today, a boy hit me but Jesus gave me the courage to hit him back'. It was necessary to suppress a smile, as one sought to respond appropriately to what the youngster had just said.

When we are wronged or feel to have been wronged, the natural response is to 'hit' back. 'An eye for an eye and a tooth for a tooth'. This can sound barbaric to our ears but it was emphasising that justice should be measured and proportionate. The punishment must not go beyond or exceed the crime. An eye for an eye—not two eyes for one eye!

Jesus, however, set a very different standard. He teaches us not to 'take' revenge' or to 'get even', but rather to choose love and forgiveness over retaliation. Throughout his life and ministry, this standard was exemplified in Jesus, It is not the natural response but must be the aim of all who are indwelt by the spirit of Christ.

The only people with whom you should try to get even are those who have helped you.

(John E. Southard)

4 September

'Will you not revive us again, that your people may rejoice in you? (Psalm 85:6)

Suggested reading Acts 2: 1-13

I was born on 17th November 1947, and that date was so significant that is was recorded on a certificate---a certificate which I still have in my possession. An unrepeatable day, the day of my birth.

Since then, I have had many birthdays and some of them have been special; for example, my 21st, my 40th, my 65th and my 70th birthday. They were times when I received cards and gifts----some of them cheeky, others memorable. A walking stick on my 65th birthday was perhaps a portent of things to come, whilst a ride on a steam train between Fort William and Mallaig contributed to a most enjoyable 70th birthday.

Birthdays are often special, memorable days but they can never be compared to the day of our birth.

Pentecost was the day when the New Testament Church was born. An unrepeatable day, when things happened which might never happen again. People from every nation under heaven heard the Apostles speak in a language they could understand. This was the day the Early Church was born; a day which can never be repeated.

But since then, the church has had her birthdays---special times when there has been a fresh outpouring of the Spirit, and the church has been revived and many converted. Not a repetition of Pentecost but a perpetuation of Pentecost. And in the dark days in which we live, how the church in Britain needs another birthday!

Revival is a sovereign act of God upon the church, whereby he intervenes to lift the situation completely out of human hands and works in extraordinary power.

(Geoffrey R. King)

5 September

> 'It was not with perishable things such as silver and gold that you were redeemed------- but with the precious blood of Christ' (1 Peter 1:18-19)

Suggested reading Matthew 6:19-24

I was employed in banking from April 1967 until August 1970---my original employer being Martins Bank, until they were taken over by Barclays Bank in December 1968. The bank's main branch was in Morecambe but there were sub branches at Bare and Heysham. These sub branches had reduced opening hours and the bank cashier was always accompanied by a guard. This was usually a retired man, wanting to earn some extra money in order to supplement his pension. These men differed in temperament but Mr. S---was a delight to work with. He was a raconteur with a great sense of humour, and he kept me well supplied with cups of tea and coffee.

One morning Mr. S---went to the bakery just opposite the bank and returned with some currant teacakes. He joined the queue at the till, and when he got to the counter, taking the teacake out of the bag, he said, 'John, can you please put this in my current account'? Other customers had an air of disbelief---were their eyes and ears deceiving them? His humour might not have had the approval of the bank hierarchy, but it would have gone down well on Candid Camera.

However healthy or otherwise our bank balances, we cannot buy or pay our way into heaven. But for those who trust in Christ, the deposit has already been paid and the investment made. Through His death for sinners on the cross of Calvary, Jesus has opened their account in heaven.

Once opened, the believer can then invest in the 'Bank of Heaven'. This we do by alleviating the material needs of the poor, but principally by supporting the spread of the gospel. Are we storing up for ourselves treasures on earth or treasures in heaven?

It is wiser to have your bank in heaven than to have your heaven in a bank.

(Anon)

6 September

'I am not ashamed of the gospel, because it is the power of God that brings salvation to everyone who believes'. (Romans 1:16)

Suggested reading Luke 24:36-49

Stuart was in my year at school, but we only became good friends, years afterwards when we had both become believers. From the day of his conversion, Stuart had a great desire to share the gospel, and he was given an unexpected opportunity.

His home telephone number was very similar to that of a local travel agent, and it was not unusual for him to be contacted by mistake. Stuart had a standard reply as callers enquired about flights to Disneyland or holidays in the Maldives or the Canary Islands.

'I cannot tell you about getting to the Maldives or the Canary Islands, but I can tell you how to get to heaven. Sometimes, perhaps embarrassed at having telephoned the wrong number, callers would stay on the line while Stuart spoke about his Saviour.

Stuart died suddenly, when still a relatively young man but is now in heaven---the place he was able to direct others to.

We might not be as natural a witness as Stuart was, but we are to be alive to every opportunity to witness. How often we are silent when the unexpected opening or the unanticipated question gives us the opportunity to speak of Jesus. We must be sensitive in our witnessing but are there times when politeness is just an excuse for cowardice?

We are not responsible for conversion but we are responsible for contact.

(A.T. Pierson)

7 September

'I warn everyone who hears the words of the prophecy of this scroll: if anyone adds anything to them, God will add to that person the plagues described in this scroll. And if anyone takes words away from this scroll of prophecy, God will take away from that person, any share in the tree of life and in the Holy City, which are described in this scroll'. (Revelation 22:18-19)

Suggested reading: Mark 6:35-44

Pat decided I needed a new pair of shoes and in order to maintain marital harmony, I agreed and off we went to the superstore. I soon chose a pair and having put them in the basket with a few other items, we went to pay at the checkout.

As we came away, I commented to Pat that the amount paid seemed rather large, in view of the few items we had purchased. On checking the receipt, we discovered my shoes had gone through twice---our basket had been added to.

I was not happy but returning to the checkout, the mistake was acknowledged, an apology accepted and the payment readjusted. I was thankful I had accompanied Pat to the checkout; otherwise, I would never have known another pair of shoes had been added to the basket.

When Jesus fed the five thousand, it was his disciples who distributed the bread and the fish to the crowd. But, they gave to the people only what they, themselves, had received from Jesus. They did not add to or take away from the basket.

There is a lesson here for every church and pastor. We must only pass on to others what we, ourselves, have received from Jesus---his Word, his Gospel, his Truth. God, at the beginning (Deuteronomy 4:2) and at the end of the Bible (Revelation 22:18-19), gives a stern warning to any who add to or take away from his Word. We must not meddle with the 'basket'.

We have no more right to tamper with Scripture than a postman has to edit our mail.

(John Blanchard)

8 September

'Set a guard over my mouth, Lord; keep watch over the door of my lips'. (Psalm 141:3)

Suggested reading Proverbs 12:14-28

I was taking part at a wedding in Hertfordshire, and having spent the night in Stafford, we continued our journey on the Saturday morning. As we approached our destination, I bought some chewing gum in order to freshen my mouth. Unfortunately, it proved to be an unwise move, as within minutes, I had bitten my tongue.

At first, I was not too concerned, as it is something I have done on numerous occasions. However, this time the cut must have gone deeper and would not stop bleeding. To say it spoilt the day would be an understatement. Speaking at the service, smiling for photographs, talking to guests and eating at the reception---all these tasks were challenging as the tongue continued to bleed.

As we set back to Stafford, the tongue had been bleeding for over six hours, and it seemed the only answer was a visit to A&E. This was not something we wanted at the end of a busy day, and so as a last resort, I put a handkerchief in my mouth and crunched it between my teeth. The two and half hour journey was spent in silence, but thankfully, the bleeding had stopped when we arrived in Stafford. A joyful wedding, but not for me the happiest of days, all because I bit my tongue.

I had an unhappy day because I bit my tongue, but ironically, many people have even unhappier days because they do not bite their tongues. Once spoken, a word can never be returned and the damage can be irreparable. My 'distress' was only for a matter of hours, but failure to bite the tongue can cause an indefinite pain. It has been rightly said 'no physician can heal wounds inflicted by the tongue'. How I, and I suspect we all need to pray 'Set a guard over my mouth; keep watch over the door of my lips'.

The Christian should learn two things about his tongue: how to hold it and how to use it.

(Anon)

9 September

' Jesus replied, "Go back and report to John what you hear and see. The blind receive sight---the deaf hear". (Matthew 11:4-5)

Suggested reading Matthew 13:10-17

I made an appointment with the optician as I was finding reading more difficult. Before my eyes were tested, I was invited to have a free hearing test. This I agreed to, although I was quite sure the problem was with my eyes and not my ears.

I sat at a desk and had to press various buttons, as different sounds were received through my earpiece. It was quite an interesting experience, but also sobering when I was informed that I had failed the test.

The eye test revealed certain deficiencies, and I was happy to be prescribed reading glasses. However, was it pride or stubbornness but I did not agree to a hearing aid? After all, I am not deaf. I can hear as well as anyone---can't I?

Physical blindness and deafness are terrible afflictions, and our hearts should go out to all who suffer in that way. And yet, there is a blindness and deafness that is even worse, which is spiritual blindness/spiritual deafness.

It is worse because, unlike physical blindness and deafness, it is self-inflicted. Humans who do not want to see or hear the truth end up not being able to see or hear the truth.

Do not close your eyes or ears to the word of God, lest there comes a day when those eyes and ears will not open. Rather come to Jesus---the Great Physician---who still gives spiritual sight and hearing.

Lord, I was blind; I could not see. In your marred visage any grace:
But now the beauty of your face. In radiant vision dawns on me.

Lord, I was deaf; I could not hear. The thrilling music of your voice:
But now I hear you and rejoice. And all your spoken words are clear.

(William T. Matson)

10 September

'I am the living bread that came down from heaven. Whoever eats this bread will live forever'.

(John 6:51)

Suggested reading: Luke 9:10-17

Feeding families has changed dramatically since I was a boy. Today, in many families, at mealtimes children seem to expect a choice. Unhelpfully, I often comment that in the 1950s we had a choice: either we ate what was put in front of us or else we went hungry.

With health and safety regulations and dietary requirements, there have also been changes in church catering. Vegetarian, vegan, and gluten-free options are now part of menus.

When Pat bakes a cake for church functions, it is necessary to set out the ingredients. On one occasion, on asking me to type them out, I mischievously included arsenic among the ingredients! However, it is no bad thing that great care is taken in the preparation and serving of food, as many people do have allergies and sensitivities.

When Jesus fed the 5000, there was no menu, no vegetarian or vegan options---it was just bread and fish. But no one refused the one food that was offered. 'They all ate and were satisfied'. (Luke 9:17)

Jesus is 'the living bread that came down from heaven' and he alone is able to satisfy the spiritual hunger that is in the human heart. 'Whoever---man or woman, rich or poor, educated or uneducated---eats this bread will live forever'. Have you tasted and eaten? Have you trusted Jesus as saviour?

None but God can satisfy the longings of the immortal soul: as the heart was made for him, he only can fill it.

(Richard C. Trench)

11 September

'Blessed are those who hear the word of God and obey it'.
(Luke 11:28)

Suggested reading Matthew 7:21-29

It was a dark, wet November evening, but that was no excuse for failing to stop at an unmarked road junction. The resulting collision with a taxi brought considerable damage to the vehicles, but the drivers, whilst shaken, were not injured. The police were soon on the scene, and having been breathalysed, I was offered the choice of a court appearance or a Driver Alertness Course. I plumped for the second option---I suppose you could call it a 'crash course'!

Some weeks later, as I made my way up to Penrith, I felt annoyed at myself and also the authorities. Having driven for over thirty years, what could a Driver Alertness Course possibly teach me? I joined a class of a dozen other similarly disgruntled drivers.

The instructor quoted constantly from a book I had heard of but not read for over thirty years---the Highway Code! Speed limits, stopping distances, traffic signs, and road markings---almost everything the driver needed to know was to be found within the pages of this book. Reluctantly, I had to admit that many of the bad habits I had developed over the years stemmed from my disregard for the Highway Code. I trust I returned down the M6 a wiser and safer driver than the one who had travelled up a few hours earlier.

The Bible—the Word of God---is increasingly being rejected, and the result is a moral landslide, a moral 'crash' impacting on families and communities. Sadly, believers are also adversely affected when they fail to submit to the Scriptures. Our constant need is to get back to the Bible, and to ensure that our conversation and conduct is consistent with what is written there.

I passed my driving test and forgot all about the Highway Code, but ultimately my neglect contributed to my downfall. As a believer, I must not make that mistake with the Bible. Neglect will lead to backsliding, whilst careful study will lead to spiritual growth and blessing.

Sin will keep you from this book, or this book will keep you from sin.

(John Bunyan)

12 September

'Do not cast me from your presence or take your Holy Spirit from me'. (Psalm 51:11)

Suggested reading 1 John 2:18-27

In one of my cars, the petrol gauge stopped working and twice I found myself out of petrol, before the gauge was repaired. Later, my problem was not a faulty gauge but rather the paucity of petrol stations in rural areas. There was a time when petrol could be purchased in most villages but in recent years, such garages have largely disappeared.

This meant, looking nervously at the petrol gauge. I had several anxious journeys, and yet, I was often surprised how far my car could run on empty. Thankfully, today's cars are much more precise in providing such information and there is really no excuse for running out of petrol.

I was surprised 'how far my car could run on empty' and the same can be sadly true of pastors, teachers, Christian workers. We are not close to the Lord, we are not filled with his Spirit, and yet, sometimes, we can continue ministering for months without people knowing that we are 'running on empty'.

We can be busy and active but the work is being done through human strength and not through the power of the Spirit. How vital it is to spend time with the Lord and each day, to seek a fresh infilling of His Spirit.

There is one thing we cannot imitate; we cannot imitate being full of the Holy Ghost.

(Oswald Chambers)

13 September

'I plead with Euodia and I preach with Syntyche to be of the same mind in the Lord. (Philippians 4:2)

Matthew 5: 21-26

I had travelled seventy miles to take the services at an evangelical church. I was aware there had been difficulties and throughout the day, I was conscious of tensions in the church. However, I was not prepared for what happened after the evening service.

We had remembered the Lord's death at His table, but within minutes of announcing the benediction, voices were being raised and I could hear the church officers arguing in the vestry. A sad end to a difficult day.

I drove back to Ingleton downcast in spirit but more important---how must the Lord Jesus, the Head of the Church have felt?

Jesus said that we needed to be at peace with one another before we came to his table. The Apostle Paul said, 'whoever eats the bread or drinks the cup of the Lord in an unworthy manner will be guilty of sinning against the body and blood of the Lord'. (1 Corinthians 11:27) These are warnings that believers need to take to heart and if obeyed, they will keep us from gross hypocrisy.

We can only echo the words of the Apostle James: 'Out of the same mouth come praise and cursing. My brothers and sisters, this should not be'. (James 3:10) May the Lord save us from such hypocrisy.

Solemn prayers, rapturous devotions are but repeated hypocrisies unless the heart and mind be conformable to them.

(William Law)

14 September

'Let us throw off everything that hinders and the sin that so easily entangles. And let us run with perseverance the race marked out for us'. (Hebrews 12:1)

Suggested reading Psalm 55:16-23

Today, I suspect most people have weighing scales in their bathrooms, which certainly was not the case in the 1950s or 1960s. I get on the scales most mornings, as excess weight is now known to be a contributory factor in many illnesses.

As youngsters, two or three times a year, my brother and I would put coins in the slot and stand on those weighing machines, which were once a feature of many shops. Being twins, there was never much difference in weight between us, so one day, it was a surprise to notice that Jim was several pounds heavier than me.

The mystery was soon solved when we discovered Jim had got on the scales with a shopping bag in his hand. This was the reason for his 'extra' weight.

Excess weight is not good for us either physically or spiritually. When we are first converted, we all come with 'baggage'----hurts, problems, attitudes from the past. But, as we are sanctified by the truth, as we grow in grace, so it is that many of these things are dealt with and we are not as 'weighed ' down by them as once we were.

This means that being rid of unnecessary 'baggage', we are better able to 'run with perseverance the race that is marked out for us'.

I am not what I might be, I am not what I ought to be, I am not what I wish to be. I am not what I hope to be; but I thank God I am not what I once was, and I can say with the great apostle, 'By the grace of God I am what I am.

(John Newton)

15 September

> 'To fear the Lord is to hate evil; I hate pride and arrogance, evil behaviour and perverse speech'. (Proverbs 8:13)

Suggested reading Ecclesiastes 12:9-14

I was enjoying an evangelistic church meal and was wondering whether to have a second helping of 'bread and butter' pudding. The temptation proved too strong and 'asking for more', I commented 'the diet will start tomorrow'.

This initiated a conversation with a lady, who never puts weight on, irrespective of what or how much she eats. She is, in fact, of interest to the medical profession, as they seek to investigate this unusual phenomenon.

'It must be great', I said, 'to eat anything and know you will not put weight on'.

'Not exactly', the lady responded, 'when there is no fear of putting weight on, you can become careless and eat foods which are not good for you'.

A downside, I had not considered.

As I later pondered on this conversation, I was struck by a spiritual application. When there is no fear of God, people become careless and commit sins that are harmful to them and grievous to God. Is this not sadly evident today? There is no fear of God in the nation and so churches are deserted, moral standards fall and crime increases.

'To fear the Lord is to hate evil' but when, there is no fear of the Lord, then 'pride and arrogance, evil behaviour and perverse speech' (Proverbs 8:13) flourish.

Solomon also said 'The fear of the Lord is the beginning of wisdom' (Proverbs 9:10) and 'Fear God and keep his commandments, for this is the duty of all mankind.' (Ecclesiastes 12:13) We must pray for our nation to come to its senses and to again have respect and reverence for God.

As the embankment keeps out the water, so the fear of the Lord keeps out uncleanness.

(Thomas Watson)

16 September

> 'Don't you know that you yourself are God's temple and that God's Spirit dwells in your midst' (1 Corinthians 3:16)

Suggested reading: Ephesians 5:25-33

The ringing of church bells is an invitation to public worship. Sadly, at one church known to me, those who ring the bells never stay for the service of worship. They invite others to do what apparently, they have no desire to do.

On holiday in Lincolnshire, I got into a conversation with a man who was very active in his local church. However, he confessed he had no real interest in the spiritual side but he wanted the church to remain open as a community asset. Ringing the church bells, wanting a church to remain open----these things might be commendable but it is to mistake the true meaning of the church.

Biblically, the church is not a building but a people,----a people who personally believe in Jesus Christ. 'Aquila and Priscilla greet you warmly and so does the church that meets at their house'. (1 Corinthians 16:19) The believers---the church---met in a house and that was the practice in the New Testament. As numbers increased, houses became too small and buildings became necessary.

We thank God for our church buildings. It is here we worship God and hear the scriptures preached but let us not forget that the true church is people, not the building.

I believe a local church exists to do corporately what each Christian believer should be doing individually---and that is to worship God. It is to show forth the excellencies of him who has called us out of darkness into his marvellous light.

(A.W. Tozer)

17 September

>'By faith we understand that the universe was formed at God's command, so that what is seen was not made out of what was visible'. (Hebrews 11:3)

Suggested reading Job 38:1-11

Our home is just four miles from the picturesque town of Ilkley, with its stunning scenery and moorland views. It is well known because of the familiar folk song 'On Ilkley Moor Baht'at ' and also because of its association with Charles Darwin.

After completing 'The Origin of Species' in 1859, Darwin stayed at a hydropathic spa hotel in the town for several weeks. Darwin Gardens and the Darwin Walk provide a memorial to his life and work.

Not everyone, however, is quite so keen to remember the English naturalist and his contribution to evolutionary biology. A blind believer has a guide dog, Arwin, but apparently when the dog came to him, it was called Darwin not Arwin. He was renamed because his owner did not want a daily reminder of the man whose writings have influenced and misguided multitudes.

The theory of evolution has resulted in many rejecting God as Creator and therefore, of necessity, the early chapters of the Book of Genesis. If humans have and are evolving, then they are not fallen creatures, they do not need a saviour, and they are not answerable to any superior being. Inevitably, this impacts upon human behaviour, with abortion and euthanasia acceptable, if we are just a 'higher form of animal' and not made in the image of God.

Some have tried to reconcile creationism and evolution but they are attempting the impossible.

The serious scientist's comment on Genesis 1 is 'I have nothing to say, I was not there'.

(Graham Miller)

18 September

'It is time to seek the Lord' (Hosea 10:12)

Suggested reading Luke 17:22-37

In the 1960s, banks opened Monday to Friday from 10 am to 3 pm and on Saturdays from 9 am to 12 pm. Queues often formed, and so it was important that the doors were opened promptly on time. And this was one of the responsibilities of the office 'junior'.

Barry was a lovable but somewhat eccentric office 'junior', and one morning the doors had not been opened.

'Barry, it is ten o'clock', said the chief cashier.

'Thank you, Mr Hughes', said Barry and continued what he was doing.

I had to gently explain to Barry that Mr Hughes was not so much telling him the time but asking for the bank doors to be opened.

What time is it? The Bible tells us and yet many take no notice and just continue what they are doing. Nothing has really changed, for that was the response of the people in the days of Noah. For 120 years he preached righteousness, he spoke out against sin, he warned of judgement to come, he built an ark, but tragically when the flood came, most of the people perished.

Jesus said, 'Just as it was in the days of Noah, so also will it be in the days of the Son of Man'. (Luke 17:26) What time is it? If we have never done so; 'it is time to seek the Lord'.

It is difficult for me to understand how an intelligent person can spend all of time building for this world and have no time for the future world.

(Billy Graham)

19 September

'God saw all that he had made and it was very good'. (Gen 1:31)

Suggested reading 2 Peter 3:10-18

On several occasions, I have been on panels at churches for Question Times, but in the late 1980s, I was invited to be on a panel that was way out of my comfort zone. The A65 Settle bypass was about to be built, and a group of 'eco warriors' were concerned as to what it would do to the environment.

I have no idea why I was asked but mindful of 1 Peter 3:15, I took my place with three others---including a town councillor---on the panel at Settle Town Hall. Most of the questions centred on the cost and the environmental impact of the development---not, I confess, my specialist subjects.

They agreed when I commented that we are stewards of God's creation and therefore, responsible for what we pass on to future generations. They were, however, rather more silent when I emphasised that worship of the Creator is vastly more important than worship of creation.

Much to the frustration and anguish of the 'eco warriors' the road was built, but remembering how Settle town centre used to be a bottleneck, I have always been thankful for the bypass.

As believers we have to care for God's creation and act responsibly to preserve natural resources. This is a Biblical mandate and we must not ignore it. However, with many, environmentalism is now a 'religion' and 'saving the planet' not 'saving the soul' is their chief preoccupation.

And whilst we should be concerned with 'global warming' the Bible affirms that creation, as we know it, is heading for 'global burning'. (2

Peter 3:10) Therefore 'we are looking forward to a new heaven and a new earth, where righteousness dwells'. (2 Peter 3:13)

Build your nest in no tree here----for the Lord of the forest has condemned the whole woods to be demolished.

(Samuel Rutherford)

20 September

'Give my greetings to the brothers and sisters at Laodicea, and to Nympha and the church in her house'. (Colossians 4:15)

Suggested reading 2 Corinthians 4:1-6

I can count over thirty churches, where I have preached, which are no longer places of worship. Many are houses but I can think of two which were demolished and are now car parks. It is always sad to witness a redundant church building. There are, however, buildings which have moved in the opposite direction and this was true of the church I pastored in Ingleton.

Once the village Co-op, the premises were a car showroom before being purchased by believers for £8,200 in 1974. Not a huge sum today but a large amount for a small group with limited resources.

On gaining possession, the necessary alterations were carried out and the premises were ready for the Harvest Thanksgiving services on Sunday 8 September 1974. A secular building turned into a place of worship---not the other way round.

The building was converted and the believers were grateful to the Lord for such a provision, and yet this was just ' a means to an end'. The great desire was for men and women to be converted through the preaching of the gospel.

This, we were privileged to see, with the change in some being far more radical than a showroom being turned into a church building. Indeed, Paul compares the change to be as great as what occurred at the time of creation. 'For God, who said, "Let the light shine out of darkness" made his light shine in our hearts to give us the light of the knowledge of God's glory in the face of Christ'. (2 Corinthians 4:6)

May we see not just buildings being converted into churches but sinners being converted into saints.

Conversion is no repairing of the old building; but it takes all down and erects a new structure.

(Joseph Alleine)

21 September

> 'As for you, you were dead in your transgressions and sins----but because of his great love for us, God, who is rich in mercy, made us alive with Christ---' (Ephesians 2:1, 4-5)

Suggested reading Ephesians 5:1-11

Shortly after my conversion, I had tickets to see the 6' 8" American singer, Solomon King. I was very much into '60s pop music and I had bought his hit record 'She Wears My Ring'. This had reached No.3 in the UK charts and had been a hit in over forty countries.

I went, as arranged, with a friend to the venue where the singer was performing, but before Solomon King came on stage, a so-called comedian was the warm-up act. Immediately, he subjected us to a barrage of obscene jokes which, whilst others found funny, I did not. After a few minutes, I said to my friend, 'I am not listening to this', and so we walked out and I never did hear Solomon King.

I was disappointed to miss the pop singer but afterwards, I was encouraged by the realisation that this was evidence I was a 'new creature in Christ'. Weeks before I might have disapprovingly listened to the comedian but not now---I was walking in newness of life.

The Apostle Paul said, 'But among you there must not be......any kind of impurity....this is improper for God's holy people. Nor should there be obscenity, foolish talk or coarse joking which are out of place'. (Ephesians 5:3-4). At conversion, we are given a new nature, and these things, mentioned by Paul, should increasingly be abhorrent to us.

I do not understand how a man can be a true believer, in whom sin is not the greatest burden, sorrow and trouble.

(John Owen)

22 September

'Then Samuel said, "Speak for your servant is listening". (1 Sam. 3:10)

Suggested reading Luke 8:16-21

I was watching an interview on television, but it was difficult to hear because of a telephone ringing in the background. No-one took any notice and so, in frustration, I turned over to another channel.

To my amazement, despite change of channel, the telephone was still ringing. It was only then I discovered that the sound was not coming from the television but from Pat's mobile phone.

As I went to answer it, the phone stopped ringing and perhaps we had missed an important call. I had been distracted by the television and wrongly presumed the call was for someone else.

There are times when, for the same reasons, we fail to hear the voice of the Lord. Either we are distracted by other things, or we foolishly think the challenge is for others and not for us.

Jesus counselled that care is needed both in what we hear (Mark 4:24) and how we hear (Luke 8:18a) May we be able to say with Samuel, 'Speak for your servant is listening'.

Speak to me by name, O Master! Let me know it is to me;
Speak that I may follow faster, with a step, more firm and free
Where the shepherd leads the flock,
In the shadow of the rock.

Master, speak and make me ready, When Thy voice is truly heard,
With obedience glad and steady, Still to follow every word,
I am listening, Lord for Thee;
Master, speak, O speak to me.

(Frances Ridley Havergal)

23 September

'Do not give the devil a foothold'. (Ephesians 4:27)

Suggested reading 2 Corinthians 11:5-15

Having taken an afternoon service at a church in North Yorkshire, I got into conversation with a middle-aged lady. She was a believer but her husband was not, and his disinterest sometimes caused difficulties in their home.

The lady proceeded to tell me that, once a week, she was calling at the home of a widower in the town. He was a believer and they were praying and reading the Bible together.

What she wanted to know was, 'Am I doing wrong'?

I think she already knew the answer, otherwise she would not have asked the question. If it wasn't wrong, it certainly wasn't wise and if it wasn't sin, then it wasn't sensible.

She graciously accepted what was said and I trust that she acted upon it.

Satan is always seeking to gain an advantage over the believer and we must not 'aid and abet' him. Going to certain places, engaging in certain activities, mixing with certain people might just give Satan the opportunity he is looking for. Paul wisely exhorts, 'Do not give the devil a foothold'.

Sometimes Satan is a 'roaring lion' (1 Peter 5:8) but is he not more dangerous when he masquerades as an 'angel of light'? (2Corinthians 11:14) He entices us with something that seems to be good----visiting a lonely widower-----but he intends to do us ill. If Satan is not to 'outwit us', we must not be 'unaware of his schemes'. (2 Corinthians 2:11)

We are in a spiritual battle but we can be victorious. 'Submit yourselves, then, to God. Resist the devil and he will flee from you. Come near to God and he will come near to you'. (James 4:7-8)

Satan is very clever; he knows exactly what bait to use for every place in which he fishes.

(A.W. Pink)

24 September

'Although I want to do good, evil is right there with me'. (Romans 7:21)

Suggested reading Genesis 4:1-7)

My father was a heavy smoker, as were many men of his generation. Indeed, not knowing the risk to health, there was a time when smoking was actively encouraged.

Dad often had sweets in his pocket and these were never more appreciated than during a Sunday service. As the sermon began, dad would tap his pocket and my little hand would pull out midget gems or other such sweets. Invariably, amongst the sweets, there would be traces of tobacco----thankfully, this early introduction to tobacco never made me want to be a smoker.

Nevertheless, there was evidence of his smoking, even in the sweets offered to me.

Sadly, because we are sinners, something similar is true of everything we offer to God. Whether it be our money or our good works, all that we offer is tainted and spoiled by sin. That is why we need to rest and trust in the finished work of Christ--- the only sacrifice that was perfect, without sin and acceptable to God.

Cain brought the work of his hands and that was rejected by God, whilst Abel's offering was acceptable because he was trusting in the shed blood of a sacrifice. Only works covered by the blood of Jesus are ever worthy of being offered to God.

Our best works before we are justified are little better than splendid sins.

(J. C. Ryle)

25 September

> 'Let us purify ourselves from everything that contaminates body and spirit, perfecting holiness out of reverence for God' (2 Corinthians 7:1)

Suggested reading: 1 John 1

I have always appreciated trees and this was a factor in purchasing our retirement bungalow. An old railway embankment, resplendent with trees, borders our back garden.

The downside is the coming of autumn (the fall) brings an avalanche of leaves which soon fills the gutters of the bungalow. If not cleared away, the leaves can trap water, giving the potential for roof or structural damage.

Ben's Gutters have just put a leaflet through the door. 'We are cleaning gutters in your area. Maybe you would like yours cleaned too?' I think I will have to make a phone call.

As believers, we still sin because the marks of 'the fall' are present within. Pride, jealousy, gossip, bitterness and many other sins can all stop the flow of the Spirit. We need daily cleansing and it is available as we confess our sins and plead the precious blood of Jesus.

If sin comes into the life of the believer, he should immediately become concerned about it. It should cause him to rush to the Lord in confession and repentance.

(Donald Grey Barnhouse)

26 September

'Fear of man will prove to be a snare, but whoever trusts in the Lord is kept safe'. (Proverbs 29:25)

Suggested reading Matthew 10:16-31

When I was a paper boy, I was twice bitten by dogs---the first time by a corgi and the second time by a Jack Russell. This had a negative effect on me, and until my daughter got a Boston terrier, a few years ago, I was always wary, even scared of dogs.

And yet, there were times, when my children were young, I did not show fear. Indeed, I would say to them, 'It won't hurt you'. It won't bite you. There is nothing to be afraid of'. What had happened? Why was I suddenly so 'brave', when confronted by a dog?

The answer is clear. My fear of dogs had been superseded by a greater fear; the fear of transferring my feelings to my children, or perhaps the fear of appearing to be a wimp in front of my children! One fear had been replaced by another.

As believers we can sometimes almost be paralysed by fear when faced by men and women. What will they say? How will they react if they know I am a Christian? Will it mean I am side-lined or ostracised? Perhaps better to lay low, say nothing and retain my friendship with them.

There is only one antidote to the 'fear of man' and that is to have a true and a healthy fear of God.

Fear Him, ye saints, and you will then
Have nothing else to fear;
Make you His service your delight,
Your wants shall be His care.

(Nahum Tate/Nicholas Brady)

27 September

'If the trumpet does not sound a clear call, who will get ready for battle'?

(1 Corinthians 14:8)

Suggested reading Revelation 3:1-6

On holiday, walking past a church in Derbyshire, I noticed a pet service being advertised, but this was a pet service with a difference. If you did not have an actual pet, you were invited to bring a teddy bear or some other cuddly toy and they, too, would receive a blessing.

Passing another church, on the notice board, there was a poster proclaiming Good News. It wasn't, however, what I might have expected---a verse from the gospels? No, the poster said 'Good News---New Loos'.

Some churches have a wayside pulpit where they helpfully display a scriptural verse or a pithy, thought provoking saying. However, I was saddened when one wayside pulpit began with the letters OMG. I contacted the minister and to his credit, the saying was removed.

It is easy to be critical and I do not doubt these churches were acting with good motives, but what message are we giving to the passing multitudes? We have an Almighty God, a Wonderful Saviour, a glorious gospel---is this not compromised when we talk of teddy bears and new loos, and fail to reverence the Lord's name?

I looked for the church and I found it in the world; I looked for the world and I found it in the church.

(Horatious Bonar)

28 September

> Jesus said, 'I have not come to call the righteous but sinners to repentance' (Luke 5:32)

Suggested reading James 1:19-27

On moving into our first home, we were blessed with good neighbours, one of whom was a single lady called Vi. Being on her own and with no living relatives, it was not surprising that she doted on Skippy, her Pekingese dog.

One morning, Pat was in the front garden, talking to Vi, who had Skippy in her arms, when they were joined in conversation by a lady passing by. Suddenly the lady gasped 'Ouch! He bit me' to which Vi replied, 'No, Skippy never bites anyone'.

Pat saw it, the woman felt it but Vi denied it, because she could see no wrong in her pet dog.

There is, however, a far worse form of self-deception, described by the Apostle John, 'If we claim to be without sin, we deceive ourselves and the truth is not in us'. (1 John 1:8) It is so easy to see sin in others, but if we fail to see any sin in ourselves, that is the worst form of self-deception. It not only makes us proud and judgmental of others but it excludes us from God's salvation.

There is nothing Jesus can do for the self-righteous, for the person who thinks they are 'without sin'. Jesus came to call 'sinners to repentance' but tragically, through self-deception, many are deaf to His call.

Self-deceivers will prove in the end self-destroyers.

(Matthew Henry)

29 September

'Dear children, let us not love with words or speech but with actions and in truth'. (1 John 3:18)

Suggested reading Acts 20:32-38

During my thirty years as a pastor, I was often humbled by the kindness and generosity of the Lord's people.

The first summer I was in Ingleton, a holiday visitor from Kent asked me to choose up to twenty books from a Christian publisher, and paid for all the purchases. Some of those books are still on my shelves today.

A couple gave me a small caravan, which was pitched in the corner of the church car park. For many years, this was my study, and it was an oasis where I could be quiet and prepare the Word of God.

In the 1980s, cars were not always easy to start and this was a challenge until a church member offered me, free of charge, the use of a garage. This provision saved me time and a great deal of frustration on many a wintry morning.

A believer in the Midlands arranged for a CD player to be delivered so that I could listen to Christian music and to sermons, which he had found helpful and challenging.

These are just a few examples of many kind and generous acts. We appreciated every gift but also the spirit in which they were given. They were not paraded 'with trumpets' (Matthew 6:2): rather it was a case of 'do not let your left hand know what your right hand is doing'. (Matthew 6:3).

It is gratifying to know that such kindness is recognised by the Lord Himself for Jesus promised 'anyone who gives you a cup of water in my name because you belong to the Messiah will certainly not lose their reward'. (Mark 9:41)

As believers, may we be characterised by kindness and generosity. In so doing, others will be encouraged, and we, ourselves will be blessed for Jesus said 'It is more blessed to give than to receive'. (Acts 20:35)

God's great desire is to give. When man follows God's example, he receives a divine blessing because he demonstrates that he is one of God's children.

(Simon Kistemaker)

30 September

'Therefore God exalted him to the highest place and gave him the name that is above every name'. (Philippians 2:9)

Suggested reading Matthew 1:18-25

When I started my education in the 1950s, the school was full of Johns, Michaels, Peters, and Davids----not the 'weird and wonderful' names which sometimes seem to be inflicted on children today.

There was, however, one boy with a somewhat distinctive name because he was called Chester. Apparently, he had been given this name because his parents had met in Chester. He must have been thankful that his parents had not met in Giggleswick or Ashby-de-la-Zouch.

Our adopted son, Aaron, came to us already named, but when my wife asked his natural mother why she had chosen that name, Pat was in for a surprise. In the hospital, the mother had been given a book of baby names and 'Aaron' was the first name in the book.

Today, much or little thought might be given to naming children, but that was not the case in Bible times. Names were given because they had meaning, and the names 'Immanuel' (Matthew 1:23) and 'Jesus' (Matthew 1:21) describe both who was born at Bethlehem and what he came to do. Jesus is 'God with us' and his great mission was 'to save his people from their sins'.

Jesus was well named for he is a unique Person who came for a unique purpose. The Incarnate Son of God who was born and died in order to accomplish our salvation. Truly, his Name 'is above every name'. (Philippians 2:9)

Except the names given to God and our Saviour, there is no sweeter word than salvation.

(William S. Plumer)

BIBLE READINGS OCTOBER

1 October

'Not everyone who says to me, "Lord, Lord", will enter the kingdom of heaven, but only the one who does the will of my Father who is in heaven'. (Matthew 7:21)

Suggested reading Matthew 10:5-16

A Friday evening in July and the doorbell rings. On the step is a distressed man, and we immediately invite him in. He has a tragic, if rather an improbable, tale to tell. Having come over from France, he is due to attend a course at Lancaster University on Monday.

Four weeks ago, his wife died suddenly, and though he did not feel like attending the course, his friends have encouraged him to do so However, in his sorrowful state, he has not sorted out his finances, and though money is waiting at the bank on Monday, he has no money for the weekend.

As he tells his tale of woe, he weeps real tears and then asks if we can pray about his situation. This we do and the man, with real passion, pours his heart out to the Lord. He also explains how important it is for him to have fellowship with believers, and asks what time the services are on Sunday.

Eventually the inevitable question comes--- can I lend him some money which he will definitely repay? To say I 'smell a rat' would be an understatement, but knowing what the Bible says about 'entertaining angels without knowing it', I always give such people the benefit of the doubt.

Consequently, I telephone the local youth hostel, and after getting confirmation they have vacancies, I give the man money for an overnight stay. I arrange to meet him next morning outside the youth hostel, and off he goes thanking the Lord for this 'wonderful provision'.

Believers are sometimes seen as being 'naïve ' or 'an easy touch' and we do need to 'be as shrewd as snakes and as innocent as doves'. (Matthew 10:16) However, in a fallen world, inevitably there will be times when we are taken advantage of, and yet I would rather err on the side of compassion than be hard and mean-spirited.

A lie is a snowball. The longer it is rolled on the ground, the larger it becomes.

(Martin Luther)

2 October (continuation of 1 October)

> 'These people honour me with their lips, but their hearts are far from me'. (Matthew 15:8)

Suggested reading Matthew 23:1-15

I telephone the youth hostel on the Saturday morning and---surprise, surprise-- there has been no sight of the man. Despite this, I still keep the arrangement and he turns up at the allotted time of 8.30 am. 'Have you had a good night in the hostel'? I ask mischievously. Not at all taken aback, he tells me another amazing story.

As he had been making his way to the hostel, he had got into conversation with a couple who were also Christians. When they heard he was spending the night at the youth hostel, they had insisted he stayed the night with them. 'What were they called and where did they live'? I enquire. He is quite unable to answer either question but is rejoicing that the Lord has met his need.

By now, the 'rat' is certainly smelling and I tell my 'friend' I am not in a position to help him any further. The man raises no objection, thanks me for my kindness and assures me he will be at the service in the morning. We shake hands and go our separate ways.

That evening, I feel most guilty when I get a phone call from the vicar of Ingleton. 'John', he says, 'I just want to warn you because I think we might have a con man in the village'. On leaving me, it appears the man had then told his tale at the vicarage and left £25 the richer. Several months later, the vicar was contacted by the police as the 'crying conman' had committed offences throughout the country.

The conman may have deceived many but he is not able to deceive the One who will be his Judge. Indeed, the Bible has a stern warning for the conman. 'Do not be deceived: God cannot be mocked. A man reaps what he sows. Whoever sows to please their flesh, from the flesh will reap destruction'. (Galatians 6:7-8)

'Repent of this wickedness and pray to the Lord in the hope that he may forgive you for having such a thought in your heart. For I see that you are full of bitterness, and captive to sin'. (Acts 8:22-23)

(Apostle Peter to Simon the Sorcerer)

3 October

'But the fruit of the Spirit is love, joy, peace, forbearance, kindness, goodness, faithfulness, gentleness, and self-control'. (Galatians 5:22-23)

Suggested reading 2 Peter 1:3-11

When I worked in the Jobcentre, it was not unusual for jobseekers and claimants to come into the office and air their grievances. One afternoon, the silence was broken by a man ranting and raving about the benefits his son had or had not received.

I thought the voice sounded familiar and sadly the man was a member of a church where I sometimes preached. To save his, or was it my embarrassment, I kept low until the matter had been resolved and the man had exited the premises.

By contrast, Jack was a humble, gracious Christian gentleman, always with an encouraging word for the preacher. My estimation of him only increased when his wife said 'The Jack you see on a Sunday is the same Jack I see every day of the week'.

It is not just the unconverted but also the believer who can be guilty of hypocrisy. Am I one thing in church on a Sunday but a different person at home or at work, the rest of the week? If so, I am a poor witness and great harm is done to the cause of Christ.

In Ephesians 5:18, Paul urges believers to 'be filled with the Spirit' and then, in the rest of the chapter, emphasises this will be seen in the home and in the workplace. Wives, husbands, children, fathers, servants and masters will all be better people because they are walking with Christ and are filled with his Spirit.

The natural man cannot be expected to love the gospel but let us not disgust him by inconsistency,

(J. C. Ryle)

4 October

'The Lord is good to all; he has compassion on all he has made'. (Psalm 145:9)

Suggested reading Matthew 5:43-48

I long since stopped watching professional football but still enjoy a Saturday afternoon non-league fixture. The not so enjoyable part is the bad language which, more often than not, does not come from the spectators but from the players themselves

On a day of sunshine and showers, I am watching a most competitive match, when a decision goes against a player, and he comes out with an unnecessary blasphemous expletive. As he does so, a most beautiful rainbow encircles the ground---so beautiful that a number of spectators photo it on their mobile phones.

To many, it is something of great beauty but to me it is far more than that---it is a reminder of the promise given to Noah many centuries ago. A reminder of God's great faithfulness.

Jesus said, 'He causes his sun to rise on the evil and the good, and sends rain on the righteous and the unrighteous'. (Matthew 5:45) The God who gives the sun and the rain, irrespective of whether humans love and worship Him, also gives the rainbow for all to enjoy.

Theologians call this Gods' common grace'----universal blessings, not deserved which are extended to all mankind. Air to breathe, food to eat, water to drink, the beauty of creation, art, music, sport, creative ability, family, friends etc. etc. These and many other gifts are tokens of God's universal kindness and goodness---examples of his 'common grace'. Despite the footballer's expletive, we still had the rainbow to enjoy.

Common grace places everyone continually in God's debt---and the debt grows with every moment of life.

(John Blanchard)

5 October

'What good is it for someone to gain the whole world, yet forfeit their soul? Or what can anyone give in exchange for their soul'? (Mark 8:36-37)

Suggested reading Luke 12:13-21

Fortnightly, on a Tuesday afternoon, we had a Ladies Meeting at the church, and men, though not invited, had a significant part to play. Many of the ladies were elderly, and it was often a team of men who provided them with transport to the church.

One day, I was driving my passenger to church, when she pointed towards a house and said 'I don't agree with that'. Her focus was a FOR SALE sign with the words UNDER OFFER emblazoned upon it.

'What don't you agree with'? I asked.
'I think', she said, 'they should offer what is being asked for and not try to offer less'.

Not having the time or energy to explain what the sign really meant, I let the statement pass, without comment.

To obtain our souls, Satan offers the world---the world of pleasure or the world of possessions. Sadly, there are many who accept his offer, not realising they are being short-changed. For even if he could offer the whole world---and he can't---that is way under the true value of the human soul.

Our souls are immortal---they will never ever die---and it is foolish to sell our souls to the devil. They need to be entrusted to Jesus; He died to save our souls, and in His hands they are safe and secure for time and eternity.

The real value of an object is that which one who knows its worth will give for it. He who made the soul knew its worth, and gave his life for it.

(Arthur Jackson)

6 October

'We put no stumbling block in anyone's path, so that our ministry will not be discredited'. (2 Corinthians 6:3)

Suggested reading 1 Thessalonians 2:1-12

In the 1980s and 1990s, upwards of forty children attended our weekly children's meeting. It was a privilege to spend time with them and to teach them Bible stories.

There was, however, a downside. When the school or cubs or brownies were having a sponsored walk, then a steady stream of children made their way to our home. They wanted 'Uncle' John and 'Aunty' Pat to sponsor them.

We could have said 'no' or sent them away but we never did. Why? We did not want to put any hindrance or obstacle in their way. We did not want to cause any unnecessary offence, and so we were prepared to tolerate the inconvenience and the financial expense.

The Apostle Paul said; 'Be wise in the way you act towards outsiders; make the most of every opportunity'. (Colossians 4:5) If Jesus died to save sinners, I must be prepared to deny myself for sinners. To some, the Christian message is offensive (Galatians 5:11); therefore, it is imperative that there is nothing offensive about us.

Whether witnessing to children or to adults our 'walk' is as important as our 'talk'; our behaviour as important as our beliefs. Let us seek 'to put no stumbling block in anyone's path, so that our ministry will not be discredited'.

You deny Christ when you fail to deny yourself for Christ.

(Anon)

7 October

'For whoever keeps the whole law and yet stumbles at just one point is guilty of breaking all of it'. (James 2:10)

Suggested reading Galatians 5:1-6

Recently, I was contacted by DVLA Swansea and threatened with a £100 fine because my vehicle was not registered with the Motor Insurance

Bureau (MIB). This I found strange, as I had the documents to prove that my insurance was up to date. Despite this, the £100 fine was still applicable because I was not registered with the MIB.

After prolonged correspondence with DVLA and my insurers, I eventually discovered the cause of the problem. The 'E' of my registration number had been erroneously transcribed as an 'F', and so consequently my vehicle was unknown to the MIB.

Now an 'F' is as near to an 'E' as you can get, but this minor error meant I was subject to a £100 fine. Thankfully, after intervention from my MP, the fine was repealed.

The Apostle James, in our text for today, is not suggesting that all sins are equally heinous but just as murder breaks the law, so also does exceeding the speed limit. God's standard is perfection, and because we have all 'stumbled', we are all guilty in His sight. Sins, I look upon as being 'small' are nevertheless proof that I have broken God's law. I need a Saviour and because He is the only One who never stumbled, Jesus Christ is the Saviour I need.

The law of God will not take ninety-nine for a hundred.

(William Secker)

8 October

'We love because he first loved us'. (1 John 4:19)

Suggested reading John 6:60-71

When we lived in Morecambe, we often saw people walking their dogs on the beach. Most were on a lead, until they got to the beach, but then they were unleashed and given their freedom. Now, living in West Yorkshire, we frequently see the same sight. Dogs running in the fields and woods, having been taken off their leads.

Now, in theory, with that kind of freedom, the dogs could bolt off and never be seen again. But that never happens. The dogs run ahead--- sometimes a good distance ahead---- but they always return to the side of their owner. Why?

Though not bound by a lead, most dogs are bound by something much stronger----a love, a devotion to their owner. That is why, again and again, they return to their owner's side.

As believers, we are not bound to Jesus by a written contract but by something far deeper. We are bound by a love, a devotion, and though at times we might wander, again and again we return to the side of our Master.

When some, who had professed to be His disciples, turned back 'Jesus asked the Twelve, "You do not want to leave too, do you"? Simon Peter answered him, "Lord to whom shall we go? You have the words of eternal life". (John 6:67-68)

Knowing who the Lord is and what He has done for us, there is no-one else to whom we can or would want to go.

And round my heart still closely twine
Those ties which naught can sever,
For I am His, and He is mine,
For ever and for ever.

(James Grindlay Small)

9 October

'-----they are blind guides. If the blind lead the blind both will fall into a pit'. (Matthew 15:14)

Suggested reading Psalm 33:1-12

In the 1960s, my school day began with a hymn, a Bible reading and a prayer, and as students, it was required that we fully entered into this act of worship. Indeed, if the headteacher thought we were not singing the hymn with conviction, he would stop us and we had to start again.

Move forward forty years and I have been asked to speak at a morning assembly at a secondary school in North Yorkshire. No hymn, no Bible reading, no prayer and I am given 5-10 minutes to speak. The children are polite and reasonably attentive but the teachers----they sit, apparently marking papers and showing a total lack of interest.

The teachers might resent having to be there but having been invited by the school, surely common courtesy demands I am given a hearing.

Jesus spoke of 'blind guides' and sadly, where moral and spiritual values are concerned, that was true of those teachers. It illustrated, also, how secular as a nation, we have now become.

'Do not be deceived: God cannot be mocked. A man reaps what he sows'. (Galatians 6:7) This is an unchanging Biblical principal and we are reaping today what has been sown in more recent years. The fruit of atheism, evolution, ignorance of Scripture is now to be seen in the many disturbing acts, taking place in society today.

We are failing our children if we just give them knowledge, without moral and spiritual guidance.

Education without religion, as useful as it is, seems rather to make man a more clever devil.

(C.S. Lewis)

10 October

'The Lord----is patient with you, not wanting anyone to perish but everyone to come to repentance'. (2 Peter 3:9)

Suggested reading Matthew 4:12-22

Having lived in rural areas for many years, I have never liked driving in busy city centres, and it is now something I rarely ever do. Let me tell you 'the straw that broke the camel's back'.

One morning I was driving in the city, when I came across some roadworks and my daughter said, 'Dad you will have to take the next turn left'. This I did and ended up in an underground car park.

The only way out was to turn round and come back the way I had come in, but it was not so straightforward. I needed a ticket and so, even though I was not stopping, I had to buy one. Having bought the ticket, I was now able to go out the way I had come in.

I had gone wrong. I had to admit I had gone wrong. Then I had to do a U-turn and go in the opposite direction to the one in which I had been going.

That is an illustration---albeit not a perfect one---of repentance. Before I could turn round or change direction, I had to buy a ticket. And that is why it is not a perfect illustration; because, where repentance is concerned, I do not have to buy the ticket. No, the price has been paid for me. It has been paid by the death of Jesus Christ on the cross of

Calvary. And so now I can repent, I can come back to God, because Jesus has done all that is necessary.

Repentance is, fundamentally a change of direction, a turning from sin to God.

(James Philip)

11 October

'We are co-workers in God's service'. (1 Corinthians 3:9)

Suggested reading Luke 14:1-14.

One morning a young woman came into the Job Centre and excitedly told me that she had got work as a domestic servant? Why such excitement? The post was at Buckingham Palace---she was to work for the monarch.

Another morning, a group of workmen came into the office but they were not excited at all. They had been working for a sub-contractor on a building site, but when they went to pick up their wages, they discovered he had disappeared. They had worked all week for nothing.

When we work for Jesus, we are in the employment of the Sovereign Lord, the King of Kings and he is the very best of Masters. No matter how menial the task, the important thing is not what we are doing but rather Who we are doing it for.

Furthermore, our wages are never in doubt. Jesus promises that we will be paid, if not now, then 'at the resurrection of the righteous' (Luke

14:14). And Paul assures us that 'our labour in the Lord is not in vain'. (1 Corinthians 15:58)

What an incentive to be busy and active in the service of Jesus.

God is a sure paymaster, though he does not always pay at the end of every week.

(C.H. Spurgeon)

12 October

'----the whole world is under the control of the evil one'. (1 John 5:19)

Suggested reading Psalm 51

For a number of years, I was associated with Ingleton Cricket Club. I was secretary, umpire and an occasional player for the midweek team.

How did every game of cricket begin? Not when the first ball was bowled but rather when the two captains went out on to the field and tossed a coin.

If our captain won the toss, he would come back to the pavilion and say either 'we are batting' or 'we are bowling'. It was the captain's decision but a decision made on behalf of the entire team. I might have preferred to bowl but the choice was not mine. The captain's decision became my decision.

In the Garden of Eden, Adam tossed the coin for all humankind. He was our representative, and in rebelling against God and siding with Satan, he took every member of the human race with him. This means his fall is my fall, his guilt is my guilt, and his condemnation is my condemnation.

We sin because we have each inherited from Adam a sinful nature and this is emphasised throughout the Bible. David says, 'Surely, I was sinful at birth, sinful from the time my mother conceived me' (Psalm 51:5) Paul says, 'sin entered the world through one man'. (Romans 5:12) John says 'If we claim to be without sin, we deceive ourselves and the truth is not in us'. (1 John 1:8)

Sinners by choice, sinners by practice and all because we are sinners by nature. Adam's disastrous decision has affected us all but thank God the situation can be remedied through the sacrificial death of the 'second Adam' (1 Cor. 15:45)

Man lost his freedom in the Garden of Eden. He is free to sin, but he is not free not to sin.

(Brian Edwards)

13 October

'He seized the dragon, that ancient serpent, who is the devil or Satan and bound him for a thousand years'. (Revelation 20:2)

Suggested reading Job 1:6-12

As a pastor in a rural area, I often visited farms and became acquainted with a number of dogs. This was a somewhat unnerving experience as, until comparatively recently, I was always wary of canines.

Most farms had a border collie which were working dogs, used for herding sheep, cattle and other animals. Easy to train and with a good work ethic, they were an asset to the farmer, but also a family pet for his wife and children.

Farms tended to be isolated dwellings and so, there were other dogs which acted as a deterrent to unwanted visitors. I recall some which were tethered to a post and barked aggressively as I passed. How thankful I was that they were not free to roam but nevertheless, I still kept a safe distance from them.

Praise God, Satan is bound and has his restrictions and limitations. He had Divine permission to attack Job, but was commanded 'on the man himself, do not lay a finger'. (Job 1:12) Likewise, Satan was permitted to attack Peter but the temptation was not to be totally overwhelming---'your faith may not fail'. (Luke 22:32) We neither underestimate or overestimate Satan's power for, though mighty, he is not Almighty.

Praise God, Satan is bound but do not put yourself in the place of temptation---do not misjudge the length of the chain!

The devil is like a mad dog that is chained up. He is powerless to harm us when we are outside his reach, but once we enter his circle, we expose ourselves again to injury or harm.

(Augustine)

14 October

'Look, he is coming with the clouds and every eye will see him, even those who pierced him'. (Revelation 1:7)

Suggested reading Mark 13:24-31

One Sunday afternoon, I was distributing gospel leaflets on Morecambe promenade, and I got into conversation with a lady who had been a Jehovah's Witness for thirty-five years. She was pleasant, not at all aggressive, and whilst disagreeing on numerous issues, we had an amiable dialogue.

On discussing the 'end times', she related how the Second Coming of Christ was an invisible, spiritual event which had occurred in 1914. Before leaving, I urged her to put on one side all Watchtower material, and to read for herself, what the Bible had to say about the Second Coming.

Some eighteen months later, this lady sought me out, and what a joy it was to discover that she was now a true believer and at great personal cost, had severed all connections with the JWs. As she had read 1 and 2 Thessalonians, she had come to see that the Second Coming of Christ was a visible, audible event which had still to take place.

His first coming was private, unseen, unheard but not his Second Coming. 'For the Lord himself will come down from heaven with a loud command, with the voice of the archangel and with the trumpet call of God'. (1 Thessalonians 4:16) 'Every eye will see him'. (Revelation 1:7)

He came the first time to be our Saviour; He comes a second time to be our Judge. We need to trust him as Saviour before we are ever, prepared to meet him as Judge.

Many people will be surprised when Jesus comes again---but nobody will be mistaken.

(John Blanchard)

15 October

'We all, like sheep have gone astray, each of us has turned to our own way'. (Isaiah 53:6)

Suggested reading Luke 15: 11-16

After Pat and I had been accepted as foster parents, Christopher was the first child who came to us. He was just six days old, when we picked him up from the Royal Lancaster Infirmary. His mother was an unmarried girl from Northern Ireland, and she had been sent over to stay with an aunt; the intention being that she should have the baby and then give him over for adoption.

Christopher's mother and great aunt came to see him every two to three days, and it was immediately obvious the mother was bonding with the baby. To our delight, after five weeks, the mother decided she could not possibly give Christopher up for adoption and she was determined, whatever the consequences, to return to Ireland with him. Thankfully, her parents accepted the situation, and Christopher had soon captured their hearts.

His mother kept in regular touch, and when he was ten years of age, she brought Christopher to our home. It was a joy to see such a pleasant, well-mannered young man. Unfortunately, shortly after this, we lost contact, and for over twenty years we heard nothing, although we often thought and talked about Christopher. Our 'son' had gone astray.

We have all wandered away from our Heavenly Father, and become 'lost' as we have sought to navigate our way through a complex and painful path. But God has not abandoned us, and is 'filled with compassion' (Luke 15:20) towards His rebellious children. Therefore, the moment we seek, God, we find he is already seeking us.

Man, made in the image of God has a purpose---to be in relationship to God, who is there. Man forgets his purpose and thus he forgets who he is and what life means.

(Francis Schaeffer)

16 October (continuation of 15 Oct.)

'You will seek and find me when you seek me with all your heart'. (Jeremiah 29:13)

Suggested reading Luke 15:17-32

Moving forward to 2017, Pat was contacted by the owner of Settle Play Barn, where she had, for some time, been organising craft activities. A man from Northern Ireland had contacted Rob, asking for Pat's phone number. Rob was understandably wary, but when he told Pat the man was called Christopher, she guessed it was our long lost foster son.

A few days afterwards, the telephone rang and it was Christopher with a sad and surprising story. His mother had recently died from cancer, and going through her papers, he had discovered for the first time, that he had been fostered as a baby. This was something his mother had never told him, even though as a ten-year-old he had visited us in Ingleton.

Having made this discovery, Christopher was determined to make contact with his 'first' parents, and had eventually come across Pat's name on the Settle Play Barn website. He intended coming over to England with his partner and child, and was eager to arrange a meeting—something which we readily agreed to.

And so, the great day arrived---a Wednesday morning at 10.30 am, outside Costa in Lancaster. We waited several minutes, but no sign of Christopher, until a phone call confirmed he was already upstairs in the building. Nervously, we climbed the steps, and there were hugs and tears as we embraced the reunion. The time raced by as we recalled his first days in Ingleton, and Christopher brought us up to date on his education, work and family. It was an emotional, memorable time, and we will never forget finding the 'son' that was lost.

In Costa, a seeking foster child met his seeking foster parents. In the parable of the prodigal, a seeking son met his seeking father, and in the life of every believer, a seeking sinner has met with his seeking Heavenly Father. God is a seeking God who pursues sinners---seek Him 'with all your heart' and discover that, all the time, He has been seeking you.

You made us for yourself, O Lord, and our hearts are restless till they rest in you.

(Augustine)

17 October

> 'We must all appear before the judgement seat of Christ, so that each of us may receive what is due us, for the things done while in the body, whether good or bad'. (2 Corinthians 5:10)

Suggested reading 1 Corinthians 3:3-15

One of my line managers, in the civil service, was an amiable fellow, and he would often join us in our coffee and lunch breaks.

Once a year, he would invite me to have a 'jar' with him, but this was not a convivial, friendly drink---it was something a little more serious because JAR was a Job Appraisal Review, where one's work performance over the past twelve months was assessed.

It could be a nervous interview because assessment of the past had a bearing on future promotion prospects.

Believers, as well as unbelievers will stand before the judgement seat of Christ. This is evident from the words of the Apostle Paul. He does not say 'you' or 'they'; he says 'we must all appear before the judgement seat of Christ'. He says 'we' and in so doing, Paul includes himself.

However, for believers, the judgement will not be to establish their eternal destiny; it will rather be to evaluate their deeds. Did I build with gold or did I build with straw? (1 Corinthians 3:12) Was I motivated by self-interest or was my chief aim the glory of God?

Human tribunals deal with crime; they have punishments but no rewards. The divine tribunal has both.

(A.Plummer)

18 October

'Because he himself suffered when he was tempted, he is able to help those who are being tempted'. (Hebrews 2:18)

Suggested reading Hebrews 4:12-16

With dementia apparently on the increase, many husbands and wives are now having to care for their spouses, and this can come at a heavy personal cost. The physical and emotional demands can be quite exhausting.

I was greatly challenged by an eighty-two-year-old man, whose care for his wife, diagnosed with Alzheimer's Disease, was quite exceptional. Day and night, he cared for her, with little or no respite.

One day his GP told him that his wife was in the best care home in the district---her own home. A testament to the man's devotion and commitment to his wife.

When I got married, I too promised 'in sickness and in health', but I have never yet had to prove my commitment as that man has. Up to now, the vow I made has been largely theoretical, but his has been experiential. He has known the pain and stress that such commitment brings.

This is why Jesus had to be tempted. He could only be our Great High Priest by first experiencing what we experience. His temptation, therefore, was not something theoretical---it was real and demanding. It had to be 'for we do not have a hight priest who is unable to sympathise with our weaknesses, but we have one who has been tempted in every way, just as we are---yet he did not sin'. (Hebrews 4:15)

Touched with a sympathy within,
He knows our feeble frame;
He knows what sore temptations mean,
For he has felt the same.

(Isaac Watts)

19 October

'Jesus replied, "Foxes have dens and birds have nests, but the Son of Man has no place to lay his head". (Matthew 8:20)

Suggested reading 2 Corinthians 8:1-9

I was speaking at a Christian conference in South Wales, and was accompanied by Pat and Aaron. It was a long, tiring journey and, on arriving at the centre, we went to the foyer to see which room had been allocated to us.

Our room was No.11 but against Aaron's name were the words 'no food/no bed'. As he was fed through a tube into his stomach 'no food' was applicable, but though Aaron spent his days in a wheelchair, he did require a bed at night.

This was gently pointed out to the Centre Manager and he immediately arranged for a suitable bed to be provided. Thankfully, we were all accommodated in the same bedroom.

No such arrangement was made for Jesus. He multiplied the bread and the fishes, He could have turned 'stones into bread' but He was often hungry. There was 'no room in the inn' when Jesus was born, and this was to continue throughout his thirty-three years on earth. It was a life of self-denial and sacrifice.

' ----though he was rich, yet for your sakes he became poor, so that you through his poverty might become rich'. (2 Corinthians 8:9)

The Saviour of sinners knows what it is to be poor.

(J. C. Ryle)

20 October

'This is love for God; to keep his commands. And his commands are not burdensome'. (1 John 5:3)

Suggested reading Psalm 19

It was a mild autumn afternoon, and after taking our daughter's dog, Desmond, a walk in the woods, we drove to a roadside café. Having the dog, and with the weather remaining favourable, we decided to sit outside. Securing Desmond to the leg of the table, we enjoyed a coffee and a scone but, unknown to us, this was the calm before the storm.

In releasing Desmond from the table, we inadvertently released him altogether, and he immediately revelled in his newfound freedom. Pat and I ran after him, shouting his name and brandishing treats, but Desmond thought it was a game and he was having great fun. However, we knew what he didn't--- the café bordered a busy 'A' road. Soon, having jumped the wall, Desmond was dodging the traffic.

My heart was in my mouth, expecting his imminent demise. Climbing over the wall, I attempted to alert oncoming motorists. Seeing me in the road, Desmond vaulted back over the wall, and raced round the car park, as though he was a greyhound.

The owners of the café, seeing the commotion, came out and succeeded where we had failed, enticing Desmond with a handful of treats. As he paused to eat, I was able to grab him, put on his lead, and after thanking the café owners profusely, I took him to the safety of the car.

Desmond was none the worse for his experience, but this was more than could be said for Pat and I. Our hearts were beating rapidly, and it was the next day before we could even tell our daughter how near we had been to returning from the walk without her dog.

There are those who think the commandments of God were given to restrict us and to make us miserable, but nothing could be further from the truth. We need boundaries and restrictions because total freedom ultimately brings disaster. Breaking 'free' of God's commandments has resulted in heartache for individuals, families and nations. To the believer, God's commandments are not restrictive but liberating. He made us and, therefore, He alone is the one who knows how we ought to live.

Man is most free when controlled by God alone

(Augustine)

21 October

'For Christ also suffered once for sins, the righteous for the unrighteous to bring you to God'. (1 Peter 3:18)

Suggested reading Isaiah 53:1-6

In 1972, I interviewed at the Jobcentre an eighteen-year- old man, the brother of our next -door neighbour. He was a polite teenager, with a good attitude to work, and I felt he would soon be in employment. It was, therefore, a huge shock to read shortly afterwards that he had been arrested and charged with murder. His trial was later in the year and he was given a life sentence.

Some six months afterwards, a young man registering for work and benefits gave me the name of the man convicted of murder. I knew this was not his real name, but I showed no emotion, registering the young man for work before referring his claim to our fraud department. It eventually transpired that the man was wanted by the police, and that is why he had registered for work under an assumed name.

The man took the place of a murderer, but not for the best of reasons. He hoped to avoid detection by the police, and saw it as a means of obtaining welfare benefits.

The Lord Jesus Christ really did take the place of a murderer. The middle cross was intended for Barabbas but Pilate---weak and cowardly---gave way to the cries of the crowd.

Jesus, however, did not just take the place of Barabbas---He took the place of all who will repent and trust in Him. He became our substitute, our saviour--- God punishing His Son, so that we might go free. Have we thanked Him? Have we trusted Him? Is Jesus your substitute and Saviour?

When Jesus bowed his head,
And dying took our place,
The veil was rent, a way was found
To that pure home of grace

(John Elias)

22 October

'Believe in the Lord Jesus, and you will be saved' (Acts 16:31)

Suggested reading Luke 13:22-30

Our twin grandchildren were born in Switzerland and Pat went over to see them, just days after they were born. Later, we both travelled to Zurich to celebrate their first and second birthdays.

On their second birthdays, we were in Zurich, on a Sunday, and went with Andrew and his family to an English-speaking Baptist church. There was a good congregation as, every week, it is swelled by visitors to Switzerland. Some---like us--- are visiting relatives, whilst others are on holiday or on work assignments.

The custom, at the beginning of the service, was for visitors to stand and to say where they were from, and why they were in Switzerland. On this particular Sunday morning, there were people present from many different countries, and for a variety of reasons.

Andrew saved us from having to get to our feet by briefly stating the reason for our presence.

In heaven, as in the church at Zurich, there will be believers from all over the world----' from every nation, tribe, people and language' (Revelation 7: 9) --- but they will all be there for the self-same reason. 'These are they who have---- washed their robes and made them white in the blood of the Lamb'. (Revelation 7:14)

None will be there because of their works and none will be there because of family associations---all will be there because they came to trust in 'the Lamb of God, who takes away the sin of the world'. (John 1:29)

Christ brings the heart to heaven first, and then the person.

(Richard Baxter)

23 October

'Be very careful, then, how you live---not as unwise but as wise, making the most of every opportunity, because the days are evil'. (Ephesians 5:15)

Suggested reading Colossians 1:9-14

Putting cases into the loft, the ladder went and so did I---dislocating and breaking my wrist.

Ever since that traumatic event, my wife and I have exercised extreme carefulness: no cleaning windows, changing a light bulb or getting anything off a high shelf, unless Pat is firmly holding the ladder.

It makes me feel as though I am an old man and dependant on others, but I do not complain as I know it to be the sensible course of action.

This word is full of moral and spiritual danger, and as believers we have to walk with care It is all too easy to become self-sufficient and careless, but 'pride goes before destruction, a haughty spirit before a fall'. (Proverbs 16:18) Am I as careful in my spiritual walk with the Lord, as I am when up the ladder?

It has become common practice to say to a friend or family member, when parting, 'take care'. The Apostle Paul put it in a rather more straightforward way when writing to the Corinthians, 'If you think you are standing firm, be careful that you don't fall'. (1 Corinthians 10:12)

Men fall in private, long before they fall in public.

(J. C. Ryle)

24 October

'If you are offering your gift at the altar and there remember that your brother or sister has something against you, leave your gift there in front of the altar. First go and be reconciled to them, then come and offer your gift'. (Matthew 5:23-24)

Suggested reading Ephesians 4:25-32

It was a Sunday morning communion service, and the minister having read from 1 Corinthians 11:28, 'everyone ought to examine themselves before they eat of the bread and drink from the cup', invited the congregation to quietly reflect upon these words.

Suddenly, the silence was broken, when a woman got up from her seat, crossed the aisle and hugged another member of the church. Unknown to us, there had been some unresolved tension between the two of them, but what a joy it was, to see repentance and reconciliation, as they remembered the death of their Saviour.

Paul said, 'Be kind and compassionate to one another, forgiving each other, just as in Christ, God forgave you'. (Ephesians 4:32) It was at the cross, through the death of Christ, that God forgave us, and when we realise how much we have been forgiven, can we withhold forgiveness from others?

Not just at a communion service but constantly we have to 'fix our eyes upon Jesus' (Hebrews 12:2) because this is often a hard and unforgiving world and, if we fail to look to Him, we can so easily be influenced by the spirit of the age. We preach a message of reconciliation, therefore, as believers we must ever seek to be reconciled one to another.

I say to the glory of God and in utter humility that whenever I see myself before God and realise even something of what my blessed Lord has done for me, I am ready to forgive anybody anything.

(D. Martyn Lloyd-Jones)

25 October

'When people are brought low and you say 'Lift them up'! Then he will save the downcast'. (Job 22:29)

Suggested reading Psalm 23

To most people the word 'rigged' means that an election or a sporting contest has been manipulated in a dishonest way. However, that was not my first introduction to the word. As my grandmother grew older and found it difficult to get out of her chair, she would often say 'I'm rigged'.

When I moved to the rural area of Ingleton, I learned this was an expression used of a sheep that had turned on its back and could not get up again. The sheep was 'rigged' or 'cast down'.

Apparently this Yorkshire dialect word has Nordic roots in the word 'riggwelter' ----'rygg' meaning back and 'velte' overturn.

Sometimes, as believers, because of sin or circumstances, we can feel that we are on our backs and not able to get up again. We are 'rigged'. We are 'cast down'.

This was the experience of both Old Testament and New Testament saints. Indeed, David said 'Why, my soul, are you downcast? Why so disturbed within me'? (Psalm 42:11)

How reassuring to know that as a shepherd tends a sheep that is 'rigged', so we have a Good Shepherd who tends and comforts His sheep. We can say with David, 'The Lord upholds all who fall and lifts up all who are bowed down'. (Psalm 145:14)

No Christian should feel 'under' the circumstances, because the circumstances are under God.

(John Blanchard)

26 October

'Blessed is the people whose God is the Lord'. (Psalm 144:15b)

Suggested reading Isaiah 1:2-9

Having been up most of the night with a man suffering a mental breakdown, I eventually secured an appointment with a hospital psychiatrist. It was early evening and I was feeling somewhat tired and despondent.

My mood changed when the door opened and I was greeted by an African man, with a beaming smile. 'Are you Christians'? He asked. How he knew I have no idea, but when we said we were, the psychiatrist prayed with us and commended the situation to the Lord.

'When I was in Nigeria', he said, 'I used to talk to my patients about the Lord, and knowing this was the country of John Wesley and George Whitfield, I just presumed I would be able to do the same in Britain. But I am not allowed to'.

I could only share his dismay---how tragic when a nation departs from God.

When a nation departs from the living God, there is always a price to pay. This was true of Israel in the Old Testament and it still holds true today. 'Do not be deceived: God cannot be mocked. A man reaps what he sows'. (Galatians 6:7). This is a Biblical principle and having sown 'the wind' are we not now reaping 'the whirlwind'? (Hosea 8:7)

And yet, there is hope because we have a God of amazing grace and great compassion. Therefore, we can pray with the prophet 'Lord, I have heard of your fame; I stand in awe of your deeds, Lord. Renew them in our day, in our time make them known; in wrath remember mercy' (Habakkuk 3:2)

What God has done in the past, He can do in the future. He can stem the tide of wickedness, revive His work, extend His kingdom, glorify His name. O that Britain might again see that 'righteousness exalts a nation'. (Proverbs 14:34) and 'blessed is the people whose God is the Lord'. (Psalm 144:15b)

The best definition of revival is 'times of refreshing---from the presence of the Lord'.

(J. Edwin Orr)

27 October

'Come now, let us settle the matter", says the Lord. Though your sins are like scarlet, they shall be as white as snow; though they are red as crimson, they shall be like wool'. (Isaiah 1:18)

Suggested reading Isaiah 64:1-7

I first grew a beard in the mid-1970s and I have had once ever since. From time to time, Pat has suggested I remove the beard, maintaining it would make me look much younger. So far, I have resisted all her attempts.

However, I do still shave, using a cut-throat razor and on one occasion, I carelessly gashed my neck. The cut was quite deep and I had to change my shirt because it was stained with blood.

We soon discovered that blood stains can be very stubborn and they were only removed with difficulty.

Blood stains and yet it is only blood---the blood of Jesus Christ---which can wash and cleanse from the dirt and filth of sin. The question asked in Revelation 7:13 'These in white robes---who are they'? is met with the answer in Revelation 7:14 'These are they who----have washed their robes and made them white in the blood of the Lamb'. (NKJV)

Amazing but wonderfully true. The blood of Jesus applied to 'filthy rags' results in 'white robes'.

Christ hath crossed out the black lines of our sin with the red lines of his own blood.

(Thomas Brooks)

28 October

'For lack of guidance a nation fails, but victory is won through many advisers'. (Proverbs 11:14)

Suggested reading Proverbs 3:1-10

Having felt a call to Christian ministry, I was happily employed in the civil service, waiting on the Lord for his leading. Most Sundays, as a lay preacher, I was taking services in a number of different churches.

One Sunday evening, in 1976, I was conducting worship at Ingleton Evangelical Church and unknown to me, there were two experienced pastors in the congregation. As we shook hands at the end of the service, one of them put his hand on my shoulder and said, 'I think you should be in the ministry'.

Even though this had never been said to me before, I gave it little thought until some three years later. It was then that I had a phone call, and a subsequent visit from two elders, asking me to prayerfully consider becoming the pastor of their church. The elders were from-------- Ingleton Evangelical Church!

'Coincidence', would be the cry of many, but not for one moment do I think so. God guides principally through his Word applied to our hearts by the Holy Spirit, but He also guides through our circumstances and the counsel of godly people.

When we are undecided or facing a challenge, it is wise to consult with mature believers. They may agree or disagree with our proposed action but we do well to prayerfully assess their advice.

Guidance is both internal----the Word and the Holy Spirit and also external----circumstances and godly counsel. 'Trust in the Lord with all your heart and lean not on your own understanding; in all your ways submit to him, and he will make your paths straight'. (Proverbs 3:5-6)

Guidance is not normally ecstatic or mystical. It is always ethical and intensely practical.

(Sinclair Ferguson)

29 October

'Father, I want those you have given me to be with me where I am, and to see my glory, the glory you have given me because you loved me before the creation of the world'. (John 17:24)

Suggested reading Revelation 21:1-8

For several years, after my mother died, I still called at her house to see my brother. The garden was the same, the furniture was the same, and yet it was not the same house. And it was not the same, for the simple reason, mother was not there.

That was the reason why I used to call; not to see the garden or the furniture, but to spend time with her. Mother was the attraction of the house. And, without mother, the house did not have the same appeal.

I am sure this is how many of us feel when we pass houses where parents, grandparents or relatives once lived. We have nostalgic memories, but the house no longer has the attraction that once it had.

The same will be true of heaven. There will be many things that will thrill us but the real attraction will not be the pearly gates or the jasper walls. No, the real attraction will be Jesus.

Yes, 'there will be no more death or mourning or crying or pain' (Revelation 21:4) but best of all, 'God's dwelling place is now among the people, and he will dwell with them' (Revelation 21:3) Heaven is far more than the absence of distress, it is the immediate presence of Christ.

'Where I am' was the description of heaven given by Jesus and it is the best description of all.

Heaven will chiefly consist in the enjoyment of God.

(William S. Plumer)

30 October

'Teach us to number our days aright, that we may gain a heart of wisdom'. (Psalm 90:12)

Suggested reading Romans 13:11-14

On a Saturday, when Andrew and Joanna were youngsters, Pat and I tried to spend time with them. On this particular Saturday, I dropped Pat, Joanna and Aaron off in Pontefract town centre, whilst Andrew and I proceeded to watch Morecambe FC play football at South Elmsall.

We had arranged to meet back in Pontefract at a quarter past five, but arriving at the agreed venue, there was no sign of Pat, Joanna and Aaron. It was in the days before mobile phones, and as the minutes ticked by, I wondered if Aaron had suffered an epileptic fit and been taken to hospital.

We waited and waited until, at just after six, the 'wanderers' appeared. They were quite relaxed and oblivious to the panic they had caused. Why? Well, Pat had gone into a shop and noticing the clock said 'half past three', she had adjusted her watch accordingly. However, Pat had not appreciated that this was the October night when clocks were put back one hour, and in preparation for next week, the shop had already made the adjustment.

Consequently, Pat thought she was in time for our 17.15 rendezvous, when in fact, it was already almost 18.15. Pat thought she knew the time but she didn't, and believing she had plenty of time, Pat had wiled away the last hour.

Paul says that, as believers, we do understand 'the present time' (Romans 13:11) We understand that every passing day brings us one day nearer to heaven or to the return of Christ. The unbeliever, however, not expecting either heaven or the return of Christ, does not know what time it is, and therefore sees no need to 'put aside the deeds of darkness'. (Romans 13:12)

Clocks go back in October, but in the spiritual sense, no one can turn the clock back. The day we depart this world or the day Jesus comes again has already been fixed by God. Therefore, the believer should spend every day as though it were his last, whilst the unbeliever should urgently 'seek the Lord while he may be found; call on him while he is near'. (Isaiah 55:6)

What is past cannot be recalled; what is future cannot be insured.

(Stephen Charnock)

31 October

'To enjoy the fleeting pleasures of sin'. (Hebrews 11:25)

Suggested reading Genesis 3:1-7

When I was a child, Thursday was always 'baking day', and during school holidays, my brother and I would 'help' our mother. The cake mixture was put in a bowl and with our individual spoons, it was our responsibility to stir the mixture.

But, on one memorable occasion, as we stirred we also tasted, and as we continued to stir, we also continued to taste. Not surprisingly, when mother came to see how we were doing, she was faced with two spoons, an empty bowl, but no cake mixture.

We were not forced to eat what was before us, nor did we need any persuading. Not at all. The mixture was attractive, tasty, tempting---it just seemed the normal, the natural thing to do.

As Adam and Eve discovered, sin is often attractive and desirable: otherwise it would not be a temptation. However, temptation only becomes sin when we yield to Satan's evil suggestion.

I suspect, having 'gorged' on the cake mixture, that later my brother and I had a sickly feeling. Pleasurable at first but then the consequences. To Adam and Eve, the temptation seemed irresistible but for them and for us, the consequences were to be horrendous. A fallen world, broken relationships---paradise turned into a 'vale of tears'.

We must ever remember this when temptation appears so attractive and desirable---the pleasure comes before the pain.

If you don't want to trade with the devil, stay out of his shops.

(Vance Havner)

BIBLE READINGS NOVEMBER

1 November

'Contend for the faith that was once for all entrusted to God' holy people'. (Jude 3)

Suggested reading Colossians 1:15-20

Many years ago, I was talking to the principal of a ministerial training college. He told me that Abraham had to find a message for his generation, Jesus for His generation, Paul for his generation. Therefore, we had to find a message for our generation. What a sad comment.

One morning, I was handed a booklet by a Jehovah's Witness. As I flicked through the pages, I remarked. 'I can't find Jesus---where is He'? I had to keep my face straight when the man responded, 'If you turn to the index, then you will find Him'. Another sad comment.

These comments revealed ignorance of two fundamental truths. We have an unchanging gospel and Jesus, Himself, is the very heart of that gospel.

We have no need to find a new message for this or any other generation. The one true gospel has been entrusted to believers---'once for all'----and it is this we must contend for, and pass on to future generations. The Apostle Paul said, 'I want you to know, brothers and sisters that the gospel I preached is not of human origin. I did not receive it from any man, nor was I taught it; rather I received it by revelation from Jesus Christ'. (Galatians 1:11-12)

Jesus is the very heart of the gospel---He is the theme of both the Old Testament and the New Testament. On the road to Emmaus, with the two disciples, Jesus, 'beginning with Moses and all the Prophets, explained to them what was said in all the Scriptures concerning himself'. (Luke 24:27) He is the Incarnate God. The Second Person of the Trinity. The Great I Am. 'In everything, he might have the supremacy'. (Colossians 1:18)

Christianity----is the revelation of God, not the research of man.

(James. S. Stewart)

2 November

'This is how we know we are in him: Whoever claims to live in him must live as Jesus did'. (1 John 2:6)

Suggested reading Ephesians 6:1-9

Having been given tickets, I went to the Yorkshire Television studios in Leeds, to watch a recording of Through the Keyhole.

David Frost introduced the programme and a panel of three celebrities were given a guided tour of a property. Attention was drawn to certain clothing items, ornaments, pictures etc. in the house, and at the end of the tour, Lloyd Grossman asked the familiar question, 'Who lives in a house like this'?

The identity of the well-known owner of the house was revealed to us, the audience, before the panel then attempted to answer Lloyd's question.

If a TV company was to spend a week in my home, not focusing on my possessions but on the books I read, the TV programmes I watch, the way I treat my wife, the amount of time I spend in prayer and reading the Bible, what would be the answer to 'Who lives in a house like this'? A hypocrite? A backslider? A committed Christian?

It is sometimes said that 'no one knows what goes on behind close doors', but the Lord does. Therefore, what matters is not what I might appear to be on a Sunday, but my true character throughout the rest of the week, in my home, at work or in leisure activities. Having trusted Jesus as Saviour, we must now seek to live as Jesus did, and though we will always fall short of his perfection, it must always be our goal.

What thou art in the sight of God, that thou truly art.

(Thomas a Kempis)

3 November

'Always give yourselves fully in the work of the Lord, because you know that your labour in the Lord is not in vain'. (1 Corinthians 15:58)

Suggested reading Mark 13:32-37

At school, there were occasions when we knew that a teacher was going to be away and a 'supply' teacher would deputise on that day. Knowing he was going to be absent, the teacher would leave us plenty of work to do while he was away---perhaps a book to read or an essay to write. He was determined we should not be idle.

However, what I often noticed was this: when the teacher was away, we were never quite as keen or as enthusiastic as we were, when the teacher was present. There was plenty of work to do, but without the teacher, we somehow lost the motivation, the incentive to do it.

We did not mind the teacher being away!

Jesus knew this would be the temptation facing his followers, in every generation, once he had returned to heaven---'when the cat is away the mice play'!

Certainly, he has left sufficient work for us to do----a world to evangelise---but are we sufficiently motivated to do it? Again and again, Jesus urged his disciples to be diligent and industrious in the time between His Ascension and His Second Coming.

He has also given us His Spirit to empower us---are we making the most of every opportunity (Colossians 4:5) or just coasting until He comes?

My talents, gifts and graces, Lord
Into thy blessed hands receive;
And let me live to preach thy Word,
And let me to thy glory live;
My every sacred moment spend
In publishing the sinner's Friend.

(Charles Wesley)

4 November

> 'Do you not know that your bodies are temples of the Holy Spirit, who is in you, whom you have received from God? You are not your own; you were bought at a price. Therefore, honour God with your bodies'. (1 Corinthians 6:19-20)

Suggested reading 1 Peter 1; 13-21

I remember preaching with a friend outside a football ground, as queues gathered for a cup tie. My friend, using a football analogy, explained how for years he had been on the side of Satan, committing every foul in the book. He then told how he had changed sides, when he had been signed up by Jesus and converted.

At that precise moment, a heckler in the crowd asked the very question we wanted to hear:

'How much did He give for you'?
'He gave everything', my friend replied, 'He gave Himself upon the cross to save me from sin and death and hell'.

How true.

We cannot earn, merit or work for our salvation---'the gift of God is eternal life in Christ Jesus our Lord' (Romans 6:23) Salvation is for us a free gift but it does not come cheap. It was purchased, at a tremendous price, when Jesus took the guilt and the punishment for our sins upon himself.

'It was not with perishable things such as silver or gold that you were redeemed from the empty way of life handed down to you from your ancestors, but with the precious blood of Christ, a lamb without blemish or defect'. (1Peter 1:18-19)

We need to remember each day, 'You are not your own; you were bought at a price'. (1 Corinthians 6:19)

There was no other good enough
To pay the price of sin;
He only could unlock the gate
Of heaven and let us in.

(Cecil Frances Alexander)

5 November

'Repent then and turn to God, so that your sins may be wiped out, that times of refreshing may come from the Lord'. (Acts 3:19)

Suggested reading Isaiah 44:1-5

The river Doe and the river Twiss are two small rivers that join together just below the village of Ingleton, to form the river Greta, a tributary of the river Lune, which eventually flows into the Irish Sea.

One calm autumnal afternoon, as I walked by the Greta, the river was slow and tranquil, with twigs and sticks floating on the surface of the water.

The next day, I did the same walk---but now---what a difference. The river had almost become a torrent, and was gushing by, taking logs and branches with it.

What had happened? Overnight, there had been hours of heavy rain and it was this which had made of the difference to the river.

Today, the Spirit of God is at work in Britain; otherwise, no-one at all would be converted. The Spirit is present, but often gospel work is slow and nothing much seems to be happening.

How we need Pentecostal showers! How we need 'times of refreshing---from the Lord' (Acts3:19) to turn the stream into a torrent. Only then will sin be washed away and multitudes swept into the kingdom of heaven.

God has done it in the past, let us plead with Him to do it in the future.

Revival is divine intervention in the normal course of spiritual things. It is God revealing Himself to man in awful holiness and irresistible power.

(Arthur Wallis)

6 November

'Then he opened their minds so they could understand the Scriptures'. (Luke 24:45)

Suggested reading Psalm 119: 9-24

Mr. B, our Religious Education teacher had been a Congregational minister and though not an evangelical, he was a kind and genial man. He was also an occasional sports teacher and at times, he would take us for rugby or cricket.

To his credit, he never started a RE lesson without saying 'we must begin with prayer'. And he would commit the lesson and pupils to God in prayer.

As youngsters, we sometimes joked he should have prayed for us before we went on to the rugby pitch. We felt more in need of prayer on the field than we did in the classroom.

I have forgotten much of what he taught us----and that is perhaps not altogether a bad thing---but I can still remember his prayers.

Are there not times when we perhaps pray more for our physical and material wants than we do for our spiritual needs?

Jesus taught us to pray 'Give us today our daily bread', so it is certainly not wrong to ask for our physical and material needs to be met. The challenge is—do we pray regularly and with the same intensity for our spiritual needs?

Before we read the Bible or attend worship, do we pray with the Psalmist, 'open my eyes that I may see wonderful things in your law'? (Psalm) 119:18)?

Before we go to school or work, do we pray 'lead us not into temptation, deliver us from evil'?

As each new day begins, do we ask that it might be a day when we 'grow in the grace and knowledge of our Lord and Saviour Jesus Christ'? (2 Peter3:18)

Do we take to heart the words of Jesus: 'Seek first his kingdom and his righteousness, and all these things will be given to you as well'? (Matthew 6:33)

The main thing is to make sure that the main thing remains the main thing.

(Anon)

7 November

'Therefore, just as sin entered the world through one man, and death through sin, and in this way, death came to all men, because all sinned'. (Romans 5:12)

Suggested reading Genesis 3: 17-24

'Do not put the suitcases back in the garage loft until I am there to help you'. These were the clear instructions of my wife, as we returned from our holiday in Scotland.

That evening, having travelled from Fort William during the day, I obeyed, but in the morning, I took matters into my own hands. Pat was not about, so I climbed the ladder, put the suitcases back in the loft and then, as I came down, I fell off the ladder and crashed to the floor. My descent was much quicker than my ascent!

'Help, Pat, I've fallen', I cried----and the result, a badly dislocated, broken wrist which required surgery. Oh, the pain and the misery because I disobeyed the wife¬

Ironically, all the pain and misery in this world is the result of Adam having obeyed his wife. 'She also gave some to her husband, who was with her, and he ate it'. (Genesis 3:6) Adam obeyed Eve but in so doing he was disobeying God. 'You are free to eat from any tree in the garden, but you must not eat from the tree of the knowledge of good and evil'. (Genesis 2:16-17)

People often wonder why this world is as it is but the answer is to be found in the early chapters of Genesis. Adam fell into sin and this has resulted in a broken world and a dislocated society. And that is why, today, we have 'man at enmity with God', 'man at war with man' and 'creation groaning' (Romans 8:22) There is no other explanation.

Oh, the misery and pain brought upon the human race because Adam disobeyed his Maker and fell into sin.

Man is not evolving upwards towards a knowledge of God. He was created with a knowledge of God and has been going down the other way ever since.

(Vince Havner)

8 November

'The God of heaven will set up a kingdom that will never be destroyed------It will crush all those kingdoms and bring them to an end, but it will itself endure for ever'. (Daniel 2:44)

Suggested reading Hebrews 12:18-29

It was the late 1950s, and a retired couple moved into the house next door. The following morning, there was a knock on the door, and we were faced with an anxious neighbour.

'Are these houses safe'? He stammered.
'Yes', my mother replied, 'why do you ask'?
'Well', he said, 'a train went by last night, and everything on the mantlepiece shook'

With my father having been a stationmaster and living in station houses, we had become immune to any shaking caused by a passing train. And so, we were able to assure our troubled neighbour that there was nothing to be concerned about.

On reflection, our houses were behind the Lancaster to Morecambe railway line, and whilst most trains just trundled by, the one exception was the Ulster Express, usually powered by a Royal Scot Class engine, which roared by at 10.30 each evening.

An awesome earthquake took place at Mount Sinai, but that is just a pale shadow of what lies ahead. Before us lies the dissolution of all things when God will undo and remake not only the earth but heaven as well.

How comforting and reassuring to know, our future can be built on something that can never be shaken: the Kingdom of Christ. As we trust Jesus as Saviour and submit to Him as King, we have a golden future and are secure for time and eternity. What are the passing, transient pleasures of this world, compared to eternal happiness in Christ?

The earth shall soon dissolve like snow. The sun forbear to shine. But God, who called me here below. Will be for ever mine.

(John Newton)

9 November

'In their hearts humans plan their course, but the Lord establishes their steps'. (Proverbs 16:9)

Suggested reading Psalm 37:23-40

I had reached the age of thirty but still had no driving licence. With a wife and two children, finances were rather tight, and with a good bus service in Morecambe, there was no real need to drive. In addition, friends were most supportive when I needed transport for preaching appointments.

The situation changed somewhat, when I gained a promotion at work, and for a number of jobs, a driving licence was an essential qualification. I, thus, began to take driving lessons and after one failed attempt, I passed the test in January 1979.

To my surprise and disappointment, no suitable vacancy became available, but in May 1979, I was approached by Ingleton Evangelical Church to prayerfully consider becoming their pastor. Ingleton was a rural area, with limited public transport, making car ownership something of a necessity. I was appointed pastor in October 1979, and without my own transport, pastoral visitation would have been incredibly difficult.

I learned to drive, thinking it would be beneficial to my career in the Civil Service, but the Lord knew that I needed to be able to drive for an altogether different reason.

How amazing is the providence of God but what is providence? Well, the basic meaning is set out in the first seven letters of the word-----p-r-o-v-i-d-e. God provides everything that is necessary for His purposes to be fulfilled in us. He might do so in ways unknown or mysterious to us, but always in ways which will be for our good and for His glory.

Either directly or indirectly, every providence has a tendency to the spiritual good of those who love God.

(Matthew Henry)

10 November

'For God so loved the world that he gave his one and only Son, that whoever believes in Him shall not perish but have eternal life'. (John 3:16)

Suggested reading 1 John 3:11-20

For most of my lifetime, Christmas greetings have come, occasionally by means of a telephone call but usually through a Christmas card. However, in recent years, we have received numerous greetings by e-mail.

In 2016, we received one which was rather disturbing. We thought D and B were our friends but their greeting said 'with OUT love'. As 't' is next to 'r' on the keyboard, I hope I was right in assuming that the intended greeting was 'with OUR love'.

Thankfully, our friendship has remained intact, so I am confident it was just a mistake on their part.

That first Christmas time, God sent far more than a card or an e-mail; He sent 'his one and only Son'. The One of whom He said, 'This is my Son, whom I love, with him I am well-pleased'. (Matthew 3:17)

God sent Jesus to take upon Himself human form at Bethlehem, in order that He might take upon Himself human sin at Calvary. The amazing love of God for a sinful and undeserving world, so 'that whoever believes in Him shall not perish but have eternal life'.

O love of God, how strong and true!
Eternal and yet ever new:
Uncomprehended and unbought,
Beyond all knowledge and all thought

(Horatius Bonar)

11 November

'No-one will be declared righteous in God's sight by the works of the law; rather through the law, we become conscious of our sin'. (Romans 3:20)

Suggested reading Galatians 3: 21-29

I was driving down the motorway, keeping to the 70mph speed limit, but for many miles cars had been speeding past me. But suddenly, everyone began to slow down. Why? An accident? Road works? Volume of traffic? No---in the distance---a police car. That police car---the presence of the law---had a restraining impact on speeding motorists.

In a similar way, a knowledge and understanding of the Ten Commandments acts as a restraint when men are tempted to do wrong. How imperative it is, therefore, that a knowledge of the commandments is passed on to future generations. Otherwise, our nation will continue in its downward spiral

I spoke at a nursing home service on the Ten Commandments. In conversation afterwards, an elderly lady thanked me and said, 'Preach the Ten Commandments and there is no need to preach anything else.

A sad comment, for whilst the Ten Commandments can restrain sin, they cannot remove sin. Indeed, the commandments reveal our sin and our need of Jesus---the only One who ever kept them perfectly and yet, amazingly, died for those who had broken them. 'The law was our guardian until Christ came that we might be justified by faith'. (Galatians 3:24)

God's law was given to reveal sin, not to remove it.

(John Blanchard)

12 November

> 'For since the creation of the world God's invisible qualities---his eternal power and divine nature---have been clearly seen, being understood from what has been made, so that people are without excuse'. (Romans 1:20)

Suggested reading Psalm 104:1-18

Visiting a garden centre, we unexpectedly met a Christian friend and his wife, who we had not seen for some considerable time. Having had a coffee together, we then went our separate ways.

Afterwards, we were just behind our friends as we queued at the check out to pay for our respective purchases.

Looking at his plants, Keith said to the assistant, 'Aren't they beautiful? Do you know the Maker'?

And then, offering the young woman a gospel, he asked, 'Have you ever read his book'?

Garden centres with their delightful sights and smells are always a joy to visit, and yet I suspect few ever recognise the hand of the Creator. Undoubtedly, many marvel and enjoy the beauty of flowers and plants but are taken up with 'created things, rather than the Creator'. (Romans1:25)

Not all of us can witness in the way my friend did, but how refreshing to be reminded that God has spoken through His creation. He has, however, spoken more intimately through His Word, and perhaps spiritual seed sown in the garden centre that day will yet bear fruit.

The heavens declare Thy glory, Lord,
In every star Thy wisdom shines;
but when our eyes behold Thy Word
We read Thy Name in fairer lines.

(Isaac Watts)

13 November

'The thief comes only to steal and kill and destroy'. (John 10:10

Suggested reading John 8:42-47

Arriving home early one afternoon, we were met by a distressed elderly neighbour who had a most disturbing story to tell. That morning, a man had knocked at his door, offering to prune the trees in his garden, and our neighbour had given his agreement.

Two hours later, having done the work, the man had demanded £500 in cash. Mr, C. did not have that amount of money in the house, and on being told this, the man had put him in his vehicle and driven him to the bank. Frightened and confused, Mr. C. had withdrawn the money and given it to the man.

The fraudster obviously felt he was on to a good thing, telling Mr. C. that there were tiles on his roof which needed fixing and he would be back in the morning. Mr. C. was crying as he related the story, blaming himself for being so 'foolish' and dreading the prospect of the man reappearing in the morning. I telephoned the police, who took the details and told me to immediately contact them in the unlikely event of the man returning.

The fraudster displayed all the marks of Satan: deceiving, stealing and destroying. And this is precisely what Satan has done to the human race. He has deceived multitudes into denying his existence and the existence of God. He has robbed children of their innocence, men and women of their dignity. He has destroyed families and relationships, with his activity all too evident in our world today.

Satan promises the best, but pays with the worst; he promises honour and pays with disgrace; he promises pleasure and pays with pain; he promises profit and pays with loss; he promises life and pays with death.

(Thomas Brooks)

14 November (cont.)

'The one who does what is sinful is of the devil, because the devil has been sinning from the beginning. The reason the Son of God appeared was to destroy the devil's work', (1 John 3:8)

Suggested reading Colossians 2:9-15

To my amazement, at a quarter past eight the next morning, the man drew up in his vehicle. I telephoned the police, and within minutes, three police vehicles were on the scene. Such was the activity that another neighbour called, thinking something catastrophic must have happened.

The man was arrested, and his van and equipment seized. It later transpired that he was out of prison 'on licence', having previously been convicted of defrauding elderly people.

I understand that the man was returned to prison, but I am not convinced that will be the end of his offending. At least, for the time being, he is detained and not able to continue his evil work.

The final word was not with the fraudster but with the police, who overpowered him and took his equipment. On the cross, Jesus disarmed and triumphed over Satan, and now all who trust in Christ share in His conquest. They are saved from the penalty and the power of sin, awaiting the day when they will be free from the very presence of sin.

The devil is still active but he is a defeated foe and his end is certain. 'The reason the Son of God appeared was to destroy the devil's work'. We praise God that, in Christ, the work has been, is being and will be fully accomplished.

Satan, as in his first temptation is still on the losing side.

(William Gurnall)

15 November

'My steps have held to your paths; my feet have not stumbled'. (Psalm 17:5)

Suggested reading Psalm 119: 129-136

My first wrist watch was a gift from my grandparents, when I passed the eleven plus examination. At that time, this was often the way in which children were rewarded and encouraged by parents and grandparents.

In the 1950s, watches had the sole purpose of telling the time, but that is far from being the case today. Besides telling the time, they now monitor your health, set out the number of steps you have taken in a day and are, generally, a mine of information.

For good health, the target has been set at ten thousand steps a day, and my watch vibrates on the rare occasions when I accomplish that feat. However, I understand that the ten thousand steps target is not rooted in science, and research suggests there are health benefits in lower levels of activity.

I have to confess I now look at my watch more to check my steps than I do to tell the time!

Our steps may have a bearing on our physical health, but they undoubtedly impact our spiritual health. Where we go and how we walk---either in the spirit or the flesh---determines what kind of a believer we are.

As we walk according to the Scriptures ((Psalm 119:133) and follow the example of Christ (1 Peter 2:21), so it is that we are kept from stumbling. (Jude 24) In the words of David, 'The Lord makes firm the steps of the one who delights in him'. (Psalm 37:23)

If you would walk with Jesus, follow the path of obedience. Saints have never had fellowship with Jesus when they have disobeyed him. Keep his statutes and observe his testimonies.

(Charles H. Spurgeon)

16 November

'There is no one righteous, not even one; there is no-one who understands; there is no one who seeks God'. (Romans 3:10-11)

Suggested reading Romans 7: 14-25

As a pastor in Ingleton, I was frequently asked to countersign passport application forms and photos. This I never minded doing, as I saw it as part of my service to the village community.

On the back of the passport photos, I had to write, 'I certify this is a true likeness of ------   ------'. Applicants were happy for me to write these words, and yet how often they protested 'Isn't it awful'? 'I don't look like that'. 'That's not me'.

But yes, it was them for, though the photos may not always have been flattering, the camera never lies!

The Bible tells us what we are really like and it is not an attractive picture. Therefore, our natural inclination is to say 'That's not me', and in our minds, we 'airbrush' ourselves.

Sadly, this is to escape from reality because the Bible does not lie. 'The heart is deceitful'. (Jeremiah 17:9) "There is no-one righteous'. (Romans 3:10) 'All have sinned'. (Romans 3:23)

It is only when we have accepted this true diagnosis of our condition, and come to Christ that He can begin to change us. However, even then, the picture will not be 'perfect' until either, we get to heaven or Jesus comes again. 'When Christ appears we shall be like him, for we shall see him as he is'. (1 John 3:3)

This life was not intended to be the place of our perfection but the preparation for it.

(Richard Baxter)

17 November

'Here is a trustworthy saying that deserves full acceptance: Christ Jesus came into the world to save sinners'. (1 Timothy 1:15)

Suggested reading Isaiah 9:2-7

Today is my birthday but I once had a birthday which I will never forget—because everyone else did. I woke early in the morning and Pat was very chatty, but no mention was made of my birthday. And so, after a while, I sang, 'Happy Birthday to me. Happy Birthday to me. Happy Birthday, dear John. Happy Birthday to me'.

Pat was apologetic, but she had no need to be because only the previous evening, she had been diagnosed with a potentially serious medical condition. It was, therefore, quite understandable that this dominated her thinking.

Just before 8 am, the telephone rang and it was my daughter. Joanna never forgets her dad's birthday and so cheerfully, I picked up the phone. 'How is mum'? Joanna asked. Mother and daughter then proceeded to talk for ten minutes and then the phone was put down. Cue for me to sing again, 'Happy Birthday to me. Happy Birthday to me-- ---------'

Early that evening, the phone rang again and it was my son, Andrew. This is amazing, I thought, he never remembers any birthday. 'Hello Andrew', I said. 'Hi, Dad', he responded, 'do you have my MOT certificate'? We chatted for a few minutes but no mention was made of my birthday, and on putting the phone down, again I sang, 'Happy Birthday to me. Happy birthday to me----'

My birthday had all but been forgotten, but in truth, I was not too concerned---I have reached an age where I perhaps prefer it to be forgotten, rather than be remembered. Far more serious is the fact that, increasingly, the birth of Jesus is being forgotten. More and more Christmas songs are now secular, and it is not easy to find a Christmas card, which has any reference to His birth. Christmas is now being celebrated as Xmas or a Winter Festival---the Incarnation of Jesus being all but ignored.

This is serious because when His birth is forgotten, so too is the purpose of His birth. 'Christ Jesus came into the world to save sinners'. Not just at Christmas time but every day, we need to remember that Jesus is a unique Person who came for a unique purpose.

Christ took our flesh upon him that he might take our sins upon him.

(Thomas Watson)

18 November

'In whom we have redemption, the forgiveness of sins'. (Colossians 1:14)

Suggested reading Matthew 18:21 -35

I was asked to take a funeral service in Leicester and not relishing a Monday morning drive, I decided to travel by train. The lady at the ticket office could not have been more helpful, advising me as to which was the cheapest way to travel.

The journey itself, with three changes, was not easy and with temperatures touching 30 degrees, I felt decidedly hot and uncomfortable. Thankfully all the trains were on time and the destination was reached safely.

The bereaved family kindly paid for my rail ticket and in due course the money was credited to my account.

As believers, we are on a journey from earth to heaven with numerous 'stops' and 'starts', and there are times when the route is difficult and uncomfortable. Wonderfully, our ticket has been paid for; not by ourselves or any human being---that is quite impossible. The ticket has been paid for by the Lord Jesus Christ and His death upon the cross.

What a price he paid and with it comes the absolute assurance that all, who are trusting in Him, will safely arrive at their heavenly destination.

The Lord Jesus has paid too high a price for our redemption to leave us in the enemy's hand.

(Charles H. Spurgeon)

19 November

'Now we are all here in the presence of God to listen to everything the Lord has commanded you to tell us'. (Acts 10:33)

Suggested reading Acts 20:7-12

I have memories of many of the men and women at my boyhood church in Morecambe, even if not always for spiritual reasons.

When the sermon started, the organist Mr. R. got up from the organ stool, to sit next to his wife in the choir. Within minutes, he was in the 'land of nod', and remained so until, as the sermon concluded, he was vigorously nudged in the ribs by Mrs. R. In my imagination, I used to imagine the congregation singing the final hymn, unaccompanied, with Mr. R. still asleep.

Another 'sleeper' was Fred----a chimney sweep and property repairer by day, which also included the Lord's Day. He worshipped every Sunday night but usually arrived just before the sermon started. Perhaps, even sooner than Mr. R. Fred was asleep, and he too was dependant on the good offices of his wife, to arouse him for the last hymn.

On a Church Anniversary weekend, Fred related how, as a baby, he had been brought to the church by his mother, and had slept throughout the services. A man was heard to quip, 'Nothing has changed, Fred---you still do'.

Sometimes 'sleeping in church' is excusable if a person has a medical condition or, for example, has come off an overnight shift, but otherwise it is an insult to God. The Word of God is being faithfully expounded, but needy souls do not hear it because they are asleep.

In Acts 20, when Eutychus fell asleep as Paul preached, there was a temporary consequence. But for sleeping souls, there can be not just temporal but also eternal consequences. Let us not insult Almighty God and do possible harm to our souls, by ever using worship as an excuse to catch up on our sleep.

The seeming peace a sinner has is not from the knowledge of his happiness but the ignorance of his danger.

(Thomas Watson)

20 November

'So you also must be ready, because the Son of Man will come at an hour when you do not expect him'. (Matthew 24:44)

Suggested reading Luke 12:35-48

At the height of the coronavirus pandemic, we started to get a fortnightly supermarket delivery. And, in those uncertain times, we much appreciated this regular supply of food.

The allotted time for delivery was always between 10 am and 12 pm, but invariably it was nearer to 12 pm than 10 am. However, one morning, we were taught a valuable lesson for having 'nipped' out for a few minutes, and returning at 10.05 am, we discovered the delivery van had already been and gone.

There was a note behind the door but none of the provisions we had ordered. We missed out because the delivery had been sooner than we had expected.

Through our presumption and carelessness, we missed out on temporary, earthly provisions, but there is a far greater danger. Through presumption and carelessness, we can miss out on eternal and spiritual benefits.

The Second Coming of Christ is affirmed by the Apostles, pronounced again and again by Jesus Himself, and yet, multitudes think it either will not happen or will not be in their lifetime. The Bible is quite clear that Jesus can come at any time, and therefore, we need to be ready all the time.

Since he may come any day, it is wise to be ready every day

(Hudson Taylor)

21 November

'Let us not give up meeting together, as some are in the habit of doing, but let us encourage one another---and all the more as you see the Day approaching'. (Hebrews 10:25)

Psalm 122

One Sunday, many years before the advent of Sat/Nav. I was preaching in Ripon, with hospitality being provided at a home, just a few miles away from the church. After the morning service, I followed the young family to their home and had an enjoyable time of fellowship.

As the time for the evening service approached, it was suggested I set off earlier and get to the church in good time. This I agreed to but Pat has always said I have no sense of direction, and on this occasion, how true that was.

A one-way system and my own unfamiliarity with the city contributed to the confusion, and when eventually, I did arrive at the church, a search party was about to be launched! I can still remember the time---it was two minutes after the service should have started.

On recalling the incident, a preacher explained it was better to arrive two minutes late for a service, rather than just two minutes before. His reasoning was that, if you arrive with just two minutes to spare, the church is annoyed at your lack of punctuality. But, if you arrive two minutes late, the church is so relieved to see you, they still give you a warm reception.

Sometimes, as believers, we find it difficult to 'make our way to church'. It might be a backslidden heart, tensions in the church, a preoccupation with other things, but the result is 'we lose our way' where worship and fellowship are concerned.

Invariably, when we do not want to be there, that is the time we should be there. In Psalm 73, the psalmist was beset with doubts and misgivings 'till I entered the sanctuary of God'. (Psalm 73: 17) Worship is appointed and commanded by God---it is both pleasing to Him and of benefit to us. Therefore, let us be there if at all possible.

We must meet with the Church Militant if ever we hope to meet with the Church Triumphant. Together in grace, Gods people make ready for glory.

(Malcolm Watts)

22 November

'Let me die the death of the righteous, and may my final end be like theirs'. (Numbers 23:10)

Suggested reading Luke 2:25-35

I knew a fine Christian man who, as he grew older, became anxious not about death but about dying. How would he die? What would be the means of his departure from this world? He shared these concerns with his minister, who encouraged him to 'take it to the Lord in prayer'.

Some years later, I was preaching in Morecambe when I heard that this man had passed away the previous evening. I called to see his wife and she had a wonderful story to tell.

The previous day had been their diamond wedding anniversary, and the man had read the greeting cards, entertained friends, and enjoyed a quiet family meal. At 8pm, feeling rather tired, he had retired to bed. When his wife later took him a drink, she discovered he had quietly passed into the presence of Christ. A wonderful end to a wonderful day, but also a wonderful answer to prayer.

What a Friend we have in Jesus, All our sins and griefs to bear!
What a privilege to carry, Everything to God in prayer.
O what peace we often forfeit, O what needless pain we bear,
All because we do not carry, Everything to God in prayer.

Have we trials and temptations? Is there trouble anywhere?
We should never be discouraged: Take it to the Lord in prayer.
Can we find a friend so faithful, Who will all our sorrows share?
Jesus knows our every weakness: Take it to the Lord in prayer.

(Joseph Medlicott Scriven)

23 November

'So in everything, do to others what you would have them do to you, for this sums up the Law and the Prophets'. (Matthew 7:12)

Suggested reading 'Mark 10:46-52

Torch Trust exists 'to enable blind and partially sighted people to encounter Jesus, grow in their faith and thrive in Christian community'. For a number of years, I have been privileged to speak at their meetings, and also to be in attendance at Torch holidays. Without exception, these have always been challenging and encouraging experiences.

Blind and partially sighted people are generally treated with patience and respect but that is not always the case. Taxi drivers refusing to have guide dogs in their vehicles and motorists shouting abuse at pedestrian crossings; these are just some of the indignities which the blind and partially sighted occasionally face.

In cafes and restaurants, buttering toast, cutting up meat, putting milk in coffee, locating the salt and pepper pots etc. etc. etc. These are everyday tasks to which most of us do not give a moment's thought, but that is not so with the blind and partially sighted. Whilst, in shops, purchases have to be explained, touched or smelt before they are bought.

It is not just their lack of bitterness and complaining which I find heart-warming, but their spirit of thanksgiving. I can truthfully say it is amongst their ranks that I have fond the most appreciative of believers. Thankful for each new day, for fresh air, sunshine, food, kindnesses received, and supremely, thankful for their Saviour Jesus and for Christian fellowship.

What a challenge. Limiting and restricting their disability might be but no bitterness or complaining. A rebuke to many of us when we become stressed and irritated by minor frustrations in life. What an encouragement. Spiritual sight is so much more important even than physical sight. Many of these dear people, having 'seen' Jesus with the eye of faith, now walk in newness of life. Their contentment and joy--- an encouragement to behold.

So much has been given to me, I have no time to ponder over that which has been denied.

(Helen Keller)

24 November

'Like the rest, we were by nature objects of wrath'.
(Ephesians 2:3)

Suggested reading 2 Samuel 12; 13-23

When he was only a few weeks old, the brain of our adopted son, Aaron, was severely damaged. This meant he was not able to speak and lacked capacity when it came to understanding.

One year, we were on holiday, staying at a cottage in Derbyshire, when an elderly believer said something which I had never thought about before. 'How wonderful to think', she said, 'that Aaron has never knowingly sinned'. It was wonderful. Too many times I have sinned, knowing quite well what I was doing, but Aaron, during his twenty-eight years, never knowingly sinned.

However, because of Adam's sin, Aaron's was still a sinner, and therefore dependant on the grace of God and the redeeming blood of Christ. It is my conviction, that all who die in infancy or without the mental capacity to understand the gospel, they are covered by the blood of Christ.

When David's seven-day-old baby died, he said, 'Can I bring him back again? I will go to him, but he will not return to me'. (2 Samuel 12:23) David knew where he was going----'I will dwell in the house of the Lord forever'. (Psalm 23:6) -----and in going to heaven, he was assured that he was going to where his child already was. We can have the same confidence about the future of infants and of all who are mentally incapacitated.

I believe that the Lord Jesus who said, "Of such is the kingdom of heaven" does daily and constantly receive into His loving arms those tender ones who are only shown and then snatched away to heaven.

(Charles H. Spurgeon)

25 November

'There will be terrible times in the last days. -------lovers of pleasure rather than lovers of God' (2 Timothy 3:1 and 4)

Suggested reading Isaiah 58:8-14

One Sunday morning the weather forecaster, having told us it was going to be a misty, foggy morning added, 'So do take care if you are driving to a car boot sale'.

His words came back to me when, later that morning, I was almost late for my preaching appointment in Chorley. For several minutes, I was held up at a roundabout, as cars queued to get into a field for----a car boot sale.

What a contrast to when I was a boy in the 1950s. There were around thirty children in the houses surrounded our home, and of those, only two did not go to Sunday School. They stood out because they did not go to Sunday School----today those figures would be reversed.

Is this not an indication of the low spiritual state of the nation when sports activities are more important than Sunday School, and when people would rather congregate at the CBS than worship at the C of E, URC or the A of G?

It still holds true that 'righteousness exalts a nation' (Proverbs 14:34), and whilst we continue to reject God and the Bible, the moral declension will continue. We will not be an exalted nation.

What greater calamity can fall upon a nation than the loss of worship? Then all things go to decay----literature becomes frivolous and society lives on trifles.

(Ralph Waldo Emerson)

26 November

> 'But while everyone was sleeping, his enemy came and sowed weeds among the wheat and went away'. (Matthew 13:25)

Suggested reading: Psalm 126

Before moving into our home in Ingleton, Pat and I spent a whole afternoon taking out the weeds in what had once been a vegetable plot. By the time we finished, our backs were aching but we were pleased to see the soil now free of weeds.

A few months later, we made our move and what was there to be seen in the garden? Dahlias? Chrysanthemums? A rose garden? Nothing of the sort. Instead weeds---hundreds of them. Weeds of every type and description.

For weeks we had done nothing but that did not mean nothing had happened. On the contrary, weeds had grown and taken over.

This is a picture of our society today. In many schools and homes, the Bible is not being taught. In some churches the gospel is not being preached. Nothing is being done but that does not mean nothing is happening. For whilst the good seed is not being sown, Satan is busy sowing his seed and the results are to be seen everywhere. Weeds of unbelief, thorns of impurity, thistles of rebellion.

In order to counteract the work of Satan, how vital it is to sow the seed of the gospel. To imitate those early believers who, when 'scattered, preached the word where ever they went'. (Acts 8:4l

Every age is an age for evangelism. God has no grandchildren.

(Eugene. L. Smith)

27 November

'Follow my example as I follow the example of Christ'. (1 Corinthians 11:1)

Suggested reading 1 Corinthians 4:14-21

Dr. Martyn Lloyd-Jones was an assistant to the Royal Physician, Sir Thomas Horder, before accepting an invitation to pastor a church in South Wales. He was then, for thirty years, the minister of Westminster Chapel in London, becoming one of the best-known preachers of the C20th.

I was privileged to hear him preach on three occasions, and was privileged to meet him in person in 1971. He was preaching at Banks Methodist Church near Southport, after the service, a group of us spent time with him in the vestry.

His books and tapes were a tremendous help to me and he was to influence me greatly in my ministry. Whatever movements arose or bandwagons were passing, 'the Doctor' just continued faithfully preaching the Word. This is what I sought to do, and though my preaching was a 'pale shadow' of his, the Lord was pleased to bless my feeble efforts.

It is good to be inspired by the example of a godly believer, and I thank God for Dr. Martyn Lloyd-Jones but there are dangers. The best of men are, at best, still men and whilst we can honour and respect them, our eyes must always be upon the one perfect man---the Lord Jesus Christ. Even godly men can stumble, and sadly, sometimes believers have stumbled with them because their eyes were on a man and not fixed on 'Jesus, the pioneer and perfecter of faith' (Hebrews 12:2)

We follow men in so far as they 'follow the example of Christ'. (1 Corinthians 11:1)

Between Jesus and whomsoever else in the world, there is no possible comparison.

(Napoleon Bonaparte)

28 November

'I am the gate; whoever enters through me will be saved'. (John 10:9)

Suggested reading Luke 13: 22-30

One afternoon, I had to take my wife and Aaron for an overnight stay at Manchester Children's Hospital. I drove to Manchester, left them at the hospital and then made my way back to Ingleton.

As I drew up outside the house, I began to feel my pockets for the house key. No key could be found either in my pockets or in the vehicle. I checked our 'secret location' in the garden, but still no key. I tried the front door and the back door without success and, as the windows were all shut, access through an open window was not an option.

I decided to telephone Pat at the hospital but as it was in the days before mobile phones, I had to walk to the local telephone kiosk. Eventually, I got through to the ward and I said to Pat, 'The house key, do you know where it is'? There was an ominous silence and then Pat said, 'Oh, I don't know what I was thinking of. I locked the door and then I put the key through the letter box'. I forget what my reply was but I hope it was gracious. I returned to my house, not quite knowing what my next step would be.

A short time earlier, we had had an extension built at the back of the house, and so I applied some pressure to the bathroom and bedroom windows. There was no movement but when I pressed against the window in the conservatory, it moved, and with even more pressure, it came open. My problem was not yet altogether solved, as the window was several feet off the ground. Hoping no-one was watching, I placed a wheelie bin under the window, clambered on to the sill, fought my way through a jungle of plants and eventually landed inside the house. And there, behind the door, was the key.

That day, there was a back window into my house but there is no back door or back window into heaven. How many are trying a back door--- seeking to be good, helping other people, going to church? All commendable things but of themselves they cannot get us to heaven. There is only one way to heaven and Jesus is that Way, only one door and Jesus is that Door.

Christ is the final word about salvation. Here, he is not only without a peer, he is without a competitor.

(G. Campbell Morgan)

29 November

'An inheritance that can never perish spoil or fade---kept in heaven for you'. (1 Peter 1:4)

Suggested reading 1 Timothy 6:1-10

Early Sunday morning and Pat gets a text message saying there is suspected fraudulent activity on our bank account, and there is a number we have to ring. We are busy, getting ready to travel to services and I say, 'probably a scam---ignore it'.

Similar texts appear during the day and when we arrive home, I notice there are four messages on the answer machine, telling us to make contact with the bank. I still think it is a scam but we decide that we will call in at the bank tomorrow.

This we do and it is no scam. Someone has been using Pat's card details in Cyprus, but thankfully, this suspected fraudulent activity has been picked up by the bank. Consequently, we have suffered no financial loss, but Pat's card has to be destroyed and she has to wait a few days, before she can be issued with a new one.

Earthly wealth is vulnerable, not least because of the cunning dishonesty of thieves. They find ever more sophisticated ways to 'break in and steal'. By contrast the treasures we have in heaven----salvation, eternal joy, Jesus Himself---these are burglar-proof and fraud-proof.

Money is a blessing if used right ----to support our families, to help the needy, to encourage the work of the gospel. But it can also be a snare and a danger, if the acquisition of earthly, material wealth becomes our central aim and motivation.

If your treasure is on earth, you are going from it: if it is in heaven, you are going to it.

(Anon)

30 November

'The word of God is alive and active. Sharper than any double-edged sword, it penetrates even to dividing soul and spirit, joints and marrow; it judges the thoughts and attitudes of the heart'. (Hebrew 4:12)

Suggested reading Jeremiah 23:25-32

I have in my possession words from Romans 14:12, written by hand on a piece of paper, over fifty years ago. The words are 'each of us will give an account of ourselves to God', and they were written by a man who attended my church and had a remarkable story to tell.

Up to the age of fifty, R. had been 'a man of the world'---an executive in the motor trade, but already divorced several times. Of his own admittance, work had been his god, and he had been part of the 'swinging sixties'. He quoted the words attributed to Einstein, in order to describe those years: 'Insanity---the ability to repeat the same mistakes whilst expecting a different outcome'.

One day, in the early 1980s, he was on a management course in Thetford, Norfolk---a financial course dealing with profit and loss accounts. As he walked by a small Methodist Church, with a 'wayside pulpit', he read these words, 'Each of us will give an account of ourselves to God'. R. was so struck by what he had read that he wrote them down, as soon as he got to the seminar.

As an executive in the motor trade, accounts were important to him, but this was an account, he had never previously thought about. For the first time, he began to think seriously about his relationship with God, and this was the start of a journey which led him to repentance and to faith in Christ.

For the next thirty years, R. lived a faithful, consistent Christian life, becoming chairman of the local Christian bookshop, taking books and CDs to churches and events over a wide area. He was eager for others to grasp the wonder of the faith, which he had embraced in mid-life.

The Bible is divinely inspired. And we must never underestimate the power of the Word of God to convict and to change human hearts. R's story is also an encouragement to churches and individuals who display scriptural verses.

While other books inform, and some few reform, this one book transforms.

(A.T.Pierson)

BIBLE -READINGS DECEMBER

1 December

'For the Lord himself will come down from heaven, with a loud command, with the voice of the archangel and with the trumpet call of God'. (1 Thessalonians 4:16)

Suggested reading 1 Thessalonians 1

Miss W. was an elderly believer who would never have a television in her home, but appreciated hearing the news and listening to church services on the radio. Being somewhat deaf, the volume was always rather loud. Visiting her, one afternoon, she had an amusing but also a challenging tale to tell.

She had been listening to the news, but had dozed off, only to be aroused by the sound of a trumpet. In her drowsy condition, she had got up from her chair and rushed to the window, quite certain it heralded the return of Christ.

The news had been followed by a brass band concert, and that was the trumpet she had heard but how wonderful to be so ready and anticipating His return.

As we enter into December, we are approaching the season of Advent, when we are reminded how God intervened in human affairs, by sending his Son to be our Saviour. But the message of Advent is not just that Jesus came but also that Jesus is coming. Therefore, we think about both his first and his second advent.

During this month, many will think of His first coming in weakness at Bethlehem, but few will consider that day when He will come again in power and great glory. Through repentance and faith, we receive Jesus as Saviour, and the purpose of His first advent is then accomplished in us.

We are now in the period of time between His two advents, and so we wait and watch and work, in order that we may be 'unashamed before Him at His coming'. (1 John 2:28)

Christ hath told us he will come, but not when, that we might never put off our clothes, or put out the candle.

(William Gurnall)

2 December

'They are darkened in their understanding and separated from the life of God because of the ignorance that is in them due to the hardening of their hearts'. (Ephesians 4:18)

Suggested reading Luke11:33-36

Pat and I were courting and having a week's holiday, we bought a 'roundabout' ticket, which enabled us to travel cheaper on the train. So, in order to initiate Pat in my love of steam trains, we travelled on the Keighley to Haworth railway. It was a gorgeous July day, and imagining myself to be the engine driver, I put my head out of the window. Not the wisest of moves for, within minutes, I felt discomfort in my right eye---no doubt a speck of soot from the engine. Pat, examining the eye, could see nothing, but the eye watered, and the pain continued throughout the evening, causing me to have a disturbed night.

The next day we caught the train to Keswick, in order to attend the annual Christian convention, but my eye was still painful. On arriving in Keswick, we stumbled across a doctor's surgery, and the receptionist said I could have an appointment at 2pm. This I gladly accepted, and in no time at all, the kind doctor had removed the speck of coal dust from my eye.

What a relief! The pain went and I could see again. We then went to the Convention, and I could benefit from the Word preached---something that would not have been possible if my eye had not been restored.

If our physical eyes are good, we can perceive objects as they really are, and move with safety and confidence. But if our eyes are defective, then our perception of objects becomes confused and we are liable to run into danger. We have a natural eye, but we also have a spiritual eye. This is the mind which guides us spiritually and morally, enabling us to glorify God. But if our minds are darkened through sin, then all of our conversation and conduct will be affected. Instead of glorifying God, we will seek pleasure, possessions and the approval of others. Do we need to go to Jesus---the Divine Optician---and ask Him to heal our spiritual eyes?

The human intellect, even in its fallen state, is an awesome work of God, but it lies in darkness, until it has been illuminated by the Holy Spirit.

(A. W. Tozer)

3 December

'Therefore, since we are surrounded by such a great cloud of witnesses, let us throw off everything that hinders and the sin that so easily entangles. And let us run with perseverance the race marked out for us, fixing our eyes on

Jesus, the pioneer and perfecter of our faith'. (Hebrews 12:1-2)

Suggested reading 2 Timothy 4:9-18

The Sports Day at the junior school in Ingleton was always a special occasion, and for a number of years, I had the privilege of starting the races. In addition to the traditional races, there were also the children's classics such as the sack race, the egg and spoon race, the three-legged race, the slow bicycle race and the tug of war. There was usually fierce competition, as children sought to gain points for their houses.

The most amusing race was always the pre-school race for the three- to - four-year -olds. They would start well, until distracted by the sight or sound of mum, dad or grandparents urging them on. It was then that they would stop or stumble, and be overtaken by the few whose eyes were still on the finishing tape.

Sadly, this can happen to believers. We can become distracted by our circumstances or the pleasures of this world, and taking our eyes off Jesus, we can stumble and fall.

Paul often compared the Christian life to a race, emphasising the need for full commitment and perseverance. ' But one thing I do. Forgetting what is behind and straining toward what is ahead, I press on toward the goal to win the prize for which God has called me heavenward in Christ Jesus'. (Philippians 3:13-14)

May we, with the Apostle Paul, press on towards the finishing tape, fixing 'our eyes on Jesus'.

By perseverance the snail reached the ark

(Charles H. Spurgeon)

4 December

'When the woman saw that the fruit of the tree was good for food and pleasing to the eye, and also desirable for gaining wisdom, she took some and ate it. She also gave some to her husband, who was with her, and he ate it'. (Genesis 3:6)

Suggested reading 1 Thessalonians 3

One of my granddaughters always had a sweet tooth. I recall one occasion when sleep was taking a hold, and she saw a 'sticky toffee' pudding on the table. For a few moments her eyes opened and flickered, but sleep eventually got the better of her.

Due to my carelessness, this trait in my granddaughter was almost to be her downfall. Foolishly, I was placing out my medication when this two - year- old came into the room. Her eyes sparkled at the sight of these sweet coloured tablets, and before I could intervene, she had popped one in her mouth.

Desperate to prevent her from swallowing the medication, I put my fingers in her mouth and managed to grab the tablet. The result was an upset granddaughter and a chastened grandfather!

As with Eve in the Garden of Eden, Satan seeks to make sin attractive and irresistible, but how often it ends in tears and sadness. Satan used the same tactic with Jesus in the wilderness. 'After fasting forty days and forty nights, he was hungry. The tempter came to him and said "If you are the Son of God, tell these stones to become bread". (Matthew 4:2-3)

How tempting that must have been for a hungry man, but Jesus resisted the devil and so can we, as we keep close to Jesus, and as we seek, each day, to be filled with His Spirit.

Unless there is within us that which is above us, we shall soon yield to that which is about us.

(P.T. Forsyth)

5 December

'A false witness will not go unpunished, and whoever pours out lies will not go free'. (Proverbs 19:5)

Suggested reading Psalm 12

In February 1970, a murder took place in Overton, a village five miles from the seaside town of Morecambe. The victim was an antiques dealer, and though he was not known to me, he was a customer of the bank where I was employed.

A young colleague at the bank lived in Overton, and as part of their enquiries, the police interviewed every resident of the village. The murder had taken place on a Tuesday evening, and the young man was asked to account for his whereabouts on that particular night. That evening, as part of his banking studies, he should have been at the local College of Further Education but, unknown to his parents, instead of going to college, he had gone to the cinema.

Interviewed, in the presence of his parents, he foolishly told the police that he had been at the college. When checks were made at the college, his deceit was soon uncovered and the young man became a prime suspect. Consequently, he arrived at work, one morning, in an ill-fitting suit as his own clothes had all been taken away for forensic examination.

It is tempting to lie when we think it is to our benefit but sin always has a negative effect upon our lives. 'White lies', 'being economical with the truth', 'exaggerating', 'half-truths' are all sins of the mouth, and we are warned 'be sure that your sin will find you out'. (Numbers 32:23)

To tell the truth results in a good conscience and is pleasing to the Godhead, for God cannot lie (Numbers 23:19) and Jesus is 'the faithful and true witness'. (Revelation 3:14) Whatever the cost, may we be enabled to 'speak the truth, the whole truth and nothing but the truth'.

Liars pervert the end for which God created speech.

(Thomas Brooks)

6 December (Cont.)

'This man was handed over to you by God's deliberate plan and foreknowledge; and you, with the help of wicked men, put him to death by nailing him to the cross'. (Acts2:23)

Suggested reading Luke 23:13-25

On the Tuesday evening of the murder, I had been with my girlfriend at the same cinema as my work colleague, and we had a brief chat at the interval. When re-interviewed by the police, he told the truth and gave my name as someone who could verify his alibi. I then had a visit at work from the Lancashire Constabulary and it was a very uneasy interview.

As bank employees, we had knowledge of the financial accounts of the deceased, and therefore had a motive for the murder. I was asked to give a signed statement and my girlfriend was subjected to a similar procedure. To be suspected of murder when innocent was an unnerving experience, and I was thankful there was no further follow-up.

A local man was later arrested and sentenced for the crime, but it was a miscarriage of justice, and after four years in prison, he was released. I cannot imagine what agonies he must have gone through: arrested, tried, found guilty and sentenced, when all the time he was an innocent man.

Later, this man was converted and having been forgiven by God, he was able to forgive those who had falsely accused him. For a number of years, I worshipped at the same church as his sister, and having become a pastor, he poignantly told of his experiences in the bestselling book Killing Time.

In 1970, the police, the judge and jury considered the man to be guilty, but Pilate and the Jewish authorities knew that Jesus was not guilty, and yet they still sentenced Him to be crucified. This was just part of the suffering Jesus endured, and yet it was all within the 'deliberate plan' of God. The innocent One had to take my guilt so that I---the guilty one--- might be counted innocent in the sight of God.

Who delivered up Jesus to die? Not Judas, for money; not Pilate for fear; not the Jews, for envy; but the Father for love!

(Octavius Winslow)

7 December

'Cast all your anxiety on him because he cares for you'. (1 Peter 5:7)

Suggested reading Luke 12:22-31

We were enjoying a family holiday in Derbyshire with our children and grandchildren. But the joy was broken on the fifth morning, when my daughter, Joanna, announced, 'We will have to go back to Leeds'. Why? Was someone ill? Had their house been broken into? No---they had forgotten to feed the goldfish.

This news was met with incredulity by most of the family, and it was suggested that Joanna could always buy more goldfish, if the fish were floating when she got back from holiday.

Joanna was not amused, and after breakfast, her husband was dispatched on a 180 mile round journey to 'rescue the perishing'. We waited with baited breath, but eventually the phone call came to tell us that the fish were still alive and swimming. My hope of a fish and chip supper had disappeared!

Joanna's care and concern for the gold fish was amusing, but God's care and concern for His children is truly amazing. Human beings are not just another animal. They are made 'in the image of God' (Genesis 1:27). They are the 'crown' of God's creation (Psalm 8:5) and therefore, he has a care for them which does not extend to fish or birds or animals.

The apostles Peter and Paul knew what it was to be tempted and tried, but these experiences only confirmed their confidence in God. 'He cares for you'. (1 Peter 5:7) 'My God will meet all your needs'. (Philippians 4:19) We can have the same confidence and assurance because our God is 'ever faithful, ever sure'.

God has made us a little lower than the angels, but he has made us a little higher than the animals.

(A.W. Tozer)

8 December

'Son, go and work today in the vineyard'. (Matthew 21: 28)

Suggested reading Hebrews 3:7-19

For many years my day began at 7am with the 'Today' programme on Radio Four. Jack de Manio, John Timpson, Brian Redhead, John Humphreys---some of the great names in broadcasting---have all introduced this early morning programme.

One morning, I was listening to the programme in bed when Pat awoke and exclaimed 'I can't believe it is Friday already'. It had been a particularly hectic week, but I had to explain, it was in fact not Friday but Thursday.

Whether it appears to drag or to race by, time is a precious gift from God---too precious to be squandered or wasted. The proverb says 'procrastination is the thief of time', and how often time is wasted because we keep putting off what we should be doing today.

It isn't just Radio Four which has a Today programme---so, too, does the Bible. The time to repent of sin is today. The time to stop backsliding is today. The time to start serving Jesus is today.

What about tomorrow? We can only assume that tomorrow must be a remarkable day, with more than twenty- four hours because so much is going to be done tomorrow.

One of these days is none of these days

(Anon)

9 December

'All Scripture is God-breathed----' (2 Timothy 3:16)

Suggested reading 2 Peter 1:12-21

'What is Christmas all about'? A number of local junior schools were invited to the church to consider this question, and we sought to answer it in a number of imaginative and appropriate ways.

It was a Friday morning and I began my contribution by telling the children what all the football scores would be, the next day, in the Premiership, Aston Villa 3 West Ham United 2, Leeds United 1 Tottenham Hotspur 0, and Liverpool 2 Arsenal 2.

The children were not impressed and told me I was guessing. They could not have been more right for when I checked on the Saturday, most of my 'prophesied' results were wrong, never mind the actual scores!

I could not tell what was to happen even tomorrow, but the Old Testament prophets foretold with pinpoint accuracy where, when and how Jesus would be born. There were two Bethlehems, but 700 years before the event, Micah was quite specific, saying that Jesus would be born in Bethlehem, Ephrathah.

Fulfilled prophecy is powerful evidence that 'prophets, though human, spoke from God, as they were carried along by the Holy Spirit'. Unassailable evidence that the Bible is the Word of God.

The Bible is none other than the voice of him that sitteth upon the throne. Every book of it, every chapter of it, every syllable of it, every letter of it, is the direct utterance of the Most High.

(John William Burgon)

10 December

'Whoever conceals their sins does not prosper, but the one who confesses and renounces them finds mercy'. (Proverbs 28:13)

Suggested reading 2 Corinthians 7:5-12

One Saturday night, I was giving out gospel leaflets in Morecambe, and I got into conversation with a man coming out of one of the pubs. During the course of the conversation, he told me it was quite probable that he would commit adultery that night, but it did not matter because he would be at confession in the morning.

Sadly, I had to tell him God would not even hear his confession because there is true repentance but also false repentance.

I was reminded of this conversation, sometime later, when listening to Gardeners' Question time, and the question was asked: 'How can I peel an onion without crying? It is an act which produces tears, but they are never tears of joy or sadness---no tears are shed because one's eyes are smarting.

Is that not a picture of false repentance? Both believers and unbelievers can claim to be sorry for their sin, but sometimes we are sorry not for the sin itself but rather for the consequences. We are smarting and it is that which produces the tears and a profession of repentance.

God demands true repentance. We gain nothing by concealing or excusing our sins, but we obtain mercy by confessing and renouncing them.

Sin may be the occasion of great sorrow, when there is no sorrow for sin.

(John Owen)

11 December

'I know that through your prayers and God's provision of the Spirit of Jesus Christ, what has happened to me will turn out for my deliverance'. (Philippians 1:19)

Suggested reading Acts 16:1-10

I had been pastoring the church in Ingleton for twelve years, when I felt that perhaps I and the church would benefit from a change. I was about to share this with my church officers when two providences stopped me in my tracks.

Conscious that we were an aging congregation, the church had been praying for young families to join us. Most unexpectedly, a young family committed themselves to the church, and I did not feel that their arrival should coincide with the announcement of my departure.

The second providence concerned the church building. Major work needed to be carried out, which would involve substantial strengthening of the whole building. It was to be a costly exercise, but I was humbled when I saw the selfless generosity of so many in the fellowship. Their sacrificial commitment to the church convinced me it could not be the Lord's will for me to go.

Thus, I stayed on in the church as pastor for another eighteen years and it was right that I did so.

Paul, with Silas and Timothy, were 'kept by the Holy Spirit from preaching the word in the province of Asia'. (Acts 16:6), but in Troas, Paul 'had a vision of a man……. begging him, "Come over to Macedonia and help us" (Acts 16:9). Paul knew the restraints and the constraints of the Holy Spirit.

God, by His Spirit, still restrains and constrains, and often He does so by the ordering of our circumstances. There will be times when circumstances dictate that we stop or delay what we were intending to do, but other times when circumstances will confirm 'This is the way; walk in it'. (Isaiah 30:21)

I dare not choose my lot;
I would not if I might;
Choose thou for me, my God.
So shall I walk aright

(Horatius Bonar)

12 December

'But if you fail to do this, you will be sinning against the Lord; and you may be sure that your sin will find you out'. (Numbers 32:23)

Suggested reading Ephesians 6:1-9

Pat's parents were visiting relatives in Australia, and it was no surprise when they brought back a boomerang for our son, Andrew. I understand there are returning boomerangs and non-returning boomerangs, but ours seemed to be a category in between.

We went into the open fields but only ever had a modicum of success. However, I suspect the problem was with the thrower, rather than with the boomerang.

The Bible reminds us that sin is a 'boomerang' and sometimes it comes back to us in this life; hence the saying 'what goes round comes round'. But, if not in this life, then certainly in the life to come. How vital to know that all our sins have been forgiven before we appear at the judgement seat of God.

However, it is not just our evil deeds that boomerang, so do our good deeds. Paul, writing to the believers in Ephesus says, 'you know that the Lord will reward each one for whatever good they do'. (Ephesians 6:8)

For many years Mrs. B. was a children and young people's worker, and a number of her charges went into full-time Christian ministry. In retirement, she was thrilled when she was so regularly contacted by her 'boys'---men who were now middle-aged or even older. In their youth, she had ministered to them, and now in her old age, they were ministering to her. The boomerang effect—her kindness and thoughtfulness being reciprocated.

Kindness always brings its own reward. The kind person will seldom be without friends.

(J. C. Ryle)

13 December

'This is how we know what love is: Jesus Christ laid down his life for us'. (1 John 3:16)

Suggested reading Galatians 3:1-14

My brother had been seriously ill in hospital for many months, and when checking his post, I discovered a final demand for a utility bill. There was no amount given, but I telephoned the company, anxious to settle the bill. Easier said than done!

Data protection meant they could not tell me how much my brother owed, and so I suggested giving my card details, and they could then put in the actual amount. Again, data protection meant this was impossible, as the amount would eventually appear on my bank statement.

To say I was frustrated would be an understatement. I wanted to settle my brother's utility bill. I wanted to give money to the utility company, but it was apparently impossible. So, deviously, I came up with a plan whereby the debt could be paid. Rightly or wrongly---you must judge---I pretended to be my brother, and the plan was going famously until they asked if I would be paying with my own debit card

Showing mental agility, I replied I would not be using my own card but my brother's (ie, mine). 'In that case', the assistant said, 'we will need your brother's permission'. 'No problem', I said, 'he's here---I will put him on'. Then, speaking in a deeper voice, I gave the required permission before pretending to hand the phone back, and giving the card details in my original voice.

The utility company was happy, and though not entirely happy, I was thankful the bill had been paid.

In order to settle my brother's debt, I pretended to be him, but there was no pretense when Jesus paid our debt of sin. He had no sin, but, when the enormous debt of human sin was placed on him, God treated Jesus as though he was a sinner. God's wrath was poured out upon his Son, as Jesus was punished for the sins of all who would repent and trust in him.

Why did Jesus do it? Because He loved us and voluntary offered to pay the price of our sins. How thankful we should be for such amazing love.

I stand amazed in the presence Of Jesus the Nazarene and wonder how he could love me a sinner condemned unclean.

(Charles Homer Gabriel)

14 December

'No-one can serve two masters. Either you will hate the one and love the other, or you will be devoted to the one and despise the other. You cannot serve both God and money'. (Matthew 6:24)

Suggested reading 1 Timothy 6:17-21

A missionary friend, after four years in Africa, returned home on furlough. His home church kindly took him out for a meal, but he confessed he was shocked by so much of the tone of their conversation. The bigger house, the new car, and the next expensive holiday---these things seem to dominate their thinking. Having ministered amongst poor believers in Africa, he questioned whether British Christians had got their priorities right.

Paul warns 'those who are rich in this present world not to be arrogant nor to put their hope in wealth which is uncertain but to put their hope in God'.

One autumn, as a youngster, I gathered a bumper crop of conkers, and had numerous competitive games with my brother. I then put the remaining conkers in an old handbag, and placed them in the garage. I forgot all about them until springtime and what a shock awaited me.

Putting my hand into the bag, something moved, and suddenly twenty to thirty field mice emerged and scampered down the drive. I felt I had become the Pied Piper of Morecambe, as mice were running everywhere. Eventually, recovering my composure, I picked up the handbag, but there were no more conker games as the horse chestnuts had either rotted during the winter or been nibbled by the mice.

A sad end to the conkers, some of which, having been polished in the autumn, had once been my pride and joy. Now, there were only fit to be disposed of.

It is not just conkers, but all material possessions will ultimately perish, and therefore it is foolish to set our hearts upon them. We thank the Lord for them, but we must never make an idol of them. Today they might be our pride and joy, but their duration is temporary. How much better to 'hope in God who richly provides us with everything for our enjoyment'.

Your priorities must be God first, God second and God third until your life is continually face to face with God.

(Oswald Chambers)

15 December

'----he will save his people from their sins' (Matthew 1:21)

Suggested reading Matthew 9:9-13

One Christmas, one of our grandchildren wrote a letter to Father Christmas. 'Dear Father Christmas, I hope I have been good enough to my brother this year'. A strange introduction? Not really because when the siblings had been squabbling, mother had said, 'Don't forget---if you are naughty, Father Christmas will not come'.

A few days later, I was asked to be Father Christmas at a pre-school party. Donning the outfit and ringing a bell, I made my entrance, and was faced by young children whose faces were a mixture of excitement and trepidation.

'Because you have all been good children', said the leader, 'Father Christmas has come to our party'. They all looked angelic and, though I know appearances can be deceptive, there was a present for every girl and boy.

Father Christmas comes for good boys and girls, but Jesus Christ came for bad boys and girls, for bad men and women. He came 'to save sinners' (1Timothy 1:15), and because we are all sinners, we are all qualified to be saved.

Sadly, some disqualify themselves because they will not admit that they are sinners. For such people Jesus can do nothing, for he says, 'I have not come to call the righteous but sinners'. (Matthew 9:13) Thankfully, for all who will confess their sin and trust in Christ, there is the promise of salvation.

Never are men's hearts in such a hopeless condition, as when they are not sensible of their own sins.

(J.C.Ryle)

16 December

'Enter by the narrow gate, for wide is the gate and broad is the way that leads to destruction and there are many who go in by it. Because narrow is the gate and difficult is the way which leads to life, and there are few who find it' (Matthew 7:13-14 NKJV)

Suggested reading Psalm 73:1-20

It is a short ride by train from Burley in Wharfedale to Bradford Forster Square, and it is a journey frequently taken by Pat and myself. The attraction for Pat is the Broadway Shopping Centre, just a five- minute walk from the railway station.

The centre, opened in 2015, has over seventy shops and also comprises a leisure complex. We usually have a look round the shops, have a snack and then make the return journey.

One day, alighting from the train, my attention was caught by a poster displayed at the station, advertising the shopping centre----CHOOSE THE BROADWAY.

In the Sermon on the Mount, Jesus warned that, when it comes to life, many have chosen the broad way. It is popular, spacious and includes various philosophies, religions and lifestyles. Celebrating and promoting self-achievement, it is a most attractive pathway but it 'leads to destruction'.

By contrast, the way to eternal life is difficult. It means renouncing sin, submitting to Christ, perhaps losing friends and status. But it is the pathway to heaven, to eternal life, to the immediate presence of Jesus.

As believers we might be outnumbered and, in the minority, but how blessed we are to be numbered with the 'few' rather than being numbered with the 'many'.

The road is not to be complained of: as it leads to such a home

(John Newton)

17 December

'I am going there to prepare a place for you'. (John 14:2)

Suggested reading Revelation 21:1-7

I am a twin, but I was born in the days long before scans and consequently my mother never knew that she was having me. She knew she was having my brother, but what a surprise---or shock---when forty-five minutes later, I appeared.

I was not expected, but I still came to a home which had been prepared because I had the warmth, the love and the care of my mother.

How much more will our home in heaven be 'a prepared placed for a prepared people'. There are many things about heaven we don't know, but as believers, we have the assurance of the Saviour's love and presence. Heaven will be a prepared, a perfect place, and it will be perfect because of the One who has prepared it.

I am not very domesticated, having always had a mother or a wife to cook my meals. Therefore, it is to my shame that, if I was to prepare a meal for you, my advice would have to be 'Don't eat it'. Whereas, if my wife was to prepare a meal, my advice would be, 'Do eat it'. How good and excellent a meal is---it is largely determined by who has prepared it.

Heaven has been prepared by the Perfect One, the Sinless One---the One who 'has done everything well' (Mark 7:37) Heaven will be heaven, paradise will be paradise because they are prepared by Jesus.

In heaven there is the presence of all good and the absence of all evil.

(John Mason)

18 December

'We believe that Jesus died and rose again, and so we believe that God will bring with Jesus those who have fallen asleep in him'. (1 Thessalonians 4:14)

Suggested reading John 11:1-16

Heather, a Christian friend, invited an African mother and her young daughter to her home for a meal, and the girl was taken up with Heather's cat, Mollie.

On a further visit, the lady asked about the cat, and Heather had to sadly explain that Mollie----because of age---- had been put to sleep.

At church, a few days later, the lady enquired, 'has the cat woken up yet'? No doubt, trying to suppress a smile, Heather explained that Mollie had in fact died.

An amusing story but it begs a serious question: 'at death do believers die or do they sleep'? Both words are used in the Bible, so what is the answer?

When a believer dies, their soul goes to be with Jesus. 'Today, you will be with me in paradise' (Luke23:43) -----the words of Jesus to the dying thief. 'When the beggar died, the angels carried him to Abraham's side' (Luke 16:22) When Stephen died, 'he said "I see heaven open and the Son of Man standing at the right hand of God-----Lord Jesus receive my spirit'. (Acts 7:56 and 59)

At death, the souls of believers are alive in the presence of Jesus. enabling Paul to say 'away from the body and at home with the Lord'. (2 Corinthians 5:8)

It is the body which sleeps at death, awaiting the Second Coming of Christ, when the dead will be awakened. 'The dead in Christ will rise'. (1

Thessalonians 4:16). They will have a new, resurrected body 'like his glorious body'. (Philippians 3:21) And redeemed souls, reunited with resurrected bodies, will dwell in 'a new heaven and a new earth'. (2 Peter 3:13)

This is the believer's eternal future.

We are more sure to arise out of our graves than out of our beds.

(Thomas Watson)

19 December

> 'Where is the one who has been born king of the Jews"? ----When King Herod heard this, he was disturbed and all Jerusalem with him'. (Matthew 2:2-3)

Suggested reading Luke 2:8-20

It was a ten-minute stroll to and from school, and so every day, I walked down Lichfield Avenue in Morecambe. It was a quiet road with residents only occasionally visible.

One afternoon, I was passing a house when a man, in his garden, shouted, 'She's had the baby---it's a boy'! I guessed from the age of the man he was not talking about his wife. He was, of course, referring to the Queen---Prince Andrew had been born, and this much anticipated birth had been announced to the nation.

That was over sixty years ago, and now with modern means of communication, the whole world knows within minutes when a royal baby has been born.

How different when the Price of Peace, the King of Kings was born. His birth was almost secret, known only to a few shepherds and wise men. It had long been prophesied, but his birth was unknown and unexpected. When the wise men asked 'where is the one who has been born king of the Jews'? No-one in Jerusalem seemed to be aware of his birth.

Christ was quietly ushered into the world at Bethlehem, and in the same way, He still enters human hearts today.

How silently, how silently,
The wondrous gift is given!
So, God imparts to human hearts
The blessings of his heaven,
No ear may hear his coming,
But, in this world of sin,
Where meek souls will receive him still
The dear Christ enters in.

(Phillips Brooks)

20 December

'Thanks be to God for his indescribable gift'. (2 Corinthians 9:15)

Suggested reading John 3:16-21

I greatly enjoyed my years as a paperboy, and was in no way put off by the early starts or the rainy mornings. The most exciting time was the run-up to Christmas; the 'tipping season' for postmen, milkmen, binmen, paperboys etc. I delivered papers in a relatively prosperous residential area, and through the generosity of the people my 'tips' were the equivalent of several weeks' wages.

These 'tips' were gifts---it was the newsagent who paid my wages---and yet, they were a token of appreciation. Whatever the weather, I tried to be punctual and keep the papers dry, which was a bonus, especially where retired people were concerned. I also avoided the paper boy's unforgivable sin---not closing the gate properly. These were all factors in my Christmas bonanza.

Jesus Christ was truly God's gift to this world. We did not deserve him and we certainly had not earned Him. On the contrary, we had rebelled against God, broken His commandments and gone our own way. It was all of God's grace that He gave us Jesus. What love, giving His Son, so that through repentance and faith, guilty sinners might have eternal life? Have we thanked Him and fully appreciated the greatest gift of all? 'Thanks be to God for his indescribable gift'.

God is far more willing to save sinners than sinners are to be saved.

(J. C. Ryle)

21 December

> 'When the set time had fully come, God sent his Son, born of a woman, born under the law, to redeem those under the law, that we might receive adoption to sonship'. (Galatians 4:4-5)

Suggested reading Luke 1:26-38)

To my credit or otherwise, I have always been a stickler for punctuality, and therefore, pleased whenever I see ON TIME displayed on a railway departure board.

On this particular day, arriving at the station, it was gratifying to see the 12.16 was ON TIME. However, my pleasure was short-lived when there was an announcement 'Due to an electrical failure all trains are cancelled until further notice'.

Consequently, we had to pay for a taxi, and we arrived home almost an hour later than had been expected.

Perhaps in Old Testament times, there were those who thought the coming of Christ had been cancelled. Should he not have come at the time of Noah, when there was such wickedness in the world? Or at the time of Moses, when the children of Israel were captive in Egypt? Or at the time of Nebuchadnezzar, when Jerusalem was captured and the Jews were exiled in Babylon? They had the promise of his coming but had it been cancelled?

Not at all. None of these were the time appointed by God. 'When the set time had fully come, God sent his Son'--- in other words at the precise time ordained by God. We can only guess why 4/5/6 BC was the appointed time. There may have been political, cultural, geographical factors, but it is only conjecture. What we do know is that Jesus came at the right time---His coming was according to the Divine timetable. And what was true of His first coming will also be true of His second.

God is never in a hurry, but he is always on time.

(Anon)

22 December

> "---she gave birth to her firstborn, a son. She wrapped him in cloths and placed him in a manger, because there was no guest room available for them'. (Luke 2:7)

Suggested reading John 1:6-18

I was a small boy when, one August, we went to spend a few days in Colwyn Bay. We had not booked in advance, intending just to have bed and breakfast for three or four days. But it was the 1950s, when British seaside resorts were booming, and so we got the same response at house after house: 'Sorry, no room, no vacancies--- we are full'.

It was getting towards dusk, and we were preparing to spend the night in the waiting room at Colwyn Bay railway station, when my father knocked on one more door. Thankfully, the lady took pity on us and somehow managed to accommodate us under her roof.

A not dissimilar situation faced Mary and Joseph when Jesus was about to be born. Bethlehem was full. No rooms were available. There was not even a railway station. No, all they could find was a stable attached to an inn, and it was there that Jesus was born.

Sadly, what was true of Bethlehem is increasingly true of many in Britain today. People are so busy, with so many demands upon them, that they cannot find any room for Jesus. How tragic---no room for the King of Kings, the Lord of Lords, the Saviour of the world.

Room for pleasure, room for business,
But for Christ the Crucified,
Not a place that He can enter,
In the heart for which He died?

(Daniel W. Whittle)

23 DECEMBER

'The Father has sent his Son to be the Saviour of the world'.
(1 John 4:14)

Suggested reading Luke 2:36-40

It is always a joy to receive Christmas cards, as greetings are received from friends, with whom there may have been little or no contact during the year. Besides the card, there may also be a letter, updating one on family news

A Christmas card came through the post with a delightful winter's scene on the front, and with a most appropriate verse on the inside. Sadly, the card was not signed, the postmark indecipherable, and to this day, we do not know who the sender of the card was.

This is sad because, unsigned, the card was indistinguishable from the hundreds of cards on display in shops at Christmas time.

To many, the birth of Jesus is no different to any other birth because they have never seen who it was that sent Jesus. He is God's Christmas gift to a sinful, fallen world.

'To us a child is born, to us a son is given' (Isaiah 9:6) Born of the virgin Mary, given by Almighty God. No ordinary babe but the God/man sent to reveal God to man, and to reconcile man to God. Jesus is a unique person given for a unique purpose, and that is why we trust him as our Saviour and we worship him as our God.

The divine Son became a Jew; the Almighty appeared on earth as a helpless human baby, unable to do more than lie and stare and wriggle and make noises, needing to be fed and changed and taught to talk like any other child. The more you think about it, the more staggering it gets.

(J.I. Packer)

24 December

'When the angels had left them and gone into heaven, the shepherds said to one another, 'Let's go to Bethlehem and see this thing that has happened, which the Lord has told us about". (Luke 2:15)

Suggested reading 1 Corinthians 1:26-31

The arrival of a first grandchild is extra special as it marks the beginning of a new generation. Pat and I were, therefore, understandably excited as we waited for Joanna to give birth.

It was to be a home birth, and one Monday morning at 7 am we got the phone call to tell us that Saul had been born. We hurriedly got out of bed, and making the journey from Ingleton to Leeds, by 9 am we were holding our newborn grandchild.

The news of the birth was quickly shared with family and friends, and, within a few hours of his birth, the postman had been invited in and was standing by Saul's cot.

I am sure this did not happen when Prince William or Prince George was born. The postman might have delivered cards or telegrams to the hospital, but he would not been invited in to see the babies.

Jesus was the Prince of Peace, the King of Kings but He was not born in a palace at Jerusalem, but rather in a manger, at Bethlehem. This meant that, without protocol or guards to satisfy, he was accessible to all--- his first visitors being a group of humble shepherds.

Had not the angel said to the shepherds, 'I bring you good news that will cause great joy for all the people'? (Luke 2:15) 'All people'----Jew and Gentile, rich and poor, young and old, educated and uneducated. Jesus came 'to be the Saviour of the world' (1 John 4:14); therefore, all are invited to come to Him for salvation.

Let earth and heaven combine. Angels and men agree.
To praise in songs divine. The incarnate Deity
Our God contracted to a span.
Incomprehensively made man.

(Charles Wesley)

25 December

'For to us a child is born, to us a son is given'. (Isaiah 9:6a)

Suggested reading Luke 2:1-7

In the weeks leading up to Christmas, Pat was speaking to the wife of a retired minister friend.

'If you ever want to get John a book on the atoning death of Jesus', the woman said, 'get him "Pierced for our Transgressions". My husband says it is excellent'.

Taking her advice, Pat duly ordered the book and kindly presented it to me on Christmas morning. I was immediately faced with a moral dilemma: did I pretend to be thrilled or did I tell Pat the truth? Two years earlier, I had given that minister a copy of "Pierced for our Transgressions".

Pat had given careful thought into the buying of that book but, unfortunately, I had already read it.

As most of us know only too well, not all gifts given or received at Christmas are appropriate, but God's gift of His Son is appropriate for all. We needed a Saviour. We could not save ourselves and therefore, Jesus Christ is the Saviour we need. He is the only one who can forgive our sins, reconcile us to God and grant to us the gift of eternal life.

'Today in the town of David a Saviour has been born to you: he is the Messiah, the Lord'. (Luke 2:11)

'Thanks be to God for his indescribable gift'. (2 Corinthians 9:15)

The Son of God became the Son of Man in order that sons of men might become the sons of God.

(John Blanchard)

26 December

'Therefore the Lord himself will give you a sign: The virgin will conceive and give birth to a son, and will call him, Immanuel'. (Isaiah 7:14)

Suggested reading Luke 1:39-56

I was invited, by a ministerial friend, to take a Bible study on the virgin birth at the home of a medical consultant. He listened courteously to what I had to say, but then acknowledged, he could not believe in the virgin birth because he was a doctor.

I gently pointed out that the gospel writer who had most to say about the virgin birth was Luke, described by the Apostle Paul as 'our dear friend Luke, the doctor'. (Colossians 4:14) He was a medical man but was, in no way, ashamed or embarrassed by the virgin birth.

My scripture teacher at school rejected the virgin birth because he said it would mean that Jesus was different from us. But surely that is the message of the New Testament. Jesus healed the sick, raised, the dead, walked on water, fed the five thousand, forgave sin. No man could do this---only the God/man.

Because Jesus was the God/man, the virgin birth was a necessity. It was a birth miraculous but natural, different but normal: a birth which included both the divine and the human element. 'Conceived of the Holy Spirit and born of the Virgin Mary'. Having a heavenly father and a human mother, Jesus was the God/man.

Those who deny that Jesus was without a human father must explain how He was without a human failure.

(John Blanchard)

27 December

'In him we have redemption through his blood, the forgiveness of sins'. (Ephesians 1:7)

Suggested reading John 6:35-40

It was a bitterly cold day, and hurrying to get our son, Aaron, into his specially adapted van, I carelessly locked the car keys inside the vehicle. This was a potentially serious situation, as Aaron was prone to fits and needed regular medication. We thought of ringing the RAC or a local garage, but it was a Saturday afternoon and time was the essence.

Eventually I said to Pat, 'Why not ring the Fire and Rescue'? And this is what we did.

Within minutes, we heard the sirens and a fire engine was with us. Four men jumped out, and when they heard of our predicament, they could not have been kinder. They went to the state-of-the-art fire engine and emerged with----wait for it---a wire coat hanger.

For half an hour they attempted to unlock the door, but vehicle manufacturers today are wise to potential car thieves and all their efforts came to nothing. Finally, they broke a side window, and when the door was opened, there was Aaron smiling, and none the worse for his experience. He had been rescued from a potentially serious situation.

Aaron did not realise the danger he was in. Similarly, in their sin and rebellion against God, men and women do not realise the danger they are in. Aaron, because of his multiple disabilities, was unable to do anything about his situation, and men and women are quite incapable of saving themselves.

For Aaron to be rescued, it needed outside intervention, and that is true for sinful men and women. That first Christmas time, Jesus came from heaven to earth, to do for us what we could not do for ourselves. He came to die upon a cross in order to save us, to rescue us from our sins. Praise God for outside intervention!

It was to save sinners that Christ Jesus came into this world. He did not come to help them save themselves, nor to induce them to save themselves, nor even to enable them to save themselves. He came to save them!

(William Hendriksen)

28 December

'When the time came for the purification rites required by the Law of Moses, Joseph and Mary took him to Jerusalem to present him to the Lord'. (Luke 2:22)

Suggested reading Matthew 18:1-11

One morning a desperate grandmother called to see me. Her unmarried daughter had given birth to a child, but the mother had no intention of having the child christened.

'What will happen', begged the grandmother, 'if the baby were to die without ever being christened'?

I explained that I did not believe the eternal welfare of a baby could ever be determined by a ritual the child was not even aware of. I hope I was able to reassure the woman, but how sad that she should be tormented by a man-made tradition.

It is my personal conviction that all children who die in infancy are 'safe in the arms of Jesus'. When David's seven-day-old baby died, he said 'Can I bring him back again? I will go to him but he will not return to me'. (2 Samuel 12:23) David knew he was going to 'dwell in the house of the Lord for ever' (Psalm 23:6), and he was assured that his son was already there.

'Jesus said, "Let the little children come to me, and do not hinder them, for the kingdom of heaven belongs to such as these". (Matthew 19:14)

There's a home for little children. Above the bright blue sky,
Where Jesus reigns in glory, a home of peace and joy.
No home on earth is like it, or can with it compare;
For everyone is happy, nor could be happier, there.

(Albert Midlane)

29 December

'But you know that he appeared so that he might take away our sins. And in him is no sin'. (1 John 3:5)

Suggested reading Romans 2:1-16

As youngsters, my brother and I were scorers for the Morecambe Grammar School Old Boys cricket team. They played in the Westmorland League---in the days when that was still an actual county. Consequently, pleasant summer afternoons were spent in places such as Windermere, Ambleside, Grange-over-Sands and Kirkby Lonsdale---places which otherwise I might not have visited.

But what did the scorers do? Well, they recorded everything that occurred on the cricket field. Every run, wicket, ball, and no-ball---all were written down by the scorer. It was the record of what each of the cricketers had done, and what was written down could never be erased or altered.

All our thoughts, words and actions are recorded, and ultimately, we are accountable to God for things done in the body. This is, for each one of us, a disturbing prospect, for we cannot cover or erase anything from our records.

However, there is good news---the good news of Christmas. Jesus 'appeared so that he might take away our sins'. Taking on human form at Bethlehem and human sin at Calvary, Jesus is able to sweep the record clean----but only through repentance and faith in Him. 'The blood of Jesus, his Son, purifies us from all sin'. (1 John 1:7)

What can wash away my sin? Nothing but the blood of Jesus.
What can make me whole again? Nothing but the blood of Jesus
O precious is the flow. That makes me white as snow.
No other fount I know, nothing but the blood of Jesus

(Robert Lowry)

30 December

> 'With the tongue we praise our Lord and Father, and with it we curse human beings who have been made in God's likeness. Out of the same mouth come praise and cursing. My brothers and sisters, this should not be'. (James 3:9-10)

Suggested reading 1 Samuel 18:5-16

Moving from junior school to secondary school can be a daunting experience for children and for my class, it was made worse by the behaviour of our science master. As he was teaching, if someone yawned, he would propel a piece of chalk in their direction. And, if anyone was not paying attention, a blackboard duster would be hurled at his intended victim.

Thankfully, Mr. P. was cross eyed, and his missiles rarely hit their intended target but what bizarre behaviour. Teaching children but at the same time, seeking to distress or even harm them. To quote James, 'this should not be', and today no teacher would get away with that kind of conduct.

King Saul was guilty of such behaviour for whist 'he was prophesying in his house-----Saul had a spear in his hand and he hurled it' at David. (1 Samuel 18:10) Prophesying and at the same time, attempting murder---'this should not be'.

As believers, can we say we have always been guiltless? James says, 'out of the same mouth come praise and cursing', and have there not perhaps been times when, having just praised God, our tongues have been employed in destroying someone's character or reputation? We cannot argue with James, 'this should not be ' and we must seek daily grace to ensure we are not guilty of such incongruous behaviour.

It is a sad fact that the tongue of professing Christians are often all too busy doing the devil's work.

(Donald Grey Barnhouse)

31 December

> 'Therefore encourage one another and build each other up, just in fact as you are doing'. (1 Thessalonians 5:11)

Suggested reading Acts 9:23-31

I recently preached a sermon on Barnabas---'Son of Encouragement' (Acts 4:36) ---and I was pleased that I had.

Before the service, I asked a man if he was still helping, as a volunteer, with a Christian organisation. He said that, after many years, he had stood down but was saddened that there had been no acknowledgement of his service. He was not seeking for praise, just for a word of encouragement.

After the service, another man said that when he had been in hospital --- 'flat on my back'---he had found telephone calls enquiring about him more effective than any the injections he had been given. He had been boosted by a word of encouragement.

We all need encouragement, and it is amazing, when we are not feeling well or under the weather, the beneficial impact which a text, an e-mail, a telephone call, a card, a bunch of flowers can have. In Acts 4 Barnabas encouraged the poor, in Acts 9, he encouraged Saul of Tarsus, in Acts 11, he encouraged new converts and in Acts 15, he encouraged John Mark. Barnabas was rightly named 'Son of Encouragement'.

As we prepare to enter a new year, let us each resolve to be a Barnabas; to be a son/a daughter of encouragement.

The church should be a community of encouragement.

(Frederick Catherwood)

www.ingramcontent.com/pod-product-compliance
Lightning Source LLC
Chambersburg PA
CBHW041134110526
44590CB00027B/4009